An Elephant in My Kitchen

Françoise Malby-Anthony was born in the South of France, brought up in Paris and has lived in South Africa since 1987. She founded the Thula Thula game reserve in 1998 with her late husband, the renowned conservationist and bestselling author Lawrence Anthony. When Lawrence died in 2012, Françoise took over the running of the reserve and is equally passionate about conservation. She was the driving force behind setting up a wildlife rehabilitation centre at the reserve to care for orphaned animals.

Katja Willemsen was born in Holland, grew up in South Africa and now lives in France. A full-time writer, she is the author of the thriller *Shepherd's Prayer*. *An Elephant in My Kitchen* is her first work of non-fiction.

Françoise Malby-Anthony
with Katja Willemsen

An Elephant in My Kitchen

What the herd taught me about love,
courage and survival

PAN BOOKS

First published 2018 by Sidgwick & Jackson

This paperback edition first published 2019 by Pan Books
an imprint of Pan Macmillan
The Smithson, 6 Briset Street, London EC1M 5NR
Associated companies throughout the world
www.panmacmillan.com

ISBN 978-1-5098-6492-8

7 9 8

A CIP catalogue record for this book is available from the British Library.

Typeset by Palimpsest Book Production Limited, Falkirk, Stirlingshire
Printed and bound by CPI Group (UK) Ltd, Croydon, CR0 4YY

Visit www.panmacmillan.com to read more about all our books
and to buy them. You will also find features, author interviews and
news of any author events, and you can sign up for e-newsletters
so that you're always first to hear about our new releases.

To my Thula Thula wild and human family,

thank you for your love and support,

and for giving me the strength

to never give up.

Contents

1

The only walls between humans and elephants are the ones we put up ourselves

Violent weather always unsettled our elephants, and the predicted gale-force winds meant there was a danger of trees blowing over and causing breaches in Thula Thula's perimeter fence. The cyclone had threatened for days, and while we desperately needed water after a scorching summer, we definitely didn't need a tropical storm. We were worried about the herd, but my husband Lawrence and I were confident that, somewhere in the vast expanse of our game reserve, they had been led to safety by their new matriarch, and my namesake, Frankie.

We hadn't seen them near the house in a while and I missed them.

Whenever they visited, their trunks immediately curled up to 'read' our house. Were we home? Where were the dogs? Was that a whiff of new bougainvillea?

Bijou, my Maltese poodle and sovereign princess of the reserve, hated losing her spot centre stage and always yapped indignantly at them. The adult elephants ignored her, but the babies were as cocky as she was, and would gleefully charge

I

her along the length of the wire fence that bordered our garden, their bodies a gangly bundle of flapping ears and tiny swinging trunks.

No matter how much we treasured their visits, we knew it wasn't safe for them to be this comfortable around humans. The risk of poachers taking advantage of their trust was too high so we planned to slowly wean them off us, or to be more accurate, wean *ourselves* off them. Not that Lawrence would dream of giving up his beloved Nana, the herd's original matriarch; theirs was a two-way love affair because Nana had no intention of giving him up either.

They met in secret. Lawrence would park his battered Land Rover a good half kilometre away from the herd and wait. Nana would catch his scent in the air, quietly separate from the others and amble towards him through the dense scrubland, trunk high in delighted greeting. He would tell her about his day and she no doubt told him about hers with soft throaty rumbles and trunk-tip touches.

What a difference to the distressed creature that had arrived at Thula Thula back in 1999! We had only just bought the game reserve – a beautiful mix of river, savannah and forest sprawled over the rolling hills of Zululand, KwaZulu-Natal, with an abundance of Cape buffalo, hyena, giraffe, zebra, wildebeest and antelope, as well as birds and snakes of every kind, four rhinos, one very shy leopard and three crocodiles.

We were very disappointed when we discovered afterwards that the owner had sold off the rhinos. At that point, there weren't any elephants either and they certainly weren't part of our plan. Not yet; definitely not so soon.

So when a representative of an animal welfare organization

asked us to adopt a rogue herd of elephants, we were flabbergasted. We knew nothing about keeping elephants, nor did we have the required *boma* – secure enclosure – within the reserve where they could stay until they adjusted to their new life with us.

'The woman must know we don't have any experience,' I said to Lawrence. 'Why *us*?'

'Probably because no one else is stupid enough; but Frankie, if we say no, they're going to be shot, even the babies.'

I was horrified. 'Phone her and say yes. We'll make a plan somehow. We always do.'

Two weeks later, in the middle of a night of torrential rain, three huge articulated trucks brought them to us. When I saw the size of the vehicles, I was hit by the full impact of what was arriving. Two breeding adult females, two teenagers, and three little ones under the age of ten. We knew enough about elephants by then to know that if there were going to be problems, they'd come from the older ones. Lawrence and I exchanged glances. *Let the* boma *hold.*

Just as the trucks pulled up at the game reserve, a tyre exploded and the vehicle tilted dangerously in the mud. My heart froze at the elephants' terrified trumpeting and screeching. It was only at dawn that we managed to get them into the safety of the new enclosure.

They weren't there for long.

By the next day, they had figured out a way to avoid the electric fence's brutal 8,000 volts by pushing a nine-metre-high tambotie tree onto it. The wires shorted and off they went, heading northwards in the direction of their previous home. Hundreds of villages dot the hills and valleys around our game reserve so it was a code-red disaster.

We struggled to find them. You'd think it would be easy to find a herd of elephants, but it isn't. Animals big and small instinctively know how to make themselves disappear in the bush, and disappear they did. Trackers on foot, 4×4s and helicopters couldn't find them. Frustrated with doing nothing, I jumped into my little Tazz and hit the dirt roads to look for them, with Penny, our feisty bull terrier, as my assistant.

'*Sawubona*, have you seen seven elephants?' I asked everyone I passed in my best Zulu.

But with a French accent that butchered their language, they just stared at the gesticulating blonde in front of them and politely shook their heads.

It took ten days to get the herd back to Thula Thula. Ten long, exhausting days. We survived on adrenalin, coffee and very little sleep. How Lawrence managed to prevent them from being shot was a miracle. The local wildlife authority had every right to demand that the elephants be put down. They had human safety issues to consider, and besides, they knew only too well that the chances of rehabilitating the group were close to zero. We were warned that if they escaped again, they would definitely be shot.

The pressure to settle them down was terrible and my life changed overnight from worrying about cobras or scorpions in my bedroom to lying awake, waiting for Lawrence to come home, scared stiff he was being trampled to death in his desperation to persuade the elephants to accept their new home. Night after night, he stayed as close to the *boma* as he dared, singing to them, talking to them and telling them stories until he was hoarse. With tender determination and no shortage of madness, Lawrence breached Nana's terror of man and gained her trust.

One hot afternoon, he came home and literally bounced up the steps towards me.

'You won't believe what happened,' he said, still awe-struck. 'Nana put her trunk through the fence and touched my hand.'

My eyes widened in shock. Nana could have slung her trunk around his body and yanked him through the wires.

'How did you know she wouldn't hurt you?'

'You know when you can sense someone's mood without a word being spoken? That's what it was like. She isn't angry any more and she isn't frightened. In fact, I think she's telling me they're ready to explore their new home.'

'Please get out of this alive,' I begged.

'We're over the worst. I'm going to open the *boma* at day-break.'

That night, Lawrence and I sat on our veranda under a star-flung sky and clinked champagne glasses.

'To Nana,' I sighed.

'To my baba,' Lawrence grinned.

The herd had become family over the past thirteen years, so we were extremely worried when the storm warnings wors-ened and the risk of the cyclone smashing into us increased with every passing hour.

Lawrence was away on business and I was on my own. He called me non-stop. *How bad are the winds now? Has it started raining yet? Are the rangers patrolling the fence?* It was the worst possible time for him to be away. Cyclones are rare in Zululand but when they strike, their devastation can be catastrophic. I found out afterwards that he'd called our insurance company from Johannesburg to double our weather-damage cover. That's how alarmed he was. I couldn't wait for him to get back.

In the middle of this chaos, at seven o'clock on Friday morning, 2 March 2012, I received a call telling me that my indestructible husband had died of a heart attack during the night. I didn't believe it. Lawrence had survived war-torn Baghdad and savage Congolese violence, and now I wouldn't be fetching him from Durban International Airport and bringing him home. I sank onto the bed, numb with shock.

The game reserve fell silent in disbelief.

'It was as if somebody switched off the plugs of life,' said Mabona, our lodge manageress.

Like a robot, I kept going. The storm was still raging and the KwaZulu-Natal emergency services had warned us that it was heading our way. I made sure the guests were safe and instructed the rangers to secure the tented camp with extra ropes and wire. Then Mother Nature gave us an incredible reprieve and Cyclone Irena veered offshore. The crisis was over. We let out a collective groan of relief and prepared to stare grief in the face.

How was I going to survive without Lawrence at Thula Thula? It felt impossible, for me and for our staff. Many thought I would take refuge in my native France. He and I had run the game reserve as a rock-solid team. Lawrence, or *Lolo*, as I called him, took on everything to do with the animals and their safety, and I handled hospitality, marketing and finance. We learned on the hop, adapted to things we knew nothing about and simply tackled each out-of-the-blue challenge that flew our way. Like adopting a herd of emotionally deranged elephants. What were we thinking?

But we managed, more than managed, with courage and craziness and plenty of laughter. We loved each other and we loved the oasis we had built in the African bush. Protecting animals, especially elephant and rhino, was the focus of our life together.

And now, from one day to the next, my partner in everything was gone. It was unthinkable, and because he'd been away when it happened, his death didn't feel real. Word spread like bush fire, and emails, calls and messages poured in from around the world. It wasn't just my grief, it was everyone's grief. Still it didn't sink in. I kept expecting a call from him.

'Frankie, I'm at the airport! Where *are* you?'

I stumbled through that first weekend in a daze. Very early on Sunday morning, I received a call informing me that the herd had surfaced and were on the move.

'They're heading south,' crackled the radio. 'Direction main house.'

That was a surprise. The last sighting of them had been during the worst of the storm alerts, when they had been a good twelve hours' walk from us – and remember, that's twelve hours powered by mammoth muscles. Now they were a mere fifteen minutes away. But to be honest, I really didn't give it any more thought. Life was a blur and I could hardly breathe for the things I had to do. Our guests didn't know what had happened and somehow I had to keep the lodge running for them.

Promise, a good-looking game ranger as skilled at rustling up a cocktail as tracking an elusive animal, was the first to see the herd and almost drove into them. They were right at the gate to the main house and reception compound, making it impossible for him to drive through. He immediately noticed something odd.

'Even the bulls are here,' he reported.

Bachelor elephants tend to stay away from the others, or, if they are close by, they stay out of sight. But that morning, all twenty-one members of the herd jostled about at the gate, clearly agitated. This was highly unusual because their visits were normally so serene.

Sometimes, if Lawrence had returned from being away, they would pop by, mill about and graze patiently while they waited for him to come out and say hello. Or if there was a baby to introduce, they would stand along the fence, radiating peace, and gently nudge the new arrival forward to meet him.

The Sunday after he died was completely different. They were restless and pacing. They walked in a disorganized jumble to the front of the house, stayed there for a few minutes then shouldered their way to the back of the house again, never grazing, always moving.

'They were disturbed but I had no idea why. I thought maybe they had had a run-in with poachers. When I got closer, I saw the telltale streaks of stress on the sides of their faces, even the babies',' Promise said afterwards, rubbing his own cheek in amazement.

An elephant's temporal gland sits between its eye and ear,

and secretes liquid when the animal is stressed, which can create the mistaken impression that it is crying. The elephants at our entrance weren't crying, but the dark moist lines running down their massive cheeks showed that something had deeply affected them. After about forty minutes, they lined up at the fence separating our home from the bush and their gentle communication started.

Solemn rumbles rolled through the air, the same low-frequency language they always used with Lawrence. Mabula, the herd's dominant bull, paced up and down with the others; just Nana stood by silently, as if waiting for Lawrence to appear but knowing he wasn't going to.

We hadn't seen them in months. Why now? Why this exact weekend? And why were they so anxious? No science book can explain why our herd came to the house *that* weekend. But to me, it makes perfect sense. When my husband's heart stopped, something stirred in theirs, and they crossed the miles and miles of wilderness to mourn with us, to pay their respects, just as they do when one of their own has died.

I grew up a city girl, a Parisian through and through, who could tell you the quickest way to Saint-Germain-des-Prés but who knew nothing at all about animals. Our family never kept pets, although we did once have a tortoise in our garden. Living and working in a city, even a beautiful one like Paris, there's no time to notice nature as you do in the bush. It's *metro, boulot, dodo*, as they say in France, when life is a relentless treadmill of *commute, work, sleep*. Yet even as I pounded the Parisian treadmill, somewhere deep inside me I always knew I would end up in a foreign country.

But living in the sticks in Africa? Not *that* foreign.

And yet there I was, in the sticks, alone, and burying my husband. I didn't know where to begin. I asked Vusi and Promise, Lawrence's trusted right-hand men, to come to the house to talk about the scattering of his ashes.

'We should move Mnumzane's bones to the dam. I want Lawrence and him to be together,' I murmured.

Mkhulu Dam was Lawrence's favourite spot at Thula Thula. He and Vusi had built it themselves and it's where he went to clear his mind, fill his soul. Mnumzane had been his favourite boy elephant who had come to us as part of the original group, a distraught youngster whose mother and sister had been shot before his eyes. Even though he was only a teenager when he arrived, just a kid really, and a troubled one too, he understood the responsibility of being the oldest male, and the very first thing he did was charge Lawrence to stop him from getting too close to his family. Lawrence admired his gutsiness so much, he named him *Mnumzane*, Zulu for 'Sir', and it became one of his favourite stories.

'He must have been terrified,' Lawrence loved to recount. 'He'd just travelled eighteen hours in a rattling iron prison on wheels and, once out of it, everything was foreign. No familiar smells, no safe hiding place to run to, just a bunch of exhausted human beings who would have represented extreme danger to him, but he still bloody well charged us. If I'd been wearing a hat, I would have raised it to him.'

Some months afterwards, Mnumzane was ousted from the herd. It's how elephants bring up their boys – they separate them and their growing testosterone levels from the teenage girls. It stops inbreeding and makes sure genes are spread far and wide. In Mnumzane's case, that didn't apply because he was an orphan with no family links to any of the female youngsters, but rules are rules in the elephant kingdom and Nana was a strict matriarch who wouldn't tolerate hanky-panky on her watch. It was heartbreaking how he suffered. He had already lost his mother and sister, and now he was losing his foster mum and siblings too. He barely ate and the only way to stop him from wasting away in misery was by tempting him with special snacks of alfalfa and thorny acacia branches, which he guzzled with the same relish a human teenager guzzles burgers.

I'll never forget the day Mnumzane decided to let Lawrence know exactly how he felt about him. This great big four-ton elephant lumbered up to his Land Rover and stood in front of him, stopping him from going further.

'I got the fright of my life,' Lawrence told me later, 'but then he fixed me with those old-soul eyes of his and lolled his giant head from side to side, as if to say *no need to be so jumpy, old man*, and I just *knew* he was telling me that he loved being with me.'

'He's looking for a new *papa*,' I teased.

'You're probably right, and it's something we have to think about. He's getting to the age where he'll need to be kept in line by someone who can pack a bigger punch than me!'

From then on, Mnumzane regularly sought out Lawrence for father–son bush chats. I don't know who loved those get-togethers more. Lawrence, the proud foster father, watching his boy grow up, or Mnumzane, the rejected teenager, flourishing under Lawrence's love and acceptance.

So it was devastating for Lawrence when this gentle giant

suddenly turned violent. Unbeknown to anyone, mind-blowing pain from an abscess was literally driving Mnumzane crazy, and when he killed a rhino then utterly wrecked a broken-down 4×4, Lawrence knew it was time. Putting him down was one of the most traumatic decisions he ever faced. He withdrew with grief and I didn't know how to console him. He even stopped joining guests at the bar, something he loved to do. Often he disappeared for hours on end and I knew he was visiting the site where his boy had fallen. We went for long drives in the bush. We sat on the edge of Mkhulu Dam and reminisced about all the things Mnumzane had done in his short time with us.

'A bloody *abscess*. A jab of antibiotics would have fixed it. I should have *known*.'

'You couldn't have. Not even you, Lolo,' I said countless times.

They were kindred spirits, those two – brave, unpredictable, funny and tender. I knew with all my heart that reuniting them in death was exactly what Lawrence would have wanted.

Only snatches of memory remain of the day we scattered his ashes. I remember the convoy of cars that seemed as long as the road itself. I remember the clouds of dust from the dirt track when we headed north to where the dam was. I remember we stood in a half-moon at the water's edge. I remember anecdotes and stories. I remember tears and laughter. I remember dark ripples in the water.

By then, I had been in South Africa for twenty-five years and I loved and embraced its melting pot of traditions and cultures, but for a few moments that day I yearned for the busy familiarity of Montparnasse where I had lived in Paris. It was the one and only time I longed for France because my life was in South Africa, and like Nana, my family were now the animals and people at Thula Thula.

Living in the bush teaches you that life is a magnificent cycle of birth and death, and nothing showed me that more powerfully than when Nana gave birth to a beautiful baby boy around the time of Lawrence's passing.

Of course, I named him Lolo.

2

Falling in love with Thabo

I stood in front of the kitchen fan, twisted my hair out of my neck and tried to focus on what my chef Winnie was saying. It was the third sweltering day of 40-degree temperatures and I was dead on my feet. We all were. But the lodge was full and we were doing our damnedest to soldier on.

'I think mango and avocado salad would be a good starter in this heat,' she suggested in her gentle way.

I nodded vaguely. Lawrence had loved mangoes. I looked up towards the noise coming from the office. Someone was broadcasting the same message over and over on the two-way radio.

'Elephant Safari Lodge, do you copy?'

Silence.

'Vusi? Mabona? Do you copy? *Nikuphi nina?!*'

The radio is a crucial bush survival tool and everyone knows how to use it. I couldn't make out who the ranger was but he sounded panicked. I was about to answer when my mobile rang.

'Is that you on the radio, Promise?' I asked.

'Françoise, poachers. Thabo took a bullet.'

I gripped the phone. Thabo, our rhino calf. 'And Ntombi?'

'She's fine but won't let us near him. We can't tell how badly he's hurt. We need Mike here urgently.'

I heard him but it didn't sink in. The two weeks since Lawrence's death had been a blind scramble of decisions and new situations but nothing had been as scary as this. I sat down, fighting off a wave of nausea.

'You still there, Françoise?'

'Just trying to figure out how to get hold of Mike,' I said softly.

Lawrence had always used Dr Mike Toft for animal emergencies. He was three hours away by car, or thirty minutes and 30,000 rands by helicopter. I hoped to God that he wasn't tied up in another crisis.

'Does Alyson know what's happened?' I asked.

'She's on her way.'

'Good. If anyone can get close to Thabo, it's her. Stay with them and call me if anything changes. Leave Mike to me.'

Alyson was our rhino calves' stand-in mum and primary carer and they trusted her completely, but that didn't mean they would let her check his wounds. Injured wild animals are unpredictable and dangerous and I hoped she wouldn't take any risks. She was a lioness when it came to her charges.

'If poachers ever hurt my little babies, I'll hunt them down and feed them to hyenas,' she threatened every time we heard about another poaching.

Little babies isn't how everyone would describe our one-ton rhino calves, but I knew exactly how she felt. I had fallen in love with Thabo at the wonderful Moholoholo Rehabilitation Centre in Hoedspruit when he was just a couple of months old. He was now a strapping three-year-old, but in my heart he was still the same lovable little calf.

Rhino calves have no horns and their soft faces look so vulnerable. They *are* vulnerable. A young rhino can't survive alone in the bush. Thabo had been found as a terrified newborn with his umbilical cord still dragging below him in the dust. How he survived even a day on his own was a miracle and no one ever knew what had happened to his family. Fortunately, when they're that tiny they haven't yet learned to be scared of humans, and that makes it easier to help them because they'll trust anyone who feeds and comforts them.

They need round-the-clock attention from caregivers who share a room with them at night, monitor their moods and body condition, feed them every few hours, and give them all the cuddles and love they're missing out on from their real mothers.

When I first met Thabo, he was already a confident little thing with perky ears and inquisitive eyes. I was invited into his *boma* to see him play by his first stand-in mum, Elaine.

'Thabo, come and say hello,' Elaine called.

Baby rhinos don't run, they half bounce, half fly. He hurtled towards her, nuzzled her, then looked up and studied me.

'*Bonjour*, little one,' I smiled.

He nestled his snout against my leg in reply. My heart melted. He was so trusting and gentle. I realized then that, although I lived on a game reserve, I had little contact with our animals. The business side of Thula Thula, managing the lodge and dealing with guests, was my domain, along with any admin to do with our animals.

When we rescued Nana and her herd, for example, I made

the phone calls, ploughed through mountains of paperwork and struggled with the maddening logistics to get them to us, but it was Lawrence who was out at the *boma* night after night, desperately convincing Nana that she was safe with us.

The minute Thabo nuzzled me with so much trust, I longed to protect him and to do more for other orphans like him. I tickled his face and stared into his innocent eyes and it dawned on me that Thula Thula was the ideal place to do exactly that. I returned home, bursting with ideas.

'I think we should build an animal orphanage,' I announced to Lawrence.

'Fantastic. Let's do it.'

But rescuing young animals is entirely different to rescuing older ones. We had experience of saving elephants but none in rescuing orphaned or abandoned baby animals. Our herd had needed Lawrence's presence and reassurance to settle them down, but little orphans need far more than just reassurance. They need hands-on love and intensive nursing, and we weren't set up for that yet. But the seed was sown and it always stayed at the back of my mind that, as soon as we had time and money, we should build our own orphanage.

A few months later, I received a phone call that set the ball rolling much sooner than we'd planned.

'We're looking for a home for Thabo,' said Moholoholo's general manager. 'Ideally a reserve that can care for him until he's old enough to be released into the bush.'

'We're *perfect* for him,' I said.

We weren't. Far from it. But life's like that. Sometimes it takes a push to make dreams come true. Lawrence didn't bat an eyelid when I told him.

'We only had a few weeks to prepare for seven elephants; getting ready for one rhino calf will be a piece of cake,' he said. 'The timing couldn't be better. I've been thinking about getting more rhinos after what happened to Heidi.'

Poachers had broken into our reserve during a storm – knowing that the noise and rain would muffle their gunshots and wash away their tracks – and killed our last rhino. Full-moon nights are usually when we're on red-alert because the moonlight makes it easy for poachers to move about without flashlights, so the attack on Heidi in the middle of a storm had caught us totally off guard. They shot her without killing her but that didn't stop them from hacking off her horn while she was alive. The horror of seeing what they did to her gentle expressive face will live with me forever. It also made us all the more determined to do everything we could to save her species.

I gave Lawrence a printout of what had to be in place before Thabo would be allowed to relocate to Thula Thula. He scanned the page and nodded.

'Easy,' he grinned.

Not *that* easy. Moving endangered wildlife in South Africa is strictly controlled and requires a special permit and a healthy bank account. We had neither. But the impossible had never put us off before.

'I'll handle the permit. You do what you can to raise money,' Lawrence said.

Within a week, we received the permit *and* raised R100,000 to pay for Thabo's transportation. Most of the money came from friends and clients who knew us and who wanted to be part of helping Thabo get to his new home.

The next hurdle was a visit from the wildlife inspectors. An hour before they were due to arrive I was a bundle of nerves.

'Have we done *everything* they asked?' I said to Lawrence.

'Relax, Frankie. They gave us the okay for our elephants; they're not going to turn us down now.'

He was absolutely right. The inspectors approved Thabo's new accommodation and outdoor area, and sanctioned the transport crate that we had specially made in Durban to their strict specifications. His adoption papers came through the same day. I was over the moon. After all the bureaucracy and waiting, little Thabo was coming at last.

Until then, the only home he had known was Moholoholo and we were worried what effect the long drive would have on him.

'Elaine would be the best person to look after him on the trip,' said the rehab centre's manager. 'She was his carer when he was a baby and he trusts her.'

'That's perfect,' I said. 'We'll pay all her costs.'

'It's a bit more complicated than that. Her internship ended a few months ago and she's gone back to England.'

I fell silent. There wasn't enough money for an international flight.

'I'll email her anyway,' I said quietly.

Elaine replied within the hour, on board to help, but she had used up her savings to join the programme in the first place and couldn't pay for the air ticket.

'I'll try and find someone else to accompany Thabo, but it's not ideal,' said the manager. 'It's a long journey for him to take without a carer he knows and trusts.'

With every day that passed, I became more terrified that

Moholoholo would decide Thabo was too young to under-take such a stressful journey with a stranger. A week went by without news. I prepared myself for the worst.

'They must have found another reserve for him by now,' I said to Lawrence.

'How much money have we raised?'

'Only half of what we need.'

At four o'clock the next morning I was up, restless and unable to sleep, so I sat down at my computer with a cup of hot tea to check for news from Moholoholo. Nothing. I didn't know whether to be relieved or worried. Up popped an email from Elaine. I scanned it, stunned. Her granny had offered to pay for her flight. Our little boy had an angel watching over him. I ran to the bedroom to tell Lawrence, my little poodle Gypsy scampering at my heels.

'She's coming! She's coming!'

He sat up and looked at me with bleary eyes. 'Who?'

Gypsy leapt onto the bed and licked his face, sharing my excitement.

'*Elaine!* She's coming to help with Thabo,' I grinned. 'She can't be away from home for months on end but she said she'll stay as long as it takes to settle him in.'

Off I went to Moholoholo with Pieter, our baby-faced ranger who didn't look old enough for a driver's licence, let alone the responsibility of bringing back our precious rhino calf, but he was the perfect man for the job, with a gentle soul and a natural flair with animals. The plan was that he would drive the truck up to the Lowveld with me, and then help Elaine and me look after Thabo on the 700-kilometre trip back home.

We arrived at Moholoholo late on Thursday night, slept for six hours and got up at the crack of dawn to start three days of intensive training in rhino calf nursing.

I fetched Elaine from Hoedspruit airport that afternoon. She was a tall, dark-haired young woman, and despite the rings of exhaustion under her eyes after twenty-four hours of travelling, she insisted I take her to Thabo straight away.

'I hope he remembers me,' she murmured.

She slipped into his *boma* while I stood at the fence and watched.

'Thabo! Hello, boy,' she called.

His head shot up and he bolted towards her, squealing in delight, little legs motoring like pistons. He crashed into her and knocked her off her feet.

'Thabo, Thabo,' she laughed. 'You've grown, you thuglet. Get off me!'

They say humans never forget their first love. Neither do little rhinos.

Two days later, we were up at daybreak to start the long trek home. Elaine prepared Thabo's favourite milk formula and placed it in a bowl inside his travel crate. He scampered inside without any fuss and off we went. His first human family waved us goodbye, in tears even though they knew this was his best chance of becoming a true bush rhino. The responsibility of helping him become the wild animal he was born to be was now ours.

A violent storm thundered around us as we crept along in the slow lane, barely able to see the road ahead in the rain.

We stopped under cover of a garage to feed him after four hours. Elaine shook her head when she saw that the only way into the crate was through a hatch in the roof.

'I'll never be able to pull myself out again,' she protested.

'It's okay. I'll go,' offered Pieter.

'But he doesn't know you. What if he won't take the bottle from you?' she fretted.

'You'll be right there to talk to him through the bars and reassure him,' I said.

Pieter lowered himself into the crate and Elaine passed him Thabo's milk bottle. Food was food for this rhino calf, and he slurped the bottle dry then banged his head against Pieter's leg for more.

'Just look at him. He's not the slightest bit bothered,' Elaine said proudly.

Just before the second feed, gale-force winds ripped the tarpaulin off Thabo's crate. We stopped as soon as we found a safe turn-off and ran to the back of the vehicle to see how he was. He looked at us quizzically. *What's all the fuss?* He was such a little trooper.

Every time we stopped for petrol, Thabo drew a crowd. People expect deep grunts from an animal his size, not toy-like sounds, and they were astounded when they saw the noises weren't coming from a puppy or a piglet but from a rather large rhino calf.

The rain was so bad that it became dangerous to negotiate the potholes and roadworks, so we reset the GPS to take us a different way. Bad mistake. Two hundred kilometres later, we realized it was routing us via Swaziland. No problem for us but a big problem for Thabo, who didn't have a wildlife passport that authorized an endangered species to leave the country.

'But we only want to drive through,' I pleaded with the border police.

'No permit, no entry.'

Bureaucracy is bureaucracy and we had no choice but to backtrack. Sixteen exhausting hours later, we arrived at Thula Thula to a welcome committee of rangers, curious guests and a very worried Lawrence. I collapsed into his arms.

'We made it.'

He held me tight. 'Well done. I knew you'd do it.'

Next challenge was getting Thabo out of the crate. His bum faced the door and he had no intention of doing a U-turn or walking out backwards. Food to the rescue. Elaine rustled up another bottle and used it to coax him down the ramp.

'Dinner time,' she cajoled. 'Come and see your new home.'

He followed his bottle out of the crate and stared dozily at the crowd of smiling but unfamiliar faces around him. Elaine knelt next to him and plopped the teat in his mouth. He closed his eyes and drank.

Tears of fatigue and relief rolled down my cheeks. Our first rescue calf was home.

Thabo chose that moment to shrug off his wooziness and run off, heading straight for the dangerously high bank of the Nseleni River. Elaine dashed after him.

'Thabo, *no!*' she yelled.

'Stop him!' I screamed.

Pieter and a second ranger sprinted after them. The great thing about South African men is that they know how to rugby tackle. They almost caught him but he was also South African, *and* in the mood for a game with the boys, because he wriggled free, dragging them through the mud behind him. Elaine darted off to fetch his bottle.

'Thabo, look what I've got,' she called, waving it in the air.

He stopped dead in his tracks, left the rangers sprawled in the mud, and trotted back to her, happily following his bottle into his new sleeping quarters, a room attached to the lodge's conference centre.

A young calf needs night-time feeds and comfort from his caregiver, so I had made arrangements for them to share a room. There were soft blankets on the floor for him and a comfy bed with the same white cotton sheets our guests used for Elaine. Not very practical of me. I had a lot to learn about looking after baby rhinos.

The first night, Thabo and Elaine were so exhausted that they fell asleep instantly. It was a good sign, and from that night, as long as Elaine was close by, he was a happy little camper. She knew from experience that he always woke up at 5 a.m., and he was so reliable that she never set an alarm. If she didn't wake up, he squealed and squealed until she did. If she pretended to be asleep, he nudged her with his snout, and if *that* didn't work, he balanced his front legs on the bed and rested his head on her stomach.

'Nothing like a heavy rhino head to force me out of bed,' she grinned. 'And he knows it'll get me up.'

On a particularly chilly morning, Elaine was still buried under her duvet and Thabo decided enough was enough. His mum was right there, so why wasn't he getting a cuddle? He heaved himself up on the bed with her. Elaine woke with a jolt on a broken bed with a very happy rhino calf snuffling his face into hers. He curled up next to her and, for once, allowed her an extra long lie-in.

Elaine never bothered with the bed again and slept on the mattress on the ground, even though she knew that uninterrupted sleep would become a thing of the past. They fought for bed space and blankets most nights and I eventually replaced her white cotton sheets with ones that didn't show the dirt quite as easily.

Looking after Thabo was better than a gym workout. He hated anything to move while he was being fed, not even a twitching toe, and Elaine quickly perfected the leap-on-table manoeuvre to get out of his way. Two hundred kilos of irritable rhino calf packs a punch. The only way to get rid of some of his exuberant toddler energy was to take him for a run. He gambolled after her like a puppy, and whenever they passed a cluster of trees he hurtled towards the closest one and hid behind it. *I can't see you so you can't see me.* Of course, she ignored the huge rump sticking out from behind the tree and played along.

His favourite place in the world – after her bed – was his wallow pool.

One minute he would be grazing quietly, the next he would zoom across the enclosure and throw himself into the mud, back legs kicking to churn up the sludge. The muckier the better. Up he scrambled and over he keeled, splashing and cavorting and peering at us through happy mud-caked eyes. You didn't have to be an animal expert to know that rhino boy loved his mud – something we encouraged because mud is crucial for a rhino's health. It's a natural sunblock, stops them from overheating and helps prevent insect bites.

Like human kids, Thabo did the opposite of what Elaine wanted him to do, and going up onto the lodge deck to say hello to guests eating breakfast was one of her big no-nos. One bump of his clumsy rump and a table would be on its side, scattering scrambled eggs and toast everywhere.

Most mornings, the two of them walked past the veranda without a hitch, but if his ears perked up and there was a spring in his step, Elaine knew trouble was brewing in Thaboland.

'Don't even think about it,' she warned.

He pretended to be on his best behaviour and ignored the deck steps but she spotted his ears turning into mini satellite dishes and jumped in front of him to distract him. He flew into a U-turn and bolted up the steps. It was too late for her to stop him. You can't negotiate with a determined little rhino in full flight.

The last time he ducked behind her and up the deck steps, he tried to headbutt his reflection in the glass doors and shattered them into a million pieces. Broken chairs and tables are one thing, but broken glass was too dangerous, and from that day a gate went up and ended his escapades on the deck.

'I think he's bored,' Elaine said. 'He needs a buddy.'

Bush play dates aren't a phone call away, so we were thrilled when Moholoholo Rehabilitation Centre said they had a female orphan ready to be rehomed.

'They're about the same age so it should be easy to introduce them to each other. She's not quite ready for release yet, but if all goes well, we can relocate her by the end of the year,' promised the manager.

My French romantic streak went into overdrive. I saw Thabo falling in love. I saw babies. I was going to be a rhino granny!

Christmas 2012, Thabo received the best present of his life – little Ntombi. Alyson, her main caregiver, had no intention of letting her young charge leave without her, so she packed her bags and came along too. Not only did Thabo get a new friend for Christmas, he also got a new mum to take over from Elaine, who had returned to England.

Ntombi had been a victim of poaching when she was only five months old. Her mother was butchered in the Kruger National Park and the poor little thing saw everything. I hate to think of the horrific memories she carried with her. When she first arrived at Moholoholo she was petrified of the humans who were trying to save her life and charged everyone who came close. She was so aggressive that she had to be fed through gaps in the fence, but with love and patience she slowly learned to trust her new two-legged family.

This is why rehabilitation centres are so important. They are safe havens where distressed and injured orphans can overcome their poaching trauma and grow into well-balanced rhinos.

The day Ntombi came to Thula Thula, we put her into the enclosure next to Thabo, with only a strong picket fence between them. I held my breath to see what he would do. He ignored her! Monsieur grazed, wallowed and snoozed, and completely ignored the young demoiselle next door. My matchmaking dream had failed.

But he didn't play hard to get for very long, or maybe curiosity got the better of him, because he sidled up to her *boma* and studied her with great interest.

'Go, my boy,' I urged. 'Start with a little hello.'

Ntombi eyed him for a few seconds then turned her back on him, clearly giving him the cold shoulder. Intrigued, Thabo trotted along the fence and rested his face against it. Ntombi looked at him over her shoulder and kept eating. After a few coquettish glances, she relented and scampered towards him. He pushed his nose between the poles. She walked right up to him and snuffled his snout.

'They're kissing!' I laughed triumphantly.

3

Poaching is war

Thabo and Ntombi became an inseparable couple over the years, so it didn't surprise me in the least when Promise radioed that Ntombi wasn't allowing anyone near Thabo. She knew he was injured and she was keeping him safe.

'How will the vet treat his gunshot wounds if she's chasing everyone away from him?' I asked Alyson and Promise.

'He may have to dart both of them,' Alyson replied. 'You'll have to decide with Mike when he gets here.'

Lawrence had always handled animal emergencies and I had no clue what to do. I glanced at my phone. Still no call from Mike. In a couple of hours it would be dark and too late to attempt treatment. I was shocked that the poachers had the gall to breach our electric fence in broad daylight. They hadn't even bothered to use silencers. Ever since Thabo and Ntombi were old enough to leave the safety of the orphanage to be free rhinos in the reserve, they had been protected by armed guards. Perhaps the poachers knew that Lawrence had just died and assumed that security would have dropped? I felt helpless and completely out of my depth.

'Please take me to see Thabo,' I said to Promise.

'Not a good idea, Françoise. Ntombi's too stressed and

another vehicle will make it worse,' he warned. 'Alyson's doing her best to calm her from the safety of the 4×4.'

'How is he? Can you see how badly hurt he is?'

'There's a lot of blood but Ntombi still won't let us close, not even with Alyson here. The problem is that the damn hyenas have smelled blood and are pestering him. Here, speak to Alyson,' he said, passing the phone to her.

She was in a state. 'I shouldn't have left them.'

'Protecting them isn't your job, and anyway, you can't be with them all the time,' I said firmly. 'Poachers don't give a damn, and if they weren't put off by the guards, you being there would have made no difference.'

'I should have been more alert,' she agonized. 'Just before I left, they both stopped eating and looked out into the distance as if they'd heard something. I bet those bastards were already there, watching us. How could I have missed that?'

'There were two armed men looking after them,' I repeated. 'If *they* couldn't stop the attack, you couldn't have either. How is he?'

Her voice broke. 'Just standing there, not moving. Spooked and in shock.'

'Let me get off the phone in case Mike's trying to get through. I'll call you as soon as I hear from him.'

I sank back into my chair in despair. Thabo and Ntombi had been doing so well on their own. About a year ago, Alyson and the rangers had started the long process of familiarizing them with the bush. They took them out on daytime walks to teach them where the watering holes were and to help them discover bush smells, vegetation and animals that they would encounter. Every night they were brought back to the safety of the *boma*, until one evening they didn't want to return. Nerve-wracking for us, but we knew it was a healthy sign and time to let them roam free. Alyson still spent a lot of time with them in the bush to make sure they were okay, and I shuddered at the danger she had been in.

I paced about the room. How would I pay the vet fees? What if Thabo died? First Lawrence, now Thabo. I'm usually good in a crisis, but I couldn't get my thoughts straight and still couldn't get my head around the fact that armed men had come into the reserve to kill Thabo and Ntombi. I only realized much later how naive that was. You can't patrol forty-five kilometres of fencing every minute of the day and night. When Lawrence was alive, security took up a huge chunk of his time. He had been closely involved with patrols, snare and fence monitoring, and dealing with all the poaching incidents. Connie, my security manager at the time, was a retired policeman who had been excellent at following instructions from Lawrence but who crumbled under the pressure of coordinating security on his own.

I've never felt more insecure and uncertain in my life. I didn't know where to start or even how to direct Connie and his security team on what to do.

Gypsy, my tiny poodle, was at my feet, panting in the heat. I felt her big black eyes on me and stroked her absent-mindedly, checking my phone. Still nothing from Mike. Gypsy didn't give up. She has a way of staring at me without making a sound that always reaches me. I looked up, gazed into her eyes. Her love touched my soul. My girl knew something was wrong.

'Ah, my Gypsy,' I sighed. 'What are we going to do?'

She had taken over as lodge princess after Bijou died of old age in 2010, but she was a gentler and humbler little poodle, a real people's princess. I had fallen in love with her when she was nothing more than a tiny ball of fur with huge black eyes that followed me around as I walked amongst the cages of our local SPCA. She shows me her gratitude every single day for having chosen her over her brothers and sisters.

I picked her up and held her against me. She licked my face to tell me I wasn't alone and that she was there for me. I buried my face in her fur, fighting back tears. She snuggled deeper into my neck. I felt her warm breath on my skin and wished I could stay in her sweet embrace forever.

But I couldn't. I had an animal in trouble and I couldn't sit back and do nothing.

'Let's get to work,' I whispered and carried her with me to the office.

She sat on the chair at the other side of my desk and kept a watchful eye on me while I drowned my anguish about Thabo in being busy.

Top priority was bolstering security in case the poachers returned. I couldn't run the risk of pulling our existing guards away from their patrol areas, so I phoned the security company Lawrence used for emergencies and they promised to dispatch two extra armed men in the morning. We weren't off the hook by a long shot because I had only enough money for them to stay for one month, but it was a start. I would protect Thabo and Ntombi even if it bankrupted me. They would not be killed on my watch.

Mike Toft called at last with the bad news that he was in the middle of another poaching crisis and wouldn't get to us that day. I told him the rangers had seen Thabo take a few steps.

'That's good news. If he's walking and not in obvious pain then the bullet probably didn't damage any bones,' he said. 'He won't be comfortable but it doesn't sound life-threatening. I'll be there first thing in the morning. Keep him safe until then.'

Our rangers aren't usually involved in security operations, which is why we employ guards who are specifically trained for this dangerous work, but they refused to leave Thabo and Ntombi and wanted to be part of their protection team.

'The guards need our help,' Vusi insisted.

Alyson was desperate to join them too, but I was worried about her safety and talked her out of it. The poachers hadn't managed to get the horns they had come for and I was terrified they would return. No one slept a wink that night. Thabo and Ntombi were skittish and didn't want the rangers close to them, so the men tried hard to give them space while still keeping them safely within eyeshot. Thabo eventually lay down but Ntombi stayed vigilant and spent most of her time chasing off hyenas. Rhinos have terrible eyesight but a superb sense of smell, so Ntombi knew these small but dangerous predators had arrived long before the rangers did, and became so distraught, snorting and stress-shrieking, that the men stepped in and helped her chase them off. By 6 a.m., two ex-military men arrived to reinforce our security. They walked bolt upright and their restless eyes constantly scanned their surroundings. What a relief. An hour later, Dr Mike Toft arrived. He immediately darted Thabo while Alyson and the rangers kept Ntombi at a safe distance.

'It's a flesh wound,' he announced.

Alyson radioed the news to me. 'The bullet missed the bone by millimetres.'

I will always be grateful that those poachers were such useless marksmen.

Good came out of this terrible attack, because it spurred me on to launch our own rhino fund. I realized that without money, my animals weren't safe and that having our own fundraising organization was the only way I could be sure always to have emergency cash on hand. Money flowed in, enough to pay the extra guards for more than a month *and* to buy extra weapons and security equipment. I hate guns, but poaching is a war and the only way to fight it is by being prepared for the worst – and that means being armed.

I will never forget those ghastly twenty-four hours after Thabo was shot, but they helped me to define the purpose of my life without Lawrence and I understood with such clarity that the mantle of protecting Thula Thula's wildlife had become mine, and mine alone.

4

Magic money tree

I often gaze out into the bush and can't believe how much meeting Lawrence changed my life. I was thirty-three and in London for a trade show. It was a freezing Friday in January and I was standing in the taxi queue outside the Cumberland Hotel, running out of time to get to my ten o'clock appointment at the Earls Court Arena. I rearranged my scarf against the wind, buried my hands in my coat pockets and hoped for a taxi miracle.

The hotel porter tapped me on the shoulder.

'Excuse me, ma'am. Would you mind sharing a cab with a guest going to Earls Court?' he asked, pointing to the back of the queue.

I saw a big man with red hair dressed in white summer trousers and a blue plastic windbreaker. I leant forward to have a better look and shook my head. I wasn't in the mood for tourists.

The porter was startled by my un-British manners but continued valiantly to search for someone more gracious. My rudeness didn't go unpunished, because half an hour later I was still standing there. Eventually I gave up and went back into the hotel to warm up, cursing my luck at being in London during its worst winter in fifty years. Who should be crossing the lobby at the same time? The tourist. He looked at me in amusement. I was mortified and said the first thing that came into my head.

'You look like a foreigner in need of help. I'll show you how to take the tube to Earls Court if you like. It'll be the quickest way to get there in this weather.'

If he thought it was funny being called a foreigner by someone speaking in a French accent, he hid it well.

'Sure,' he said. 'I just need to make a quick phone call.'

A bit of a cheek but I had been rude enough, so I kept quiet and surprised myself by agreeing to wait. We eventually headed for Marble Arch tube station and fought our way down the steps with everyone else caught out by the weather. I was worried I would lose him in the crowd but his bright-blue jacket turned out to be a useful beacon. His South African shoulders were just as useful and he easily jostled us to the right platform. We even managed to find seats. I discovered that he was in London on business and that the only touristy thing about him was that he had flown in from Florida the day before.

'Bad timing to arrive in this weather,' I bantered.

'You can say that again. I can't stand it. Where I come from, it never drops below fifteen degrees, not even in winter.'

He explained that he was meeting an exhibitor about a revolutionary product called Aquaboy, designed by a surfer to save people from drowning. It was worn on the wrist like a watch and, as long as you had the presence of mind to yank it while a ten-foot wave tossed you about like a rag doll, it would open like an underwater parachute and pull you to the surface.

I thought it was brilliant and it was my first glimpse of the passionate visionary he was. Only a mad South African could come to snowbound London to market a surfing gadget.

He fell silent and I realized he looked really ill. I wondered what was wrong but didn't want to ask. So there I was, sitting next to a strangely dressed man who looked seasick. He explained afterwards that he'd had a nasty hangover after being badly roasted by a nightclub comedian because he was South African. In 1987, apartheid still existed and white South Africans weren't very welcome abroad. Afterwards, he had almost frozen to death trying to find a cab back to the hotel. No wonder he looked queasy.

I knew nothing about his country and was curious to hear more, so to keep the conversation going I asked if he liked jazz.

'I love it,' he replied, quite eagerly for someone so sick. 'Do you know any of the jazz clubs here in London?'

'I'm going to one later with friends. Why don't you join us?'

We met in the hotel lobby at nine that evening. He had changed into jeans and a patchwork leather jacket, not really suitable for Ronnie Scott's, but I ignored my fashion alarm bells. His stories about life in South Africa fascinated me. He was a born salesman and I'm pretty sure he knew exactly what he was doing, because in the bone-biting chill of London, his country sounded like heaven.

Once back in Paris, I wondered if I would ever see him again and was quite taken aback when he announced he was coming to visit. Flying 10,000 kilometres for a date was typical of him – bold, impulsive and never letting anything stop him.

The glacial weather that had brought London to its knees when we met had eased and it was a cosy zero degrees when he landed at Charles de Gaulle.

'It's freezing here. Can't we go somewhere warmer?' he moaned after a few days.

'How about Venice? It's a boiling hot thirteen degrees there,' I joked.

'Perfect. Let's go by train.'

'The only direct trains are night trains and they'll take forever. It'll be much quicker to fly,' I protested.

'Where's your sense of fun? Have you ever been on a night train?'

'No, but—'

'All the more reason to do it. What do we care if it takes forever? It'll be fun and we'll be together!'

Twelve hours by train versus two hours by plane wasn't my idea of fun, but he was so enthusiastic I couldn't say no. The next thing, we were in a taxi weaving our way through rush hour traffic to Gare de Lyon. At the station, Lawrence came face to face with Parisian attitude at its worst.

'*Hors de question*,' snapped the woman at the ticket office. 'You're too late. The train is about to leave and you'll never get to the platform on time.'

'Tell her we want to try,' Lawrence whispered.

I persuaded her to sell us two tickets and off we sprinted to platform 3, getting there just as the train pulled away. Lawrence sped after it, frantically waving his arms, probably hoping the driver would take pity on two hopeless romantics trying to get to Venice. We felt so stupid and disappointed, but then we caught sight of each other – out of breath on a deserted platform – and burst out laughing.

'Let's go and get a refund,' he said.

'From that grumpy bag? She'll *never* agree!'

'Watch me.'

Not only did he get our money back with his two words of French, he even squeezed a smile out of her. I soon learned that Lawrence always got what he wanted.

A few months later, I boarded an Air France flight to South Africa and discovered that he hadn't given me a sales pitch at all. His country was every bit as breathtaking as he had described it, and I loved it from the moment the hot humid air clung to my cheeks when I stepped onto the steaming tarmac.

'We're going straight into the bush to a friend's game farm,' he said.

I had no clue what he meant. 'Bush?'

'You foreigners call it *going on safari*,' he teased.

We drove through the lush hills of Zululand, with sugar cane plantation after sugar cane plantation on my left and the surging Indian Ocean on my right. It was like being in an exotic postcard. Eventually we left the coast and swerved inland, negotiated the chaotic streets of Empangeni, and turned off onto a dirt road through a rural village where barefoot children, dogs and cattle shared the dusty track with us. It was different from anything I had ever seen. We stopped outside the gates of Windy Ridge.

'Welcome to my world,' Lawrence said proudly.

The guard let us in and Lawrence insisted we immediately go on a game drive.

'It's the best time of the day,' he said.

I didn't like the look of the *bakkie* – pickup truck – he wanted me to get into.

'*That's* supposed to keep us safe from wild animals?' I groaned.

'Have a bit of faith in me,' he smiled. 'I've done this hundreds of times. The animals see us as part of the vehicle and won't bother us in the slightest.'

'What about the lions?'

'There aren't any here. Come on, hop in! You'll love it.'

He was so confident that I decided to trust him. We juddered along a badly eroded track and parked near a waterhole just as six giraffes arrived. They were as tall as a two-storey building and walked with the slow, swaying steps of dancers.

'They're beautiful, so graceful,' I murmured.

'Don't be fooled. They can be very violent.'

I thought he was joking and laughed.

'I'm dead serious. Their necks are their weapons – two metres of rock-hard muscle that they wallop each other with.'

He added that a group of giraffes was called a *tower of giraffes*. I searched his face to see if he was pulling my leg, but no, he wasn't.

I had never seen wild animals before, not even in a zoo, so every animal I saw was a new experience for me. The first rhinos I ever set eyes on were at Windy Ridge. Four enormous prehistoric-looking beasts grazed about ten metres away from us. They seemed peaceful enough, but their size and horns terrified me.

Lawrence and Nana always had a special relationship.

Lawrence and myself with our chefs Tom (*left*) and Winnie (*right*).

Baby Thabo next to Elaine's bed the day he arrived at Thula Thula.
I soon learned that white sheets were not a sensible option.

Thabo and Ntombi kiss.

Our veterinary nurse Alyson with Thabo and Ntombi.

Me and our ranger Johnny with Baby Thula, Nandi's calf,
who was too ill to survive in the wild.

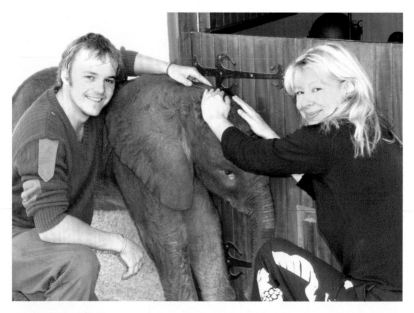

The herd at Lawrence's beloved Mkhulu Dam.

At Mkhulu Dam after scattering Lawrence's ashes.

Mabula with his alpha male role model, Gobisa.

Thabo was shot by poachers in broad daylight.

Baby Tom – the elephant in my kitchen! – after she became separated from the herd.

Baby Tom being fed by Tom, Shireen and Alyson.

The main house.

Rhino horn poisoning with the local vet, Dr Mike Toft.

Mabula doing yoga!

Our breeding colonies of white-backed vultures are under threat, as their brains are highly prized for *muthi*, traditional medicine.

Gobisa and Frankie cuddle.

Mkhulu Dam during the 2014 drought.

'You'll never guess what a group of rhinos is called,' he said.

I shook my head.

'A *crash* of rhinos,' he grinned.

If he thought that would make me less nervous, he was wrong. I crouched down in the *bakkie*.

'I think we should leave. They don't like us being here.'

'Nonsense. Look at them. They're just eating,' he replied.

'What if they attack us?'

'Why would they? They've got better things to do than hassle us.'

'But if they *did* attack, is this truck faster than them?'

He must have wondered why on earth he had brought a city girl to a game reserve.

Thirty years later, I know much more about rhinos and I understand that while they can be unpredictable, they usually don't attack unless provoked.

The biggest difference between then and now is poaching. Back then, it didn't really exist. There were no armed guards, no GPS tracking collars on rhinos, no surveillance drones flying over reserves. Being in the bush was simpler, more primitive and pure.

In those days, the rhino population was actually growing, thanks to Dr Ian Player, an internationally renowned conservationist who was a close friend and mentor to both of us. He spearheaded Operation Rhino, an ambitious initiative aimed at repopulating reserves with the southern white rhino to broaden their gene pool. It was a huge success and pulled that particular species of rhino back from the brink of extinction. What an impact our friend made, and if he were still alive, he would be devastated to see how poaching is wiping them out today. If rhinos continue to be killed at the current rate, there won't be a single one left in twenty years.

Everything was so different in South Africa. The people were warm and welcoming, the autumn weather was a sweltering thirty degrees, even the air smelled different. The smoggy pollution of Paris felt like a million miles away. I was hooked. Not only by the larger-than-life man creeping into my heart but also by the African wilderness that was stirring my soul.

Lawrence took me on that first game drive and I never looked back.

A year after we met, I gave up my job and my chic Montparnasse apartment and moved to South Africa. My work was with a chamber of commerce in northern France, and as head of international trading my role was to attract foreign investment. I travelled a lot, dealt with high-powered executives, and it never occurred to me to do anything else. Needless to say, my friends thought I was out of my mind throwing everything away to go to a country full of racists, which was quite ironic coming from the French.

Of course, I hadn't yet seen what life in South Africa was really about. I had met a wonderful, funny, crazy man living in a magnificent country and I wanted to be with him. It was that simple.

One day, Lawrence took me to Umdloti Beach on the north coast. Soft yellow sand stretched for miles and the sea was as calm as a pond, rolling onto the beach in gentle ripples.

At the entrance was a sign: *Net Blankes*: Whites Only. I frowned and scanned the beach.

'Lawrence, *why* are there no black people here?'

'It's apartheid,' he grimaced.

I knew it existed, but actually to see it written was so strange. After that, I saw the signs everywhere. At bus stops, post offices, even on benches. I had come across racial discrimination before in my travels but never like this, and it quickly crept into all sorts of unexpected corners of my life.

Housekeeping was never my strong point and I always had someone to do the cleaning, even in Paris. So when Lawrence and I lived in our first apartment, years before we bought Thula Thula, I quickly employed a young Zulu woman called Beauty to help us.

'Where are my plates and knives and forks?' she asked me on her first day.

'I'm sorry?' I frowned.

I learned that black domestics never shared eating utensils with the white families they worked for. What a shock. I showed Beauty where I kept our crockery and cutlery.

'What we use, you use,' I said simply.

Beauty was often bewildered by my cooking, especially when I prepared something French like snails in garlic sauce, but Zulu culture is very polite and she never said no to anything I made for her. Only years later, I realized that the strangeness of us working together was probably as great for her as it was for me.

My Thula Thula staff always get worried when they see me being creative in the kitchen at the lodge.

'*What* are you concocting now?' Mabona complains.

She was one of the first village girls I employed back in 2000 and has blossomed from a timid, determined-to-learn teenager into a confident young woman who has become like a daughter to me and who runs our lodge with humour and efficiency. She's beautiful, smart, sings like an angel and never hesitates to tell me what she thinks.

'Get ready to be a guinea pig,' I threaten playfully.

Which is exactly what they're concerned about. I once made crocodile meat curry with a dark chocolate sauce and although they tolerated my experiment, I saw the horror in their eyes: *what* is she making us eat now? Promise and Mabona are by far my most adventurous tasters and always game to try something different, even if they can't identify what I've put on their plates. They're also my most valuable critics because they're never scared to tell me what they like or don't like, or give me pointers on how to improve a dish.

'Tell me about your name,' I once asked Beauty.

She smiled shyly but didn't reply.

'Is there a story behind it?' I pressed.

'My first boss couldn't pronounce my Zulu name,' she shrugged.

I was baffled that Beauty wasn't her real name.

'It's what my Zulu name *Buhle* means in English, and Beauty was easier for that boss to pronounce,' she explained. 'After that, I just stayed with it.'

I called her Buhle from that day and her story jolted me into signing up for Zulu lessons. Unfortunately, no matter how hard I studied, my French accent did terrible things to Zulu and everyone begged me to stop trying.

'Your Zulu is *technically* good, much better than Lawrence's, but it really hurts our ears,' Mabona grinned. 'Rather speak to us in English.'

I had loved working in the competitive Parisian business world and when I arrived in South Africa in 1987, I was looking forward to getting stuck into something challenging, but I quickly saw that business in the tropics was different. Especially in Durban, where everyone is laid-back and more interested in the waves than what's happening on the stock exchange.

However it was a perfect environment for creativity, so I decided to try my hand at fashion and looked around for a school where I could learn how to design and sew clothes. I found one in downtown Durban and asked the woman at the front desk if they had classes for me on Mondays.

'Sorry, that day's for Indians.'

'What about Tuesdays?' I asked.

'That's for black people,' she frowned.

'Do you have a day for French people?' I asked crossly, convinced she was making it up because she didn't want me.

I finally joined a school run by an Indian man where I was the only white person. When the course finished, I invited my new friends to our apartment in Durban North for a graduation party with a Bastille Day theme. My white neighbours were quite surprised but they probably figured I was a mad foreigner and never complained.

I bought an industrial sewing machine and brought Buhle on board, teaching her everything I knew about sewing. We were a fantastic team, and later that year I sold my first fashion and accessory ranges to chi-chi boutiques in Cape Town and Johannesburg. Looking back, I was as mad as Lawrence. We both believed we could do anything we put our minds to.

One evening he came home with the news that his friend was selling Windy Ridge. He unfolded a map and circled the area around the hunting lodge. I looked at him, not sure what he was up to, but the fire in his eyes warned me that there was probably a hare-brained scheme cooking.

'It's my old stomping ground,' he sighed. 'And everything around it is wild tribal land.'

'Yes . . . ?'

'Let's buy it and turn it into a massive conservation area.'

'But we don't know anything about animals or game reserves!'

'You didn't know anything about making clothes.'

'How on earth will we pay for it?'

'We'll only buy Windy Ridge, the rest will stay tribal land. Don't you see? The local community should be part of it. We'll do this *with* them. We'll form a huge nature reserve, create jobs *and* help wildlife at the same time.'

'We're not exactly rolling in cash, Lolo.'

'That's the least of our worries. We'll find some,' he scoffed.

I couldn't help laughing every time he said he was going to *find* money. When I grew up, I was taught that you *earned* money, and I always teased him that he was hiding a magic money tree from me.

We sold our beautiful home, he talked the banks into giving us a hefty loan, and Windy Ridge became ours –

1,500 hectares of pristine bush, a rustic camp with four huts, and some very skittish game.

We did two things immediately: ended hunting and changed the reserve's name.

People had hunted there since King Shaka's days, and between gunshots and testosterone, much of the wildlife had been killed. The name had to reflect our vision of turning the killing fields into a sanctuary. We chose *Thula Thula* because it expresses the tranquillity and peace we wanted to offer the animals. In Zulu, the word *thula* – quiet – is usually said in a hushed voice: *shhhhh, thula, be still, my baby is sleeping*. It's a tender little word best known from the Zulu lullaby, *Thula Baba*.

Our next challenge was figuring out how to make our dream happen.

It's what I loved about life with Lawrence. There was never a dull moment. He wanted to make a difference and we did. The word *can't* wasn't part of our vocabulary. If we didn't know how to do something, we found out.

At night, we sat on the stoep – veranda – and soaked in the silence, with our dogs, Max, Tess and Bijou, at our feet. No throb of cars, no aeroplanes overhead, no screeching alarm sirens. And after a while, the silence talked to us and the air filled with the grunts, squeals, whistles and chirrups of animals, birds and insects.

And gunshots.

We had banned hunting but were powerless against poaching.

To this day, it's my biggest challenge. Rhino horn has become more valuable than gold and platinum. It's the new status medicine in the Far East. Some claim it heals cancer, others use it as a hangover fix, and men believe it helps virility. What nonsense. Rhino horn is made of keratin, the same as fingernails. These people pay top dollar for a product they grow on their own hands.

Lawrence and I had no idea that poaching would be such a big problem, but it didn't stop us wanting to create the biggest conservation area that KwaZulu-Natal had ever seen. It just came with a bigger price tag than we could afford.

We were still figuring out how to raise money when Lawrence received the life-changing call from Dr Marion Garaï about a small herd of elephants that was causing havoc on a reserve near the Kruger National Park. Money was tight and we had only two weeks to build a thirty-two-kilometre electric fence, plus a *boma* big enough for nine disturbed and angry elephants.

Lawrence talked to his magic money tree and then threw himself into getting the required infrastructure ready at breakneck speed. Our dream became very real, very fast. It was nail-biting, right up to the very last moment.

Shortly before the herd was due to arrive, Lawrence had to leave on an emergency trip to Germany, and while he was gone I received a call from the manager of the reserve that owned the elephants.

'You have to take the herd sooner. We can't keep them for another day.'

'You can't do that. We're not ready!'

'If they don't leave tomorrow, we'll have to shoot them.'

'They can't come now. Lawrence is overseas,' I said quietly. He was silent.

'Could you give us until after the weekend? He'll be back by then. I can't possibly handle their arrival on my own,' I begged.

He wasn't happy but he relented.

'They leave on Monday. Not a day later.'

That gave us five days. Enough time for Lawrence to get back home to finish the fence and deal with the last hurdle of getting it approved by the conservation authorities.

An hour before the inspectors arrived, Lawrence noticed that the electrical wires had been attached to the wrong side of the fence.

'If they pick it up, they'll never okay the bloody thing,' he said in despair.

I was stunned. We were ready and now the herd might be shot after all.

'Should I try and get the reserve to delay sending the elephants?' I suggested.

'It's probably too late. They'll be on their way to us already. Let's just hope our herd has guardian angels.'

I buried my face in my hands. The only reason the inspectors were here was to check for mistakes and weaknesses in the fence. They would never sanction it if the electrics were wrong.

They held the herd's death warrant in their hands.

5

Reality strikes

I paced up and down our veranda, checking my watch and wondering why the inspectors were taking so long. It couldn't be good news. We were desperate to save the herd and now through sheer bad luck and an electrician's carelessness, they would end up being shot.

My mobile phone rang. Lawrence.

'They rejected it, didn't they?' I said.

'Crack open the champers, Frankie. Our herd just won their passport to a new life.'

I yelled in delight. The inspectors hadn't picked up that anything was wrong, and the minute they left, Lawrence and his men fixed the wiring.

We were ready for Nana and her herd at last.

Monday morning, my phone rang. I grimaced when I saw who it was. The owner of the herd. The elephants were supposed to arrive that night. Had something gone wrong? Had he killed them after all?

'We had some trouble with the matriarch,' he said without preamble.

'What do you mean? Is she all right?'

'I shot her.'

'You *what*?'

'She's a bloody nightmare and would have broken out of your reserve and flattened someone.'

I was speechless.

'I took out the baby too so there are only seven elephants arriving.'

'*Why*, for God's sake? We were ready for all of them, trouble or not,' I said furiously.

'That matriarch was bad news, lady. I did you guys a favour.'

I was beside myself with anger and despair. A herd's matriarch usually inherits the role from her own mother and she is their teacher, referee, keeper of memories, travel guide and bush stateswoman rolled into one. They turn to her in a crisis, the little ones learn the ways of the wild from her, and she 'negotiates' with other herds they might come across. She is their anchor and their rock.

When I told Lawrence, he exploded. Killing the matriarch went against everything we stood for. Her owner's complete indifference to shooting her is the brutal truth behind elephant culling. He thought he was helping us.

'This is bad, Frankie. Really bad,' Lawrence said. 'How the hell did he think this poor herd would cope after losing their leader? He probably shot the matriarch right in front of them.'

I began to worry about what we had taken on. The herd was already in a bad way before this and now they would be even more traumatized *and* without a leader to calm them.

'You know, Lolo,' I said quietly. 'They need us even more now. We can do this.'

'We can,' he agreed. 'And we will.'

By the time the herd arrived that stormy night, Nana had already taken over as matriarch, with a confidence that came from knowing it was a job she had to do. The rest of the elephants accepted her with the same ease, as if they knew that Mother Nature had always intended for her to be their commander in chief.

Keeping them safe was going to cost a fortune, so finding a regular source of income became our top priority.

'What if we had a really upmarket lodge?' I said to Lawrence over croissants one morning. 'Ecotourism is the way of tomorrow. It could be a way for us to have money coming in on an ongoing basis.'

'Brilliant idea. Let's do it.'

We built seven luxury chalets under the acacia and tambotie trees on the banks of the Nseleni River and opened the Elephant Safari Lodge in June 2000. I was bursting with pride.

'How are the bookings?' Lawrence asked at the end of every day.

'Not good,' I said glumly. 'Two rooms for the weekend.'

Only a handful of guests trickled through our doors. We were so naive. People don't visit places they haven't heard of, but we had no budget for marketing. We refused to give up.

'The chalets are great. Your food is fantastic. People will start talking,' Lawrence said.

'Maybe, but at this rate, we can't even afford staff with lodge experience.'

We did as much as we could ourselves and put the word out that we wanted to employ locals, with or without experience. The Zulu bush telegraph spread like wildfire and

by the next day a long queue of young men and women looking for work had formed outside the gate. I employed the
ones who spoke the best English and began the challenge of
teaching them about office work, dealing with guests and
cooking French dishes they had never heard of.

Lawrence handled everything to do with the reserve – he
mended fences, monitored security, improved the dirt track
network and cleared the vegetation. It was back-breaking,
relentless work. We stumbled along in a constant state of
exhaustion and were just beginning to see the fruits of our
labour when war broke out in Iraq.

'I've got to go and help,' Lawrence announced.

'What on earth do you mean?'

'I can't sit here and do nothing while they bomb the hell
out of Baghdad Zoo. *Someone* needs to rescue the animals.'

I didn't even try to talk him out of it. 'How long do you
think it'll take?'

'I'm not sure. Maybe a couple of weeks.'

He was gone for six months.

The toughest problems I faced without him were human
ones. The bush is a macho environment and Lawrence was an
alpha male, respected by the men he employed. With him
away, I was just a foreign blonde who spoke funny and who
was clueless about the bush. Instead of pulling together as a
team for the good of the animals, many took advantage.

I don't know how I survived, except that I knew that I
didn't have a choice and I got on and dealt with it. If I hadn't
been a hundred per cent behind what Lawrence was doing in
Iraq, it would have been impossible. War rarely has a con-
tingency plan for human victims, and it never has one for

animals, so while I was desperately worried for his safety, I was equally desperate for him to succeed.

Lawrence left me with a new game reserve manager who thought his job description involved playing Romeo to our young volunteer vet, the daughter of a friend in France. He was the worst kind of macho.

'That perimeter fence of ours might as well be made of dental floss,' he declared. '*Anything* can get through it. We're lucky we still have animals left.'

Rather than getting on and fixing the problem, he cracked jokes about the elephants escaping. I was still traumatized from the herd's earlier breakouts and didn't need this kind of bad news from the person supposed to be in charge of them. I was also very concerned about his behaviour towards my friend's daughter. I barely slept during the first few weeks that Lawrence was in Iraq. Satellite phone conversations with him were a nightmare. Half the time, it sounded as if he was underwater, which made discussing the problems I was having almost impossible.

In short, it was chaos without him. The rangers were undisciplined. Poachers exploited the confusion. And on top of this, several of the bull elephants were in musth – a sexual condition that causes their testosterone levels to skyrocket. They were out of control, chasing vehicles and fighting one another.

And night after night, all I saw on TV was bombs and more bombs in Baghdad.

One morning I woke up and thought, *I've had enough.*

I fired the Romeo and replaced him with Vusi, one of Lawrence's most respected rangers. He didn't really have enough experience to be reserve manager, but he was a well-built, softly spoken Zulu man with solid bush knowledge and quiet gravitas. He fixed the fence, improved security and employed new rangers. Promoting him was one of the best things I did, because when Lawrence passed away he was an irreplaceable pillar of strength.

Lawrence's stint in Baghdad was my baptism of fire in running the reserve on my own, although I didn't need to become directly involved in the conservation and animal side of things – Vusi had that covered. He and I were both very relieved when Lawrence finally came home and took control of the security staff again.

In 2012, we had twenty-three full-time guards who were supposed to watch over our animals, sweep for snares and be first responders if poachers entered the reserve, and it was a shock when problems with them surfaced so quickly after Lawrence died. I was devastated when the officer investigating the shooting of Thabo told me that they suspected an inside job.

'How is that possible?' I gasped. 'Do you know *who*?'

Officer Khuzwayo shook his head.

'Our informer only said that it was someone at Thula Thula. Probably one of the guards.'

I sat back, stunned. Could one of my staff really have tried to kill my beloved Thabo? It felt so personal. Everyone knew how important Thabo and Ntombi were to me and it crossed my mind that someone might be trying to frighten me into leaving. They obviously didn't know me, because I had no intention of going anywhere. Thula Thula was my life.

'What should I do? What if he tries again?' I asked.

'I'll let you know if I hear anything,' he promised.

I immediately called the security manager into my office.

'What's going on, Connie?' I asked.

'Could be anyone,' he replied.

'Have you had specific problems with any of the men?' I prodded.

'There's always problems,' he shrugged.

I looked into his eyes and wondered if he even cared. I didn't know what to do. Our ongoing poaching problems and my instincts told me some of the guards couldn't be relied on, but I had no way of finding out which one had betrayed me. Connie wasn't interested in taking orders from me, and I couldn't speak directly to the guards because most of them didn't speak English and my Zulu wasn't nearly good enough to tackle such a delicate subject with them.

I forced myself to take one step at a time. Snap decisions taken in panic are rarely the right ones and I certainly didn't know enough about security to risk any decisions without guidance.

'Any clue at all who could have done this?' I asked Vusi.

'There's talk it was someone on the outside with a grudge . . .' He paused, as if not wanting to worry me.

'But Officer Khuzwayo's informant said the guy was still here.'

He rubbed his thumb and forefinger together.

'You think one of our guards was *bribed*?'

'It's possible,' he nodded gravely. 'I think we should make some changes to who guards Thabo and Ntombi. Why don't you ask Connie to appoint Richard as their full-time guard and then get Richard to choose who else he wants on his team?'

It was good counsel. Richard was a tall, wiry Zulu with sun-wizened skin and wise, watchful eyes. He had worked directly with Lawrence and I knew without question that he would protect our rhinos with his life.

On top of this security chaos, I had no money. When news broke of Lawrence's passing, booking after booking was cancelled. It was as if I didn't exist and people thought Thula Thula was going to collapse without him. Cash flow dried up, made worse by administrative complications with Lawrence's estate and a huge overdraft that had grown over the years. In a flash, I was back in the frightening situation that we had been in years ago, scraping together rands and cents to survive. It's a miracle we made it through, and to this day I'm dead against credit. If I don't have the money, I don't buy it.

Lawrence was gone, I had a rhino in trouble, security men I couldn't trust, and an empty bank account.

The pressure to deliver was enormous and I struggled against the scepticism of people who didn't believe in me and who didn't think I would manage. No one said it to my face but I sensed it, and over the years some have admitted that they never thought I would cope on my own. Most thought I would go back to France. But that never crossed my mind. How could I have left the Thula Thula dream that Lawrence and I had fought so hard for? I worked with the most wonderful local people who were relying on me. They were my second family and I couldn't abandon them. I had lost a husband but they had lost a man who had been like a father to them.

And then there was our special herd and the rhinos we had raised from babies. They were my family too. It was unthinkable to abandon them.

I had a lot to learn, but tragedy and adversity have ways of opening new roads of hope and opportunity, and I slowly found my feet. There were moments when I felt I was drowning, and others when I had such clarity about what to do. I clung to the image of a ship navigating dangerous seas and was determined to survive the storm.

Vusi and I set up daily meetings to go over reserve and animal issues together and to agree on priorities. If I didn't understand something, he would patiently explain it again. All the long-standing staff members were the same. I learned so much from them during that time.

One morning, Vusi told me that the conservation authorities were coming the following week to do a game count by helicopter.

'Why?' I asked.

'It's part of their environmental research for long-term bush management.'

'Can't we just tell them how many elephants we have? Couldn't we let them know that sixteen babies have been born since Nana arrived and that we now have a total of twenty-two elephants?'

'They count *all* the game, Françoise, not only the elephants.'

'But a helicopter will terrorize them. Why don't they do it from the ground and use our Land Cruisers?'

He didn't reply, which was his gentle way of saying that there was nothing we could do.

'What actually happens?' I asked.

'The men in the helicopter count the game and report the total via radio to a land-based team who record everything.'

'What do they do with all this info?'

'It's mainly to track trends. They'll send us a report once it's done.'

I hated the idea of the animals being disturbed by the helicopter but I also knew that this kind of environmental research was invaluable for safeguarding KwaZulu-Natal's wildlife.

About a fortnight after the game count, Vusi, Alyson and I met to talk about Thabo's condition. Physically, our young rhino was healing well, and he was allowing Alyson to clean his gunshot wound every day, but emotionally, he wasn't doing well at all. He was still very traumatized and had regressed back to his baby ways, needing constant love and comfort. He lost weight, cried out at night and had become worryingly lethargic.

The day before, he had lain down at the dam edge with his face completely submerged. Rhinos can't breathe underwater and although they are quite good at holding their breath, his guard Richard was so worried about him that he had taken off his trousers and sat next to him on the bank of the dam, cradling his head on his lap until he was ready to get out. Everyone did everything they could to help him get better but it still took a good year before he was over the trauma.

Alyson left and Vusi handed me the report the conservation authorities had sent him. I frowned at his glum expression.

'Are we in trouble?'

He didn't answer. I scanned the report and stared at him.

'Too many elephants? What the hell do they mean?'

'They have strict guidelines on how many elephants can live on a reserve our size and apparently our herd has become too big for the amount of land that we have.'

I struggled to take it in. When Lawrence was still alive, we had gone through two expansions that had added 3,000 hectares to the reserve.

The first had taken place in 2008, ten years after we bought Windy Ridge, and involved land that had originally been given to the *amakhosi* – tribal leaders – but it had serious water problems which made using it for cattle grazing impossible. So when Lawrence approached the leaders about needing to increase the size of Thula Thula and suggested we create a joint conservation project, they didn't hesitate to give us the green light to drop the fence between our two properties.

Lawrence loved the magnificent bush on the new land so much that a year later, he and Vusi built Mkhulu Dam there. It's where his ashes were scattered and where his beloved Mnumzane's bones lie to this day.

Two years after the first expansion, we reached an agreement with the Robarts family to extend onto their bushland south of Thula Thula.

'Vusi, we have *three* times more land than when we started. Surely that's enough?'

'The herd's also trebled in size, Françoise.'

'What about what they say here about the alien vegetation and fire breaks?'

'It's all to do with environmental planning. We have to

clear plants that aren't indigenous and create enough space along both sides of the fence to act as a fire break.'

This was Lawrence's domain and I had no idea what to do.

'Let me think about how to handle this,' I sighed.

It turned out that there wasn't much I could do or say, and even my contact on the conservation board just repeated what was in the letter. The alien vegetation had to be removed, fire breaks had to be cleared and worst of all, he confirmed that Thula Thula wasn't big enough for our herd and that we would have to make a plan to control the numbers.

That was all well and good, but *what* plan? And *how*?

'You have two options,' the man said. 'Bring in a team to cull them, or relocate some of them.'

I ended the call in tears. Culling is just another word for killing and the thought of it sent me into utter panic. And relocation? Tear apart our elephant family? Not a chance. This herd had suffered enough. Lawrence and I hadn't spent the last thirteen years protecting them and rebuilding their trust in humans to put them through another massive trauma.

There had to be a better solution.

6

Enfant terrible

To think that Lawrence and I were once concerned that we only had three breeding females, because now here I was, faced with too many elephants!

The original three – Nana, her daughter Nandi, and feisty Frankie, who Lawrence had named after me – weren't the only ones responsible for the growth of our happy brood, because a year after they arrived we rescued a fourth female.

Dr Marion Garaï is a passionate champion for traumatized elephants. She has studied them for thirty years across several continents, and her doctorate focused on trauma in young elephants. It was thanks to her initiative and determination that Nana and her herd found peace at Thula Thula, and when she heard about an elephant that was about to be auctioned off, she didn't hesitate to take action.

'What caught my attention was that this young elephant was alone. I mean, how is that even *possible*? Where was her herd?' she lamented. 'And when I delved deeper, I was absolutely horrified to discover the poor thing had been alone for a *year*. In a big five reserve. Can you imagine the horror of that? She's only twelve.'

'How the hell did she end up on her own?' Lawrence asked.

'She was originally part of a group of seven orphans, but as they got older, they caused problems and the owner basically dumped them onto whatever reserve would take them. One was even shot, probably a paid-for hunt. She's the only one left of that bunch and now he wants to get rid of her too. I'm trying to find her a home because heaven alone knows who will buy her at the auction and what could happen to her.'

'Is she a problem elephant?'

Marion paused.

'To be honest, I don't know her, so I can't vouch for her like I could for Nana, but if she *is* causing problems, it's because she's traumatized, not because she's necessarily an aggressive elephant.'

'The thing is, if he's auctioning her, he must think she's worth something,' Lawrence groaned. 'We're still paying back the banks for the loan we took out for Nana and her herd. Is she in danger of being shot?'

'Not yet. But if a hunter bids for her at the auction . . .'

'Look, we can definitely take her, but we don't have the money to buy her.'

'Fair enough. It's good to know you'll take her if you can. At least I know I have a possible home for her. She doesn't deserve to end her life at the barrel of a gun. There *must* be a way I can raise money to buy her. I'll make some calls.'

I couldn't get this young elephant out of my mind. Twelve in elephant years is similar to twelve in human years, so for her to have been utterly alone for so long was too painful to think about. And now she was being sold and could end up anywhere, even dead. Wildlife auctions are such a gamble. There was no way of knowing who would buy her.

Marion phoned a few days later with unexpected good news. The Nature Conservation officials had denied the owner an auction permit.

'But he's still determined to sell her and is going to fight the decision, so it's not guaranteed she'll come out of this alive. But at least it gives me time. I've put out feelers to an old colleague who is part of an animal welfare organization in Zurich and he says he'll chat to his board of directors about helping us with the money.'

'I'll make sure the *boma* is ready for her,' Lawrence said.

She gave a rueful laugh.

'I wish it could be resolved that quickly, but I'm afraid it's going to take a while still. Their next board meeting is a month away and the owner may have found another buyer by then.'

'A month is a month. Why don't we do a fundraiser for her with a radio station? I'm damn sure a lot of people will want to help,' he said.

'If we could buy her ourselves, that would be fantastic. I'd better make sure her owner is okay with that.'

She phoned back, heartbroken.

'He's already sold her. Some American hunter has paid big money for her. *More* than the original asking price. We've lost her.'

We were beside ourselves. She had been a hair's breadth from being rescued.

'What if we raise enough money to match the price?'

'It's too late. She's been paid for and the hunt is scheduled for 14 February. Apparently he's in a wheelchair, so I suppose a frightened young elephant without a herd to protect her is the only way he's going to get his trophy,' she said bitterly.

Hunting is a mystery to me. How humans can want to shoot magnificent wildlife is beyond me, and the fact that the hunt was scheduled for Valentine's Day sickened me. Here was a young elephant that had lost her family, not once but twice, had been shifted from one reserve to the next and, worst of all, condemned to a solitary miserable life, and now her beautiful face was going to end up above some American's fireplace.

Lawrence phoned the radio station and cancelled the fundraiser. We moped about, wracking our brains for ideas to rescue the young elephant.

Days flew by. Only a miracle could rescue her now.

Early one morning, Lawrence's phone rang. Marion. He grimaced. Every one of her calls over the past few months had brought bad news.

Not this time.

'The reserve's hunting permit expired at the end of January,' she whooped. 'The hunt's off for now. The American had to cancel his flight, but he still wants her so the owner is reapplying for another permit.'

One step forward, two steps back, but at least for the moment we were standing still.

'He hopes to have it by early March and I'm going to try and block it,' she said.

What an angel this little abandoned elephant had in Marion! Lawrence decided to start work on the *boma* straight away.

'You never know,' he said. 'It might all come together

when we least expect it and then it would be terrible if we weren't ready for her.'

He bought a new transformer for the electrical current, and then along with Vusi and a team of workers, they fixed the fence and reinforced the gate. By the end of February, everything was done. She just needed one last miracle.

On 3 March, it came through.

Her owner's application for a new hunting permit was denied. We never found out why, and we didn't care. The youngster had been given another reprieve. Now we needed to raise the money to buy her. Quickly.

Lawrence jumped on the phone to his radio presenter friend to revive the fundraiser. Bad news. The man had resigned. We went back to the drawing board. We ran fundraising competitions ourselves, offering free weekends at Thula Thula as prizes. We sent out newsletters about the elephant's plight. Some money came in, but not enough.

'I'm going to try my friend in Zurich again,' Marion said. 'It's a long shot but you never know.'

Five minutes later she phoned back. '*I have the money!*'

Lawrence and I collapsed onto the sofa, too drained to celebrate.

Three weeks before Easter, the reserve owner received his blood money and the move was immediately scheduled for the following Monday. The sooner we got her out of there, the better. Our unhappy orphan was four days away from her new home at Thula Thula.

We didn't dare get too excited. Lawrence contacted the regional authorities to finalize her transport permit. They promised to get back to him the next day.

Midday on Wednesday, the permit was rejected.

We couldn't believe it.

'We checked up on her and found out she's trouble,' the official said. 'We have enough problems on our hands without inviting more. She'll have to go somewhere else.'

We were devastated. The money had been paid, we had been on standby for weeks and now she wasn't allowed to leave. Lawrence got into his car and went to speak to the officials face to face. If we didn't get their okay by Friday, Marion would have to cancel the transport booked for Monday, and who knew what might happen to the young elephant after that.

Unfortunately, none of us had first-hand knowledge of her, but Lawrence stuck his neck out and assured the authorities that she wasn't trouble, just traumatized, and that she would be fine once she knew she was safe. Marion risked her professional credibility and backed everything Lawrence said.

'How can you be sure your herd will accept an aggressive newcomer?' the official asked.

Now we were on safer ground. The herd had only been with us for a year but we knew they were gentle and compassionate and it hadn't crossed our minds that they wouldn't welcome her.

'Because our herd has been through what she's been through. They know the horror of having their families shot in front of them. They'll understand that she's not a threat and that she *needs* them,' Lawrence said quietly.

The official ummed and ahhed and eventually said he couldn't make the decision without his boss, who was away.

Marion was at her wits' end after eight exhausting months of fighting for an elephant she had never met. If only that little calf knew how hard everyone was fighting for her life.

'The owner won't keep her past Easter,' she reported to us in tears. 'My colleagues think I'm mad and that I should just let her be hunted so she's put out of her misery.'

We refused to give up. Between the three of us, we harassed every living person we knew in conservation to help. Late on Friday afternoon, a fax stuttered out of the machine. I jumped up and watched it slide out.

The permit. Approved.

We didn't dare breathe out. This little elephant was too jinxed. Would she really be getting onto that articulated truck on Monday?

With only a few minutes left before businesses shut for the weekend, Marion finalized insurance for the relocation. That evening, we had every bit of paper, every single stamp, every last signature that we needed.

But our worries were far from over.

The elephant had to endure a twelve-hour journey from the reserve in Gauteng to us in Zululand. She was healthy and strong, but after everything she had been through, would she survive the stress?

She made it through and arrived at Thula Thula at last. Her life of hell was over.

We put her straight into the *boma* and Lawrence set up camp outside with two rangers. She hated their presence, charging Lawrence every time he approached the fence. Her animosity and fear turned her eyes black with rage.

'We have to be patient with her. She's our *enfant terrible*,'

I said, using an affectionate French expression for difficult kids.

'That's a good one,' Lawrence said wryly. 'We'll call her ET for short.'

'She's had so much trauma packed into that little life of hers. We're not going to give up on her now.'

'It's the strangest thing that with all that anger, she's so silent. She hasn't trumpeted once,' he puzzled. 'I'm worried about this girl.'

ET's rage turned into the deepest despair. Unfamiliar territory. Scary new smells. Terrifying human beings close by. It was too much for her. She stopped hiding, didn't bother to charge Lawrence, wasn't eating, and just walked round and round in listless circles. Lawrence took me to her and she barely acknowledged our presence. She had given up.

I understood completely. Humans represented danger and pain and grief. She was trapped in yet another strange environment. What could we do? You can't hug an angry elephant. Lawrence would have stayed with her for months if he'd thought that would help but she looked as if she had lost the will to live.

'We've got to get Nana here,' he said. 'If she doesn't get company soon, she's going to die of heartbreak.'

Using food and sweet talk, he and Vusi lured the herd to ET's *boma*. They had probably already sensed the presence of a strange elephant close by but they still trusted Lawrence enough to follow him to her.

The minute Nana and Frankie set eyes on the frightened teenager, they lumbered up to the fence and 'talked' to her, floating their trunks between the electric wires to touch her.

She stared at them, transfixed. They were the first elephants she had seen in a year. She tentatively raised her trunk to theirs. Quiet rumbles rolled between them. Even our macho rangers were wiping their eyes.

The rest of the herd came closer to say hello, as if it was the most normal thing to do. And it was. In their world, they never questioned her right to be with them.

'I think they're reassuring her,' Vusi murmured.

'I hope so,' I smiled.

He nodded confidently.

'They're probably telling her their story – that they too lost their families and know what it's like to be frightened and alone. They're saying, *You're going to be fine. We'll walk with you.*'

I choked back tears at the beautiful image he was painting and hoped with all my heart that he was right.

'I'm taking down the *boma* gate and letting her out,' Lawrence said firmly. 'She needs to be with them.'

He slid the gate aside and we watched from the Land Rover to see if ET would work out how to walk through. She walked past the open gate several times but didn't realize she was free to join the herd.

Nana and Frankie milled about, moving unhurriedly in front of the gate as if trying to show her what to do. ET followed them, backwards and forwards, not understanding that nothing stopped her from being with them. Her wretchedness was heartbreaking.

The herd began to leave and she let out a strangled cry. Lawrence shook his head in despair.

'Oh my God. The poor thing has no voice.'

We learned later that after she'd lost her companions in the other reserve, she had shrieked herself hoarse in fear and damaged her vocal cords forever. To this day, she can't trumpet and can only squeeze out strangled honking noises.

Just as we were about to give up for the day and close the gate again, she paused in front of it, her eyes on the disappearing herd, and walked straight through.

I was in awe of our herd's compassion and tenderness with her. They accepted this troubled youngster without hesitation, and during the first few months she was never ever alone. One of the older females was always close to her. Sometimes I think that elephants have a greater sense of community and responsibility towards one another than humans will ever have. I was so proud of our herd, and relieved that ET would never in her life be short of love again.

On Easter Sunday, Lawrence phoned Marion.

'She's doing fine and already has a mother figure in Frankie,' he reported. 'The whole herd has just come past the river in front of the lodge and she was right in the middle of them, Nana in front of her, Frankie next to her, and Mnumzane behind with his trunk on her back. She has a new family, Marion. Thanks to you.'

To this day, Frankie and ET have one of the strongest bonds in the herd.

Not that ET calmed down straight away. She remained fearful and skittish for a long time, living up to her *enfant terrible* name, and she once gave Promise the worst scare of his life.

He had jumped out of his Land Cruiser to track animal spoor and he heard her before he saw her. By the time he spun around to face her, she was coming at him, ears pinned back and trunk curled under.

'Her eyes were so damn black and angry, I couldn't look at them,' he told me afterwards. 'This wasn't one of her moods, this was a full-on charge. My 4×4 was twenty metres back and I didn't have a hope in hell of getting to it in time.'

Elephants can reach speeds of forty kilometres per hour and she was closing in fast. Running wasn't an option.

'Lawrence always told me that in a face-off with an elephant, you have to do the *last* thing your body tells you to do, so I stood my ground. What choice did I have?'

Ninety kilos versus five tons.

The distance between them narrowed. She was metres away and thundering closer. He almost choked in the dust. The ground vibrated under his feet. He focused on breathing, staying calm. If she picked up his fear, he wouldn't stand a chance.

She stopped.

He didn't move, felt her breath on his head. She towered over him. He stared at the monster legs in front of him. One tap would crush his skull. He talked silently to her. *I'm not going to hurt you. Please leave me alone.*

Abruptly she spun around and stalked off, tail high and stiff in irritation.

'You should have seen how quickly she skidded to a halt. I don't know how they do that without ABS brakes,' he joked at the bar that night.

'*Eish*,' said a guest, a farmer from Nelspruit. 'You have balls of steel, man.'

'Nah, he's just bushwhacked,' laughed another ranger, tapping the side of his head.

'I knew I couldn't outrun her,' Promise shrugged. 'Not even Usain Bolt could.'

Nothing helps settle the soul like having one's own family, and the same year ET arrived, she fell pregnant. Twenty-two months later, baby Jurgen was born.

It was the herd's fourth baby since coming to Thula Thula but for Lawrence and me, this little one was an extra special arrival – ET's life had come full circle.

7

French temperament

Frankie was named after me because, according to Lawrence, she was second in command.

'It's actually because I recognized in her someone I know quite well,' he teased.

I grinned, not taking the bait.

'That feisty French temperament . . .' he smirked.

'That feisty French temperament will take her places,' I laughed.

Frankie was a bit more than feisty. In the beginning, she had a temper and an unpredictable streak that meant we were never sure how she would behave around game drives. But time brought her confidence and inner peace, which stood her in good stead when she took over as matriarch.

I will always remember when Nana began to relinquish the reins to her in 2003, four years after they had arrived at Thula Thula. We were confused at first because Nana was still young, not even forty years old. It wasn't a power struggle because, unlike bulls, there's never a battle between old and new matriarchs.

Lawrence had picked up that there was an unusual shift in roles between them and he arrived home late for dinner one evening, very concerned.

'I saw the strangest thing,' he said, tucking into T-bone steak and *gratin dauphinois*. 'Nana was taking the herd through the trees near the dam when she seemed to go off course.' He gave a puzzled frown. 'And then Frankie took over the lead and Nana quite happily let her. I've never seen them do that before. Something's wrong.'

'Do you think she's sick?'

'I hope not. I'll go and take another look tomorrow. It'll be easier to see if there's a problem in daylight.'

We had a restless night and neither of us slept much. At dawn, he kissed me goodbye and dashed off to check on his girl. I hoped it wasn't poachers and that she wasn't suffering from a festering gunshot wound. I shuddered at the thought of losing her, or any of our herd for that matter. They were as important to us as our families. Big Jeff, our Labrador, sensed my anxiety and jumped onto the bed, cuddling his sturdy body against mine. I gave him a hug then got up, too worried about Nana for a lie-in.

Lawrence came home in the afternoon, looking grim.

'I think she has a cataract on her right eye. It's bad and looks as if it's almost completely covering the eye. I'll be surprised if she can see anything out of it at all. No wonder Frankie was helping her last night.' He shook his head. 'I can't believe I'm only finding out now.'

'Do you think we could have it removed?'

'No idea. I'm waiting for Cobus to call me back. If anyone can, he can.'

Dr Cobus Raath was a veterinary surgeon based in Nelspruit who had masterminded the relocation of the herd to us, and Lawrence knew he could trust him. It took a week before he was free to come to Thula Thula, and during the wait, Lawrence was with Nana every single day.

'Frankie and Nana's teamwork is incredible,' he reported back to me. 'They're timesharing their responsibilities. During the day, Nana can see fine with one eye so she's the boss, but as soon as it gets dark, Frankie takes over. I hope to God we can help her.'

The vet arrived with three students in tow and Lawrence immediately took them in search of Nana. I kept in radio contact with him throughout the day as they searched high and low for her. Nana had disappeared. Night began to fall and they reluctantly agreed to try again the next day. As if Nana sensed their capitulation, she appeared out of the trees and strolled across the clearing towards them.

'Hello, Nana, my baba. I've been looking everywhere for you. Where have you been?' Lawrence said; then feeling guilty as hell, signalled to Cobus to dart her.

The herd scattered and the little ones trumpeted in distress. Lawrence hammered a few gunshots into the ground to make sure they stayed away so he and Cobus could safely approach Nana. The vet swung his medical kit out of the 4×4 and they both ran towards her.

'You're right. It's a cataract, a bad one,' grimaced Cobus.

'Can you operate?'

'Not without a very real danger to the eye. I'll smother it with disinfectant to reduce the risk of further problems and then—'

'Lawrence! *Watch out!*' yelled Vusi.

Frankie was thundering towards them across the savannah.

'Cover me! I can't leave Nana out cold,' shouted Cobus.

'Get the hell out of here *now*!' cried Vusi.

The vet injected the reversal drug into Nana.

Lawrence yanked him to his feet. '*Run!*'

The two men sprinted to the vehicle and were pulled inside by the rangers. Frankie shot right past them to Nana. Chests heaving, Lawrence and the vet watched her keep vigil until the drug took effect and a very groggy Nana heaved herself back onto her feet. With her trunk draped over Nana's body, Frankie glowered at the men as she tenderly nudged Nana towards the safety of the trees.

Nana knew she was going blind and realized that she wouldn't be able to look after the herd for much longer. Safety comes before ego in this wise feminine world and she realized the time had come to hand over her responsibilities. If only world leaders gave up power as graciously.

We were so grateful for Frankie. She had been through a lot in her life but she was a tough cookie and has proven to be a shrewd and fearless matriarch. What a contrast to the highly strung elephant she had been when she almost killed Lawrence and me not long after Lawrence released the herd into the reserve for the first time.

He had decided that they were settled in enough to be let out of their holding *boma* so they could enjoy the full expanse of the reserve. Every couple of hours, he drove out to check up on them and to make sure they weren't trying to break through the perimeter fence.

'They were near the river this morning. Shall we go and see how they are? We can take the quad bike,' he suggested.

I hopped onto the back of the off-road bike, thrilled to see

the herd in the wild at last. We bumped and bucked along a
rutted track up to a viewpoint from where we could survey
the area where he thought they were. A heat haze hung low
over the reserve and the hills and savannah were a milky blur,
but Lawrence always had a sixth sense about their whereabouts and spotted them immediately.

'They're by the river and it looks as if they're on the move.
Let's give them some time to leave the bank, then we'll use
the river to get to them,' he said.

The Nseleni River runs right through the reserve – a
perfect bush freeway. It hadn't rained in ages so we drove
through the low water, laughing and holding our feet high
and dry. Lawrence revved the engine hard and powered up
the steep bank to get us out of the riverbed. I clung to him to
counteract the kickback. When I looked up, the elephants
were right there.

'*Shit*,' Lawrence grunted.

We were in the middle of them. I felt small, very exposed
and yet strangely unafraid. I knew they were wild and that
our reserve was still new to them, but I naively thought they
were happy to be with us, and happy elephants won't hurt
you, right? Wrong.

Frankie was at the back of the herd, as stunned as we were,
but then she flew between the other elephants towards us,
ears pulled back, body shaking in fury, and her eyes . . . she
has a *look*, a frown, a way of squinting out of the corner of
her eye, that turns my blood cold. None of the other elephants do it, just her.

'We've got a problem,' Lawrence muttered.

I slid my arms around him and held on. If *he* was worried, I was terrified.

We couldn't go back. We couldn't go forward. The herd was in front and the river behind, *and* we were between Frankie and two babies who were squealing and trumpeting in panic. The rest of the herd moved about restlessly, edgy and full of tension. Frankie shook her great head at us. Nana stood by silently, observing warily. I was bewildered by how agitated they were. It had never occurred to me that they would be anything but peaceful. I was about to learn a thing or two about angry elephants.

Lawrence took out his 9-mm to scare them off with a few shots in the air.

'Don't, Lolo. We don't know how they'll react.'

Frankie gave an ear-splitting trumpet and headed for us, trunk rolled under for maximum impact, eyes blazing. Those eyes alone could have killed me. Nana did nothing to stop her.

'We're in trouble,' Lawrence muttered, giving me the gun. 'Shoot if it gets bad.'

He might as well have given me a toy for all that 9-mm could have helped. I took it reluctantly, hating even to touch it. Frankie sprinted towards us. I closed my eyes. Nothing would stop her. We were going to die.

Lawrence sprang up on the bike and threw his arms overhead to make himself bigger.

'Frankie, it's okay, my baba. It's me. It's me.'

She was close. Her rage seared like lasers.

This is it, we're dead, I thought.

'Frankie, *Frankie*! My baba, it's me. It's me.'

Something in his voice – desperation? love? – reached her. I peered past Lawrence. Her trunk swung at us in wild circles but her hostility had dropped a fraction. I don't know how I knew but I sensed it.

'It's okay, my baba. It's me. It's me.'

Her ears flapped backwards and forwards, no longer pinned against her body – the deadly sign of intention to kill. Her mood was changing. I choked back a sob and cowered down. She plunged towards us again.

Lawrence stayed standing, arms high, panting.

'Frankie, it's *me*.'

She stopped right at the bike.

The world went silent, holding its breath.

Frankie glared at us from above. I saw the deep wrinkles on her skin, the fine hair on her trunk, long thin cracks in her massive tusks. One toss of them could fling us and the bike into the air like insects.

She backtracked a few paces and waited for the calves to bolt past her.

We didn't move.

She swivelled her head from side to side, showering us in dust, never taking her eyes off us.

Lawrence sank down onto the seat.

'My baba,' he whispered.

Her anger changed to surprise, as though she suddenly understood who we were, that the people she was about to kill were those who had given her a new home, the ones she was beginning to trust. Her eyes softened. *Oh, it's you.* She loped back into the bush after her son and daughter, throwing us a puzzled backward glance as she left.

Lawrence and I collapsed against each other. The herd moved off. We sat frozen, in shock, not daring to move. We had escaped being trampled by an enraged elephant. I stared death in the face that day and felt terror I'd never experienced in my life.

We realized in hindsight that the terrible racket of the quad bike must have given her such a fright that her memories of what humans had done to her blinded her to who we were. It was so careless of us to have gone out on the bike, but we had never looked after elephants before and were learning every day.

I saw these majestic creatures in a different light after that because I understood how similar they were to us. She did exactly what we would have done in that situation – protected her family from danger. I also saw that elephants are capable of insight, of realizing their mistakes. One minute Frankie was hell-bent on killing us, the next she knew we weren't the enemy and she walked away. But after that day, I became very wary of her. I had seen the black rage in her eyes and knew she could have killed us if she'd wanted to.

Wild animals are like the sea – beautiful, unpredictable, dangerous. An overdue reality check both Lawrence and I needed to learn.

8

Baby Thula

Being guardians and protectors of wildlife is not for the faint-hearted. The rewards are immense but the constant worry never goes away and when something goes wrong, the loss, the guilt, the pain, is indescribable.

Back in the summer of 2004, we had been waiting for weeks for Nana's daughter Nandi to give birth. It's difficult to pinpoint a due date with elephants because they're pregnant for twenty-two months and often we only realize they're expecting when the pregnancy is well under way. By then, it's impossible to work out how far gone they are.

That morning, the rangers reported that the calf had been born at last but that the herd was behaving strangely. Lawrence went out immediately to check. He returned at midday, ashen-faced.

'There's something wrong with her feet and she can't stand.'

I looked at him, bewildered. Several calves had been born since the herd arrived and we had never had a problem with any of the births.

'She's trying to get up and they're all there, helping her, wrapping their trunks under her body and holding her up, but as soon as they let go she collapses. I was there for hours and it's so damn hard to watch.'

'If she can't stand, how is she suckling?'

He grimaced glumly.

'She isn't. She can't get to Nandi's breasts from the ground – that means she's had nothing to eat since she was born. And in this damn heat, she won't stand a chance. We may already be too late.'

'Are they somewhere safe? Where are they?'

'On the way to the lodge, just before the river crossing, where there's not a blasted tree in sight. Nana and Nandi are using their bodies to shield her from the sun but even the herd can't stay out there for days on end. It's a disaster, Frankie. There's no way that little thing will survive.'

'You don't know that, *chéri*. Elephants are smarter than we think. They'll find a way to help her.'

'What if they feel they have to abandon her?'

'They would never do that!'

'They might have to. If the baby holds the herd back, then Nana and Frankie have no choice.'

'Then we'll save her. We can't leave her to *die*.'

He nodded wearily.

'I know that, but the calf doesn't just need feeding, Frankie. She needs an orthopaedic specialist. I don't even know if such a thing exists for elephants. We always said we would let nature take its course but . . .'

He fell silent. I knew he was right, but we'd never had to put our belief to the test before.

'Maybe they won't abandon her,' I said hopefully.

'She won't last another day without milk.' He paced up and down. 'What the hell are we going to do?'

'Go back, Lolo. See what happens and then we'll decide.'

I made him some sandwiches and he packed bottles of water into a cooler box and headed back to the herd. I glanced at the thermometer at the door: thirty-seven degrees and it was two o'clock in the afternoon. I ran after him with his cap. His skin is about as un-African as you can get, and without it he would turn into a lobster.

I was already asleep when he slipped into bed that night and woke me to say she was still alive.

'She's desperately weak but they're all still with her. They haven't given up on her yet. Please God she makes it through the night.'

At dawn, he was off again to help the calf's grandmother and mother keep an eye on the little one. He was family, after all. I phoned him mid-morning to find out how she was.

'She's still alive, only just,' he said in a hushed voice. 'But it looks like Nana has decided that it's time to go.'

Female elephants are deeply maternal and often take care of each other's babies, so leaving behind the newborn calf would be devastating for all of them.

Nana made the first move to leave and Lawrence's description of her melancholic walk away from her dying granddaughter broke my heart.

'She shuffled off with such heavy, slow steps,' he said in despair.

Frankie had already taken over as leader but Nana was still a much-loved adviser, and she was also the calf's grandmother, so it's possible that Frankie had left the decision up to her. Nana must have longed to stay and console her daughter but instead she led the herd away. It was so typical of the wise guide we loved. Her decisions were never for herself. She always put the herd first. I hope I never find myself in the position that she was in that day. This is why the role of matriarch falls to leaders who not only have the insight to make such big decisions, but also have the courage to follow them through.

And so baby Thula was left to die.

Only Nandi stayed behind, bone-weary from childbirth and the endless vigil that was going into its second day.

How on earth could Lawrence and I ignore her plight? We were committed to the theory of letting nature take its course, but in this case it was impossible. We couldn't have lived with ourselves knowing that we hadn't done everything to save her, especially after the herd had tried so hard themselves to help her.

'I'm going in with the guys to get her,' Lawrence said.

I hugged him hard, grateful for his big heart.

Knowing that Nandi hadn't had anything to eat or drink since giving birth, Lawrence loaded his Land Rover with freshly cut alfalfa and water and carefully reversed towards her. It was risky, because if she was suspicious of his intentions, she would charge him. A 4×4 looks very sturdy but it's nothing more than a tin can to a three-ton mama protecting her dying young.

The moment she caught the smell of food, her trunk shot into the air and she lumbered over to the vehicle and began to siphon up gallons of water and squirt it into her mouth.

Lawrence edged away. Nandi followed trustingly. Feeling

guilty, he stopped to let her drink. She drank and drank, quenching thirty-six hours of thirst. Then he moved the vehicle forward at a snail's pace, leading her behind bushes until the baby was out of sight.

The rangers rushed to the calf. She was so tiny, it only took two of them to lift her into their truck. Minutes later, they drove up to the house.

She was thin, listless, her newborn ears blistered by the sun, and she had open puncture wounds on her sides where her mother and aunts had prodded her with their tusks to get her to stand. I thought she would die within the hour. She lay motionless in the shade of the wild fig trees, following us with frightened eyes.

We doused her with cool water to lower her body temperature. The vet administered a drip with life-saving nutrients. I sat next to her, rubbing her face and whispering to her. *Reste avec nous, ma petite.* Stay with us, my little one.

All we knew about baby elephants was that they were highly intolerant of cow's milk. Lawrence got on the phone to the Daphne Sheldrick sanctuary in Kenya to find out how to feed her. They recommended a special mixture using coconut oil. A ranger raced off to Empangeni to buy bottles and teats and the right ingredients.

The vet gave her a second drip bag, and a third.

Miraculously, she perked up.

'If she survives the next twelve hours, she stands a chance,' the vet said. 'She's a damn big calf. It looks as if she could have been too big for her mother and her feet didn't have enough space to grow correctly, but the good news is that she doesn't have any broken bones.'

My guest room became a nursery overnight and we carefully moved her into our home. She lay on the mattress, surrounded by what I hoped was the reassuring smell of grass and hay. I couldn't take my eyes off her. Apart from her sunburnt ears and tusk wounds, her tiny body was perfect in every way, with a beautiful baby face, squirming trunk and surprisingly sturdy-looking legs. In fact, if the vet hadn't told us that there was something wrong with her feet, I wouldn't have known. She fell asleep quickly, lying on her side, with her trunk rolled up against her mouth for comfort. I could have watched her forever.

A ranger stayed with her that first night but I was up every couple of hours to check on her and to monitor the fence, panicking that if the herd realized she was with us, they might crash through it to get her. If they wanted their calf back, nothing would stop them, not even 8,000 volts.

But they didn't come for her that night. They ambled up to the house a few days later and spent the entire morning calmly grazing along the fence. We kept expecting them to become agitated and to show some sign that they wanted their crippled infant back.

Lawrence eventually rubbed his shirt and hands over the calf and went up to them, palms outstretched, to 'tell' them that she was safe. Nana, Frankie and Nandi's heads shot up and their trunks writhed between the electrified strands towards him. I stood on the veranda, more than a bit nervous. Their trunks quivered all over his hands, scenting the calf, then, far from being distressed, they looked reassured and left as serenely as they had arrived.

Lawrence walked back to me, slipped his hand into mine

and we watched them leave. We were family, the elephants and us, and they had just entrusted their calf to us. Words can't describe how moved we were, and how responsible we felt for her survival.

'We'll call her Thula,' I murmured.

Lawrence nodded and squeezed my hand. 'She's going to be fine.'

The vet was upbeat and felt confident that with daily home 'physio' we would slowly be able to move her feet into the right position in the hope that she would learn to walk. By morning, Thula had gobbled up an entire bottle of her formula. I was so happy for her, and so encouraged, because baby elephants are notoriously difficult to feed, even when they're really hungry. Their head and trunk tip instinctively to search for their mother's body and they need to feel secure before they will drink. We helped her along by hanging up a heavy piece of rough sacking – to mimic her mum's skin – and gave her the bottle from behind it.

Every day, she had 'walk therapy' and even though it was obviously painful for her to use her feet, she was determined to try.

By day three, she managed a few paces – very unstable and unsure but she did it. We were so excited, cheering her on and clapping at her achievement. She looked very pleased with herself. Before the end of that first week, she tottered across the lawn without help. I burst into tears. She was so gutsy and seemed thrilled by each of her milestones.

She and Biyela, our gardener, adored each other and spent hours outside together, with him gallantly protecting her baby skin from the sun with a huge golf umbrella. It was such a happy sight to see old Biyela and little Thula strolling across the lawn side by side.

She loved the umbrella and would sneak up behind him and curl her trunk around the handle and try to snatch it from him. Our sweet gardener would gamely launch into a tug-of-war with her, resulting in many broken umbrellas. But I didn't care. There were plenty more where they came from and I wanted to do everything I could to keep that impish gleam in her eyes.

Everyone wanted to help, and within days she had her own foster herd of humans around her. Emotional well-being and physical health go hand in hand for these helpless creatures and love is as critical to their survival as any medicine a vet could prescribe.

Her feet became stronger and stronger, and before long, she was scampering everywhere like a boisterous toddler. She became my shadow, more puppy than elephant, and there wasn't a thing in the house that little trunk of hers didn't touch.

She was fascinated by the long thing growing out of her face and flopped it about chaotically until she learned a bit more control over it and promptly set about destroying my decor.

One day, she knocked over a stool. She gazed at it in confusion then tried to walk over it but her legs were too uncoordinated and she broke it. Delighted with her new toys, she picked up the pieces and flung them into the air. My poor home. Newborn elephants don't usually master the use of their trunks that quickly, and whilst I was very proud of her,

I quickly understood that it was safer to move any precious objects and breakables out of her reach.

She loved the kitchen, and even though she didn't eat solids it didn't stop her from sniffing every one of the ingredients I was using. Max and Tess, my Staffordshire bull terriers, stood by in total bewilderment. *Why is she allowed to do that when we aren't?*

I was once cutting tomatoes and her trunk curled over the edge of the table and scooped up some of the pieces. I think the texture fascinated her, because she pushed those interesting red globs around the kitchen and created quite the Picasso artwork on the floor.

Max was right there, hoovering up the mess. He was never far from her and I was convinced that he thought she was part of his pack and knew she needed him to keep her safe.

Bijou and Tess were jealous of her and not at all happy about the way she had hijacked me away from them, but their possessiveness was mixed with motherliness because they too seemed to sense her fragility and often wandered into her room, sniffing and licking her face.

My home was quite an interesting hotchpotch of 'children' – a snobbish poodle, my two warrior staffies and a baby elephant. All living in perfect harmony.

Despite Thula's size, she was surprisingly gentle with the dogs, especially Bijou, who often walked with her in the garden. Even with her wobbly legs, Thula never once trod on her by mistake. If only she had been as careful with my furniture!

Week one slipped into weeks two and three, and we began to relax. She was a long way off from being strong enough to keep up with a running herd, but I was confident she would get there.

Near the end of the fourth week, her carer ran into the kitchen.

'Come quick! Thula can't stand!' he shouted.

I ran after him to her room. She tried to get up to greet me, squealing in pain and frustration that she couldn't. I fell to my knees and held her in my arms.

The next day, she refused her bottle.

The vet didn't know what to do. We phoned every expert we knew but no one could help. We had no idea what was wrong with her. It seemed as if her joints were sore and any movement made it worse. She became listless and barely able to lift her head.

We took it in turns to be with her, to stroke her, to tell her how brave she was and how much we loved her. I told her that her mother Nandi was waiting for her and that the whole herd were excited about the day she would be back with them. I don't know if she understood but Lawrence always believed animals understood emotion so I kept talking to her.

Back onto the drip she went. Nothing helped. She deteriorated before my eyes. It happened so unbelievably quickly.

Biyela came to the door every morning, umbrella in hand and hope on his face. I couldn't speak and just shook my head at him.

Our baby girl didn't make it.

Lawrence woke me up before sunrise exactly four weeks after she was born and told me she was gone. I couldn't believe it. How could she be gone? Just a week ago, I was chasing her through the house to get my sun hat back.

I was broken. We all were. I cried and cried. I had been so confident that she had made it through the worst. I never realized how much I loved her until she died. Her death was such a shock. Yes, she hadn't been well for a few days, but she had been thriving the week before, and it never occurred to me that she wouldn't bounce back.

She was such an optimistic and brave bundle of joy and I thought she would be with us forever. They were dark days, my sorrow was so deep, and it took me a long time to recover. Even now, years later, I choke up at the thought of her. Some creatures never leave your heart and she's still in mine, that brave little Thula.

9

Long live the king

Nandi fell pregnant again almost immediately after losing Thula, and after a long pregnancy she gave birth to a very healthy boy calf, Shaka. I was so excited and relieved when Vusi told me he was walking within hours of being born. Once you've been through the trauma of not being able to save a very sick creature, the fear never leaves you that it will happen again.

Happily, every baby born since then has been healthy, and so here I was in 2012, six years and twelve robust calves later, trying to find a way to appease the authorities who were still pressurizing me about our elephant-to-land ratio. I was doing my best to look for solutions but I was also very determined that nothing we did would disrupt their peaceful existence.

I asked Mike Toft for advice on controlling numbers in a way that didn't involve culling or breaking up the herd.

'There is something I've been investigating for a while but I won't get your hopes up yet because I need to do some more research first. How much time have they given you?' he asked.

'They didn't say,' I replied. 'And I'd rather not ask. The

next time I contact them, I want to be able to show them that we're doing everything we can to address the problem.'

'I'll get back to you as soon as I can,' he promised.

He didn't elaborate but I felt hopeful. I found it really hard to accept that 4,500 hectares wasn't enough for our herd. We often went for weeks on end without seeing them at all, not even when the rangers went looking for them, so how could our reserve not be big enough? I still had so much to learn about conservation.

Strangely, during that period the elephants visited the house almost every day. Did they know their fate was being decided? Were they reminding me that we were part of the same big family? I didn't know, but it didn't matter. I loved seeing them so often and having their calming presence so near to me.

Sometimes one of the calves would walk up to a game drive vehicle and Nana would immediately bustle up to it and stop it from getting too close. The calf would be allowed a mock charge or two for practice, swivelling its head and flinging its tiny trunk about, but then she would gently nudge it away. Rules are rules and cars were out of bounds. Lawrence would have been proud of her. He always wanted the herd to be truly wild and never get too accustomed to being around humans.

The adult females have an endless supply of patience and I've never seen any of them lose their temper with one of the babies, and believe me, they can be as much of a handful as human kids! They're curious and have too much energy for their own good.

It's one of the reasons Lawrence and I rescued Gobisa.

After Mnumzane died, the younger bulls were unmanageable. In the wild, they would have had an alpha male to teach them manners and without Mnumzane, they ran riot. Mabula was our oldest bull but at eighteen years old, he was far too young and irresponsible to take over.

'We need an adult bull to take charge of them,' Lawrence said. 'Especially Mabula. He's inherited his mother's bolshie attitude and he's getting too big for his boots. Without an alpha male to keep him in check, he could end up being a real problem for us when he's older.'

The role of dominant bull generally goes to an adult male in his thirties and while it isn't a leadership position like the matriarch's, he is crucial for controlling teenage bulls and for passing on strong healthy genes, because he usually gets the pick of the females when they go into oestrus.

One afternoon, Promise and a second ranger Siya were on a game drive with a Land Cruiser full of guests. They had seen very few animals and the guests were getting restless, so Promise was taking them to see our hippos, Romeo and Juliet. A few minutes from the dam, they drove around a corner and there was the herd, right in the road. Promise slowed to a stop and smiled at the guests.

'Here they are,' he grinned, feeling quite smug that he had found them after all.

Mabula spun towards them the minute he heard the vehicle arrive.

'That's Frankie's son,' Promise explained.

Mabula lifted his giant head and gave an annoyed trumpet. The guests were delighted and clicked madly with their cameras. He began to trot towards them. Promise shifted into reverse but stayed put. Mabula sped up, trunk swinging from side to side.

'It's just a mock charge,' Promise said calmly. 'Stay seated and don't panic.'

Mabula stampeded towards them, followed by two other young bulls. Promise began to reverse slowly. Mabula didn't slow down. Siya scrambled out of his tracker's seat and into the 4×4.

'*Eish, wena!*' he yelled at Mabula.

Promise had his foot flat on the accelerator. There was dust everywhere and still Mabula kept charging. Promise and Siya hammered the side of the 4×4 with their hands and shouted at Mabula to back off. Our teenager wasn't taking orders and knocked the Land Cruiser with his tusks. If the guests had been bored earlier, they were now getting enough adrenalin to last them a lifetime.

Thanks to Promise's level-headedness and Formula One reversing, Mabula lost interest, but when he tried the same trick a fortnight later, Lawrence was concerned.

'If we don't get a father figure for him, he's going to take this charging nonsense too far.'

He made some calls and after a lot of to-ing and fro-ing with the authorities, Gobisa arrived, a powerful bull in his mid-thirties. I took one look at him and wondered how Mabula would react.

'He's *huge*,' I said to Lawrence. 'What if Mabula doesn't listen to him?'

'Gobisa will batter him into submission,' he shrugged. 'It's the way it has to be.'

Except Gobisa had no intention of staying.

Just before midnight on his first day, we were woken to the news that he had smashed through the 8,000-volt *boma* fence. Lawrence radioed for support, kissed me goodbye and flew out the door. I sat by the phone on tenterhooks, reliving the drama of Nana's breakouts ten years earlier. What a nightmare. Lawrence kept me posted as he tracked Gobisa's path of destruction.

'We wanted a boss man and we got one,' he said. 'He's heading back to where he came from, broken through six electric fences and he's still going. We've got two choppers looking for him and Dave Cooper's got trucks and a crane on standby.'

'Be careful, Lolo,' I said. 'I want both of you back in one piece.'

'Roger that, Frankie,' he replied, his grin coming down the phone line.

A team of seventeen men in two helicopters and several 4×4s hunted the area for Gobisa, and when they found him he put up one hell of a fight. Nothing frightened him, not even the racket of the helicopter that tried to chase him out of the dense bush where he was hiding. It crossed my mind that we might be getting more elephant than we had bargained for.

'He's taken cover in the ravine,' Lawrence reported to me. 'It's now or never. If we don't get him, the authorities will shoot him.'

I knew exactly which ravine he was talking about. A long narrow gorge with minimal access. If Gobisa went in too far, neither helicopter nor 4×4 would be able to get anywhere close to him.

'How on earth are you going to save him now?' I asked.

'There's one open area that's our last chance . . . if they can dart him there, we can get him out. If not . . .'

'Don't take any risks,' I begged.

Half the day went by without news and my imagination went into overdrive. Not only had Gobisa disappeared into the ravine, but Lawrence had followed him and been injured and no one wanted to tell me. I was desperate to phone. But if they were in the middle of a rescue, the last thing they needed was a panicked call from me.

One of the longest days of my life later, my phone rang at last.

'We got him back,' Lawrence said, exhaustion in every word.

'Thank God you're okay,' I groaned.

'Bad news is the bastard got out of the *boma* again and has run off in the direction of the perimeter fence.'

'*What?*'

'Smashed right through the *boma*'s 8,000 volts. I saw it with my own eyes. This is one mother of an elephant, Frankie.'

'Come home, *chéri*. You've been going for twenty-four hours. You need rest.'

'I need my elephant back,' he grunted. 'Can't give up on the bugger now.'

Maybe it was the effect of the multiple doses of sedatives that Gobisa had been given when the men had brought him back the first time, or maybe it was pure exhaustion, but he didn't break out of the actual reserve. Instead, he disappeared into the undergrowth and hid. We had no way of knowing where, but the fact that there were no breaches in the fence meant he was still inside Thula Thula. It saved his life. Had he escaped again, the authorities would have shot him. Human lives and property were at stake and no one was cutting an enraged six-ton bull any slack.

Lawrence got hold of Gobisa's owners to tell them what had happened and to ask their advice. They were shocked and promised to send a man Gobisa knew well to help settle him in. At that point, Lawrence had his doubts that anyone could help but we were desperate and he was prepared to try anything.

'Send him,' he said. 'I need all the input I can get.'

Ndlovu arrived the next morning, a wiry Zulu with glittering eyes and a solemn manner. He and Lawrence immediately went out in the Land Rover to look for Gobisa.

'He's close. I can feel him,' Ndlovu murmured. 'He's hiding in the shadow of hills, in a forest near an old riverbed.'

Lawrence was dumbfounded. Ndlovu had described the exact location where they had last spotted Gobisa.

'How do you know?' he asked.

'His spirit reaches me and mine reaches him. We will wait.'

It had been days since Lawrence or the rangers had set eyes on Gobisa but the morning after Ndlovu arrived, he came out of hiding.

'I told you he knew I was here,' Ndlovu smiled.

'What do we do?'

'We wait.'

Lawrence and he sat in the Land Rover and watched Gobisa make his way towards them. Lawrence stiffened as Gobisa walked straight up to the 4×4. He had seen the destruction this enormous beast was capable of. Gobisa silently circled them then disappeared again.

'What was *that* about?' Lawrence said.

'He came to say hello,' Ndlovu shrugged, as if it was the most normal thing in the world for a bull elephant that had broken six electrified fences, been chased by two helicopters and a swarm of 4×4s, and then been drugged to the teeth and hauled back to base camp on a flatbed truck, to wander up for a casual hello with an old friend.

'What's our next move?' Lawrence asked.

'We wait for him to feel safe.'

'And how do we do that?'

'Look at it from his point of view,' Ndlovu said softly. 'He comes to Thula Thula and he can smell there are other elephants. He knows there must be a dominant male around.'

'Mabula is a squib compared to Gobisa,' Lawrence scoffed.

'Ah, but he doesn't know that, does he? He knows he's not feeling his best and that he must hide to protect himself from the dominant bull whose territory he's in.'

'How long will he hide for?'

'As long as it takes for the sedatives to wear off and for him to feel confident enough to explore his new terrain and gather as much information as he can about Mabula to understand whether he's a threat or not. He will smell the presence of all the other elephants but he'll be most interested in the bull that might fight him for territory. He will eventually realize from Mabula's dung that he's no danger to him. Be patient. Give him space.'

We were lucky to have such a wise Zulu man to advise us and help us understand what was going on with Gobisa. The way he explained it made so much sense and made me feel a lot less worried about him.

'Won't Mabula realize that Gobisa is here?' I asked Lawrence.

'He probably does, but if he has any sense he'll stay with the herd and keep out of Gobisa's way, because after what I saw of Gobisa, there's no way Mabula would survive a run-in with him.' He fell silent. 'I have never in my life seen such courage. This bull is going to be good for our herd.'

On Sunday, Vusi phoned to report that the battle of kings had begun. For two days, Gobisa and Mabula fought with bone-shattering, tusk-clashing fury. I knew it had to happen but I hated every minute of it.

'Where is the rest of the herd?' I asked Lawrence anxiously.

'Nana's headed north with them. They're safe but two of the younger ones have snuck back to see what's going on.'

Mandla and Ilanga watched from the sidelines, never getting involved, but learning what lay ahead if they ever took on the winner.

'Ndlovu feels that Gobisa has the upper hand,' Lawrence told me.

'Does he know how much longer it's going to carry on for?'

'As long as it takes for Mabula to back off. He's putting up one hell of a fight. Thank God Gobisa came when he did. If Mabula is already so bloody-minded at eighteen, imagine the kind of bull he would have grown into without a father figure to teach him a thing or two about being part of the herd.'

'How will we know it's over?' I fretted.

'Ndlovu says we can relax when Gobisa flicks Mabula's penis with his trunk. It's the ultimate sign of dominance.'

I was so relieved when their power struggle came to an end and Mabula survived with no serious injury other than a few surface wounds and a punctured ego.

'Do you think Gobisa was careful not to hurt him too badly?' I asked Lawrence.

'I wouldn't put it past him,' he nodded. 'Make no mistake, he had his hands full fighting Mabula, but he probably had a few tricks up his trunk that he used to prolong the battle and tire out his opponent. We got ourselves a true king, Frankie.'

Mabula never really accepted Gobisa's authority, but he had no choice while Gobisa was bigger and stronger than him, and when I look at Mabula today I know we did the right thing. He's full of sass, just like his mother Frankie, and having to submit to an older bull's authority helped ensure that his spirited behaviour was never allowed to become dangerous. Quite the contrary! He channelled that feistiness into becoming the herd's entertainer, and nothing makes him happier than being in the spotlight. If he were human, I have no doubt that he would use his South African connections to beg Trevor Noah for a job at Comedy Central.

His favourite trick is disrupting a game drive with bush yoga, but his rules are strict. No cheering, no show. He starts with a back leg stretch then raises his leg up high, slowly bends his front legs and lowers his huge head onto the ground, eyeballing the guests as he freezes in a Three-Legged Downward Elephant position.

Between cameras clicking and guest applause, Mabula knows that he has an appreciative audience, and the rangers know they're in for a long wait because once our performer gets going, there's no stopping him. The louder the laughter, the better.

His adaptation of the Corpse Pose is legendary. He plonks down on his bum, shifts about on his butt cheeks to get comfortable, then straightens out one leg and lounges onto his side in the Mabula Centrefold Pose. His comic timing is superb because if he hears the ranger shift gears to leave, he too changes gears and quickly kneels on all fours and twerks. Yes, *twerks*. Anything to prevent his fans from going. His gyrating rump makes Miley Cyrus look like a beginner.

His other favourite trick is a game of chicken.

He faces the vehicle, shakes his head and billows out his ears, getting ready to charge. The ranger knows it's a pretend charge but the guests don't. He starts with a slow trot that speeds into a stampede. Adrenalin in the 4×4 rockets. That much elephant bearing down on you at breakneck speed is terrifying, and he knows *exactly* how scary he looks.

Bearing in mind that the behaviour of a wild animal is always unpredictable, the ranger usually backs away to give him space. As soon as the 4×4 kicks into reverse, Mabula veers off to the side. Game over and he knows he's won, preening in delight as he saunters back to the herd.

Everyone in show business knows that performances don't always go according to plan, as Mabula found out the hard way.

Tambotie trees are so strong that their timber is used for gun stocks and arrows. Not an easy tree to knock down, and usually an elephant will use its entire body weight to knock one of them over, but Mabula wanted to show that he could do it with just one leg.

With his right foot against the trunk and his eyes on his audience in the Land Cruiser, he pushed with all his might. The tree bent and creaked. The guests clapped and whistled. Mabula pushed harder. The tree groaned and buckled to breaking point.

Suddenly his foot slipped and the tree boomeranged against his forehead.

Gales of laughter exploded from the vehicle.

Mabula flew into a rage, whipped around and charged. He likes people to laugh *with* him, not *at* him.

But the ranger was ready for his temper tantrum and sped off, leaving him on his own, wondering what the heck had gone wrong with his show.

10

Dangerous deals

I reread the message my assistant had left propped up on my desk.

Piet Potgieter called three times. Has rhinos and wants a meeting.

Piet Potgieter*? Never heard of him. I had no money to buy more game. Maybe he was a journalist trying to get an interview. I tapped the piece of paper then shrugged and dialled the number. One call wouldn't commit me to anything. A clipped voice answered the phone.

'Potgieter.'

'Hello, it's Françoise Malby-Anthony. You called me this afternoon.'

'Ah yes, Françoise. Thanks for getting back to me so quickly. You're quite a difficult woman to get hold of.'

'Sorry about that but I have a lot on my plate. How can I help you?'

'I have a proposal I'd like to discuss with you but preferably not over the phone.'

'What is this about?'

---

* Identities and place names have been changed to protect the location of rhinos.

'Rhino conservation.'

That caught my interest.

'Your message said you had rhinos for me. I must warn you, I'm not in the market to buy,' I said.

'I'm not selling. I have eight rhinos I'd like to rehome and they won't cost you a cent, other than maybe the transport, although I'm even negotiable on that. I'm talking big-scale rhino conservation here, but it's too complicated for a phone conversation. How about we meet the next time you're in Johannesburg so I can explain? My farm's up in the Limpopo but I'm often in Joburg on business.'

'I don't have a trip planned but I'll let you know when I do,' I said neutrally.

He didn't miss a beat.

'No problem. I'll come to you. We've heard a lot about Thula Thula and I know my wife would love to meet you. Would the last weekend of this month work for you? We could be there by midday on the Saturday.'

To say I was taken aback is putting it mildly. There's no easy route from the Limpopo to Thula Thula. It would take him two flights followed by a two-hour drive to get to me. I wondered why I didn't recognize his name but I figured it was probably because he kept a low profile. You get people like that. They do fantastic work and yet they stay out of the limelight. It would have been rude to refuse, and to be honest, by then I was more than a little curious about why he was prepared to go to such lengths to talk to me. We agreed on dates and I promised to send him driving directions from Durban airport to Thula Thula.

I lowered the phone, feeling slightly uneasy without knowing why. I put it down to his offer of free rhinos. Lawrence always said that if something sounded too good to be true, it probably was. Who gives away animals as valuable as rhinos? Eight of them would be worth about R2.8 million – an enormous amount in South Africa's struggling currency. Even in a more stable currency like dollars, it was a lot of money. I could do plenty for conservation with $330,000.

A fortnight later, the gate guard called to announce Mr and Mrs Potgieter's arrival. I glanced at my watch – five past twelve. My rhino benefactor was a punctual man.

'Thanks, Thembo,' I said to the guard. 'Please could you arrange for someone to escort my guests to the lodge and let them know that I'll be there to meet them.'

It's a short drive from my office to the lodge and of course I don't go anywhere without Gypsy, but because I walk fast and her short legs can't keep up, I usually carry her. By the time I arrived at the lodge with my little poodle in my arms, Piet Potgieter was already downing a Castle Lager at the bar. He jumped up when he saw me and Gypsy went into a barking frenzy at the bearded stranger striding our way.

Potgieter was a stocky man somewhere in his seventies, and his square face burst with confidence more suited to a young buck than an ageing bull. I nuzzled Gypsy to calm her down, then I put her on the ground at my feet. Piet Potgieter took my hand in both of his.

'It's lovely to meet you, and let me just say this: you're even more beautiful in real life.'

I searched his watery blue eyes but saw nothing. And I mean nothing. No windows to the soul there, I thought to myself. I asked my lodge hostess, Sindi, for my usual glass of cold sparkling water and a bowl of water for Gypsy, who had positioned herself between me and the man.

'Is your wife not joining us?' I asked.

'She's just freshening up. Nice place you have here.'

'Thank you. So, on the phone you said you have a farm up in the Limpopo?'

'I've got 8,000 hectares a few kilometres outside of Tzaneen. How many do you have here?'

'About half that. You're not a hunting farm, are you?'

His laugh was somewhere between a snort and a guffaw.

'I've been accused of many things but hunting isn't one of them. I breed rhinos.'

'You *breed* them? To do what with, if you're not selling them to hunters?'

'To save the species.'

I took in this grand statement and checked his eyes for fire. Still nothing.

'That's one hell of a mission,' I acknowledged.

'And you can be part of it.'

My stand on conservation was no secret. I wanted to help rhinos, one orphan at a time. Despite his rather annoying manner, I was intrigued.

'How do you mean, I can be part of it?'

He signalled for another beer and waited for it to be poured.

'I've been breeding them for about twenty years and now I have too many, so—'

'What do you call too many?' I interrupted.

'Just under a thousand.'

I hid my shock. 'That's a lot.'

'One of the largest stocks in the world,' he nodded.

I flinched at the word *stock*.

'So where does the conservation part come into it?' I asked.

'Simple. Poaching is going to kill our rhinos. The demand in Asia for horn won't change in our lifetime and if we don't do something about it, they'll disappear. I know it. You know it. Three rhinos are killed every day in South Africa alone, and at this rate they'll be extinct within a few decades. I breed them and harvest their horns, so one day soon when it's legal again, I'll flood the market and we can all sit back and watch the price per kilo plummet. Then all those—'

He stopped mid speech at the arrival of a very well groomed, very young blonde. Gypsy growled and I quickly slipped off a shoe and stroked her with my bare foot.

'Françoise, meet my Anneline,' Potgieter said.

'Hello Françoise, it's fantastic to meet you. I just loved *The Elephant Whisperer*. I *mos* cried the whole way through.'

From her accent, I deduced that Anneline Potgieter was Afrikaans. From the size of the rocks on her fingers, and the fact that she looked young enough to be his daughter, I deduced he was her sugar daddy. It didn't bother me in the least. If trophy wives and sugar daddies found a way to combine love with business, who was I to judge?

'I'm glad you liked the book,' I smiled.

'Oh my God. I love your accent! Isn't her accent sexy, Pietie?'

'We *both* have accents,' I laughed. 'Where are you from, Anneline?'

'I'm from Bredasdorp but I wish I sounded like you. You

know, we went to Paris for our honeymoon. It was so romantic, wasn't it, Pietie?'

Potgieter passed her a glass of sweet white wine.

'Here you go, *my bokkie*. I ordered your favourite wine from Klein Constantia.'

'*Ag my hemel*, I'm so excited to be here. How do you say cheers in French?' She clinked her glass against my water glass. 'When can we go on a game drive?'

'Popette, remember how I said Françoise and I first need to talk some business? Let me finish my meeting and then I promise you, we'll do whatever you want.' He gave her a quick kiss and turned back to me. 'Where were we?'

'You were explaining how harvesting rhino horns would save the species,' I said dryly.

'The way I see it is that if we dump a crapload of rhino horn on Asia, demand will drop.'

'You're saying the more horn that's available, the *less* people will want it? How does that work?'

'Basic economics. Supply and demand. Flood the market and prices drop. You see what I mean?'

'No, actually, I don't think I do. Rhino horn is used for anything from curing cancer to a status trophy in a board-room, so why would flooding the market—'

'I'll give you an example. Say your favourite food is pizza and—'

'I'm French. I don't eat much pizza.'

'Okay, frogs' legs then. Imagine they cost five hundred rand per leg and suddenly you can get them for fifty rand. What do you do? You eat yourself sick and then you won't want them any more.'

He gave me a triumphant grin. Anneline smiled proudly at him over the rim of her wine glass. I was beginning to feel like I needed a glass myself.

'Look what happened when they banned the sale of rhino horn in 2009.' Potgieter hammered his fist on the bar. 'The bloody price shot up.'

'But—'

'Here's what I've been doing about it. I've been removing my rhinos' horns for years. Better a live rhino without a horn than a dead rhino without one. You get my drift? The idea is to sell the horns to protect the rhinos. I have an army looking after mine – sharpshooters, ex-military men, a helicopter, infrared cameras, electric fencing, the lot – and it costs me an effing fortune, pardon my French.'

'I still don't understand the conservation part, because your rhinos aren't actually being rehabilitated to go back into the wild, are they?'

'Let's keep it real. They get *killed* in the wild. If we don't do what I'm doing, there won't be rhinos left to protect. My rhinos have outgrown my farm so I'm looking for game reserves to get on board to help. Me and my team will take care of the horn harvesting and here's the part that will interest you – I'll split the proceeds. You get a third, the community gets a third and I keep a third, and by the way, I don't care what you do with your third.'

He made it sound so logical, so easy. At the time, I was still struggling to pay off debts after Lawrence's death and didn't have a cent to my name. He must have known how attractive his offer was to me, and he was somehow making it sound as if I would be irresponsible if I didn't help him in some way. I desperately needed time to think.

'I'll never be able to afford to keep so many rhinos safe.'

'I'll send men to provide round-the-clock protection.'

He had it all worked out.

'The horns are worth $90,000 per kilo,' he continued. 'Bearing in mind that just one of them weighs four kilos, that's plenty bucks coming your way. And I want to give you *eight* rhinos. It's a no-brainer, Françoise. Think what you could do for the community. Think what you could do for Thula Thula.'

'But what you're saying is quite hypothetical, isn't it? Because right now, selling horns isn't allowed and I'm not interested in anything illegal.'

'It won't be for long. I've got contacts. Plenty contacts. People who'll help me change the law. Don't you worry about that. The law's going to change and then selling rhino horn will be one hundred per cent legal.'

'How can you be so sure?'

Anneline laced her fingers with his. 'What Pietie wants, Pietie gets.'

'Let's just say I've got friends in high places,' he said. 'Do we have a deal?'

I didn't know what to say. I'd done the figures in my head and what he was proposing would save my life. I would be able to clear all our debts *and* have a steady income to safeguard Thabo and Ntombi. If my calculations were right then there would eventually be enough money for me to expand the reserve and create the much-needed extra space for my growing herd. Luckily, the authorities had been very supportive of what we were doing and they hadn't brought up the issue of culling again, but the kind of money Potgieter was talking about would solve that problem too. Still I hesitated.

'How do you think your rhinos will get on with mine? Ours have never been around other rhinos,' I said.

'They'll figure it out. Don't forget, mine aren't exactly *wild*. They're used to being around other rhinos. I doubt they'll attack them, if that's what you're worried about.'

That's exactly what I was worried about. Rhinos are territorial, and after everything Thabo had been through, the last thing I needed was him fighting off strange male rhinos who were eyeing his Ntombi.

'What's the male-to-female ratio of the rhinos you want me to have?'

With an impatient flick of the wrist, Potgieter signalled to Sindi to top up Anneline's glass.

'And another Castle for me. Sure you won't have anything other than water?'

I shook my head. 'Tell me more about the rhinos I'll be getting.'

'Can't we go on a game drive before lunch?' Anneline begged in her best little-girl voice.

It struck me then what a good team they were. She had obviously picked up that he didn't want to go into detail about the rhinos and was stepping in to distract.

'I'm so sorry, Anneline, but there aren't any drives scheduled until sunset,' I said. 'So, Piet, you were telling me about the rhinos?'

'You'll get eight in excellent health, even vaccinated against Histotoxic Clostridia toxaemia.'

I didn't let on that I had never heard of the disease.

'I suppose they'll be dehorned before they get to Thula Thula,' I said.

'The horns will grow back within a year or so and then they'll start making money for you.'

I took this in without replying and he misunderstood my silence.

'Okay, okay. I can see what you're thinking. How about this? I'll make sure four of them still have their horns so you'll reap the rewards quicker.'

'It doesn't feel right,' I said quietly.

'We knock them out. They don't know what's happening.'

It wasn't at all what I meant, and his nonchalant attitude to anaesthetizing the rhinos shook me. He was right that dehorning doesn't hurt the animal, but the process remains brutal and it can go wrong – there is no such thing as a risk-free anaesthetic.

I understood then why Gypsy hadn't liked him. He wasn't the kind of conservationist Lawrence and I had set out to be.

'The thing is,' I said, 'we spend our lives educating people that the horn is worth nothing and that it has no more medical value than the keratin in their nails, so don't you think that selling the horns goes against everything we conservationists are trying to do?'

'You're not going to change the minds of the idiots who buy the stuff, so you may as well make money for your animals from them, and anyway, let's remember the objective here – once we flood the market, the price will drop and the horns won't be as lucrative for the poachers any more.'

Not before you've sold your *stock* at the current dollar rate per kilo, I felt like saying, but I kept quiet. I had no doubt that in the two decades he had been quietly breeding his rhinos, he had built up millions of dollars' worth of horn, waiting for the day that the selling embargo would be lifted. Maybe he was right that the price would drop, but I didn't for a moment believe that a product so ingrained in a society's cultural belief system would become less popular if it was less expensive. Yes, some of the status around owning rhino horn might disappear, but what about the uneducated Chinese labourer whose cancer-riddled mother is dying and who really believes that traditional medicine with rhino horn powder will save her life? Of course he's still going to buy it.

Lawrence would have laughed in Potgieter's face. The only reason he wanted to *give* me some of his rhinos was because he was running out of space. Just because he was a breeder didn't mean he didn't have to stick to South Africa's wildlife regulations, and I knew first hand how strict the rules were about the ratio of wildlife to size of reserve.

'Are the rhinos you want to give me males, by any chance?' I asked.

His eyes narrowed for a second. Bingo. He was offloading territorial males. Anneline placed her hand on his forearm.

'Are you done yet? I'm dying to meet Nana,' she pleaded.

I leapt at the opportunity to get rid of them.

'I'll arrange a private game drive for you. I could even ask the kitchen to prepare you a romantic lunch in the bush if you like.'

'*Really?* That would be great,' she squealed.

I waved them off on their game drive *à deux*, but not before Potgieter tried to extract an answer from me.

'I can't make the decision on my own,' I protested.

'Why not? You're the boss.'

'I'm still learning about conservation, and for something as big as this I prefer to talk it over with my team.'

'Are they here? Why don't you let me speak to them?'

'They aren't all here,' I lied. 'But there's a meeting planned for next week so I'll be able to get back to you pretty quickly.'

He tried again over dinner to persuade me to agree to his proposal, but by then I'd had a quick word with Vusi and Promise and they both agreed that we shouldn't touch the rhinos with a bargepole.

Firstly, none of us believed that selling rhino horn would help the species in the long term, and secondly, I didn't want anything to do with what was effectively a huge con. People who believe rhino horn has medicinal value are being duped and I wanted no part of it, no matter how badly we needed the money.

The Potgieters left straight after breakfast the next morning and I promised I'd let him know about the outcome of our meeting and then I did the French thing and just left it. And he never made contact with me either. He was a smart man and I think he realized that I wasn't just a broke blonde, desperate to say, *Yes! Bring me rhinos. Let's cut off their horns and get rich.* He thought he could lure me with bags of money and he was wrong. There's a fine line in conservation between putting animals first and turning it into a business. If you want to get rich, don't get into conservation. Everything we make at Thula Thula goes back to the animals. I spend it all on them, every last cent of it.

Potgieter's visit was yet another wake-up call for me. Ever since Lawrence's death, I'd been so focused on coping with everything at Thula Thula that I wasn't really aware of what was happening outside the reserve.

My exposure to this man prompted a big change. I began to lift my head and look outwards again, and one of the first things I did was become more involved in the conservation world, a world with which I had had very little contact until then. I quickly discovered that Potgieter cropped up everywhere as a pro-trade lobbyist.

Thank heavens I had listened to my instincts and refused his dangerous offer.

11

Courage is doing what you're afraid to do

I was on a game drive with Jos, an old friend of Lawrence's, and Elisabeth, a German journalist he had brought to Thula Thula for me to meet. Elisabeth was a striking woman in her sixties with piercing blue eyes who devoted her writing skills to telling the world about wild animals in trouble.

Even though I had rarely met Jos in my twenty-five years with Lawrence, he did everything he could to help me after Lawrence died. I don't think his mind ever stops trying to find ways to make a difference to the lives of those he cares for. He is an extrovert with a sense of humour as big as his personality and he's always smiling – except when Mabula gets too close to him, because he's convinced himself our big bull doesn't like him!

'Is Mabula in musth at the moment?' Jos asked Vusi nervously.

'For *months* already,' Vusi nodded, sending me a quick wink.

'Don't worry, Jos. We didn't tell him you were coming,' I grinned.

Jos adjusted his trademark baseball cap and squinted into

the bush. I smiled at Elisabeth and the other guests, Joanne and Bruni, who had joined our drive.

'It's fine. Mabula's nothing to worry about.'

'What does being in musth mean?' Joanne asked.

Vusi explained, 'It's when bull elephants have a surge of testosterone and even the most placid elephant can become . . .' He paused, searching for a word that didn't sound frightening.

'*Moody*,' I suggested.

'More like *crazy*,' Jos grimaced.

'It's when we don't get too close to *any* of our bulls,' Vusi said diplomatically.

'Does it happen to all of them, even the young ones?' asked Elisabeth.

'No, only once they get to about twenty years old,' Vusi replied as he manoeuvred the 4×4 through the dry riverbed and revved the engine to get up the opposite bank.

I quickly scanned the area for Frankie. This was the exact same crossing where Lawrence and I had run into the herd fourteen years earlier and it still gave me the shivers. There wasn't an elephant in sight. I sat back and tried to relax.

'How old is Mabula anyway?' asked Jos.

'Twenty-three,' I replied.

The vehicle fell silent as we bumped along the rugged terrain. You could almost hear everyone thinking, *does that mean he's had three years of practice at being bad-tempered?*

'The thing about Mabula is, he's stroppy like his mum Frankie,' explained Vusi. 'But as long as we remember we're in *his* space, and we stay out of his way when he's in musth, he actually loves us being around.' He grinned at Jos. 'He also loves a good prank, especially giving someone a fright.'

'Why does he have to pick on *me* though?' Jos muttered.

'Hello there. Look who's here,' Vusi said softly.

Thabo and Ntombi were standing in the middle of the track, side by side with their backs to us. Vusi slowed to a halt and switched off the engine. A rhino's bum is about as solid as it gets: a barrel of rock-hard muscle on stumpy but powerful legs that can outrun an elephant's. Neither rhino acknowledged our presence, not even with a quick over-the-shoulder peek.

'Something's caught their attention all right,' Vusi murmured.

I noticed him shift the gearstick into reverse. Smart man. We didn't know what Thabo and Ntombi were staring at, but a prepared man is an alive man in the wilds.

'We hand-reared these two from when they were babies,' I whispered to the guests.

'Do rhinos go into musth too?' Bruni asked.

'No, they don't,' Vusi reassured him.

'Thabo looks like he's healed completely,' Jos observed.

'He's doing well physically, but emotionally, it's taken him a very long time to get over being shot. He really took a bad knock, poor thing,' I said.

The huge, grey head of an elephant appeared from behind a tree.

'Uh-oh,' said Vusi, starting the engine.

'Mabula?' Jos asked.

Vusi shook his head and slowly began to reverse. 'Shaka.'

Jos let out a sigh of relief. Shaka is Nana's grandson and he has inherited her sweet nature. He ambled towards Thabo and Ntombi, stopping a good fifteen metres in front of them, ears swishing air over his body, trunk down and relaxed. Vusi moved back to a safer distance then cut the engine again.

'Bush stand-off,' he laughed.

'They're not going to fight, are they?' Joanne asked nervously.

'I doubt it. Thabo's too friendly for his own good and just wants to say hello.'

Thabo took a few steps towards the young bull.

'I wish he wouldn't get in Shaka's way like that,' I frowned. 'That's the problem with hand-reared wild animals, they don't grow up with bush manners.'

'But what are the alternatives for animals that are orphaned like he was?' Elisabeth asked.

'A proper animal orphanage where human contact is kept to a minimum. We'll have one here some day,' I said confidently.

Ntombi had ambled after Thabo and the pair of them were now very close to Shaka, who hadn't moved at all. He looked down at them with a bemused expression as if to say, *I think I have right of way here, buddies.* The widest part of his trunk was more than twice the size of Thabo's back legs. One swipe, and he could knock either rhino off its feet.

'What about Shaka, how old is he?' Joanne asked.

'Only seven, also very young.' I smiled despite my concern. 'Look at them – just a trio of curious youngsters eyeballing each other in the playground.'

'I think now would be a good time to leave,' Vusi said. 'If those two little tanks decide to turn around and bolt for the hills, we do not want to be in their way!'

It was pouring with rain that evening so we ate inside, and

over my chef Winnie's latest dish – crayfish bouillabaisse – Elisabeth and Jos peppered me with questions. They were passionate about wildlife and determined to see how they could help.

Will Thabo and Ntombi have babies one day? Would you take in more elephants that needed rescuing? Is poaching getting worse?

'What are your plans for Thula Thula?' Elisabeth asked.

'To carry on Lawrence's dream of creating one of the biggest reserves here in KwaZulu-Natal. And I would love to do more to help rhino calves whose mothers have been killed by poachers, but it's a big project and there's no money for that just yet. I've got my hands full keeping Thabo and Ntombi safe.'

One of Elisabeth's questions stayed with me for days after she left. She had asked how I was managing on my own after Lawrence died. The truth was that I had survived by simply getting up every day and doing what had to be done. I was utterly out of my comfort zone, small decisions felt overwhelming, and there was so much to learn. Rumours had continued to fly that I was going back to France and even the bank kept checking with me that I wasn't leaving.

One thing I was grateful for that first year was that no one at Thula Thula stopped talking about Lawrence. He always cropped up in conversations.

'Remember how he would say he was bringing two guests for dinner at the lodge and then arrive with twelve?' Mabona reminisced with me. 'And telling him *I'll try* wasn't ever good enough. He taught me to go out and make things *happen*.'

I loved how Vusi would quietly disagree with me about something then go on to explain what Lawrence would have done, and the way Promise would tell a story in the bar at night and mimic the way Lawrence used to tell it.

We weren't the only ones affected by his passing. People from all over the world contacted me to say what an impact his books had had on them, and the stream of supportive messages that came to me throughout 2012 was so comforting. Lawrence had no idea how many lives he had touched and he would have been deeply moved by the kindness shown to me by complete strangers.

The anniversary of his death came too quickly, and before I knew it I was planning a small memorial for him on Saturday, 2 March 2013 at his beloved Mkhulu Dam. I wanted a simple and relaxed get-together that Lawrence himself would have enjoyed. No big speeches, no tears, just his closest friends and family celebrating his life together. His mother, brother and two sons Jason and Dylan joined us, along with friends from far and near, and of course everyone from the game reserve.

The sky was pale blue, and on the horizon storm clouds were gathering. I looked around at the beautiful faces standing in a half circle facing the spot where we had scattered Lawrence's ashes. Vusi, Mabona, Promise, Siya, Alyson, Winnie, Tom, Sindi, Fortunate, Biyela, Victor and many more – my Thula Thula family. Between us, we had held it together and made it through the year, somehow keeping the wheels turning. I was so thankful for every single one of them.

The dam was full and I could just make out the gleaming partly submerged bodies of our hippos Romeo and Juliet. A herd of Cape buffalo drank at the water's edge on the other side, lifting their heads occasionally to fix us with austere stares from underneath magnificent curved horns that looked like helmets. Lawrence had loved bringing me here. We weren't often able to carve out time alone and we had cherished our sundowners together, just him and me, watching the animals until it was too dark to see.

I said goodbye to everyone and spent the rest of that weekend alone with Gypsy, Gin and Jeff. They sensed my sadness and nuzzled me gently, paws touching some part of me, warming my skin with their love, shepherding me to sleep with their soft snores. On Monday morning, I reluctantly headed for Durban for a week crammed with appointments. The storm that had threatened during the memorial had turned into nothing more than a drizzle and an eerie mist hovered between the Zululand hills as I slowly drove along the coastal road. Trucks transporting anything from timber to vehicles roar along that road so I always take my time and allow plenty of extra margin to get to my first commitment of the day.

I raced from meeting to meeting and arrived after five o'clock at the apartment Lawrence and I had owned, a second home where we stayed whenever we had business in the city. I poured myself a glass of cold Sauvignon Blanc, pulled open the sliding doors and went outside onto the covered veranda. Seagulls swooped low over the ocean in front of me and a troop of monkeys jabbered away in the palm trees close by, no doubt eyeing the open door behind me and trying to figure out if they could bolt through to steal fruit from my kitchen.

Inside, my phone pinged. I ignored it. The day had been exhausting and I wanted half an hour of peace before tackling the build-up of emails and messages. The waves rolled in gently, scattering white froth over the rocks then sliding back again. I never tire of looking at the Indian Ocean. The waves can pound with brutal power in the morning then caress with infinite tenderness by afternoon.

Ping. Ping. Ping.

Whoever was trying to get hold of me was very determined. I frowned in frustration and went to look for my phone.

Promise. My heart lurched. Was something wrong?

They're at the main house!

Who? What did he mean? Had I missed a meeting?

I clicked open the first photo he had sent.

The herd. Surrounding my house at Thula Thula. It was still drizzling and their backs glistened like ebony in the fading light. I opened photo after photo. There was Nana, standing at the fence with her daughter Nandi, both staring towards the house. And Mabula, his trunk tip scouting out the electric fence. I smiled to myself. He was checking the current before trying to stretch over the wires to the acacia tree on the other side. Our youngest calf, Victoria, was huddled against her grandmother Frankie.

They came back! Can you believe it? Promise messaged.

I stared at his words, stunned. Exactly a year ago, on 4 March 2012, the weekend of Lawrence's death, the herd had inexplicably come to the house too. It was one of those strange phenomena in the bush that is impossible to explain scientifically but every one of us at Thula Thula knew they had returned because of Lawrence. Elephants mourn their dead for a long time. Years after Mnumzane died, they would return to where his bones lay and linger for hours, dark streaks lining their cheeks from their temporal glands, touching and picking up the bones in an elephant ritual that we didn't understand. They have a sense of time beyond our comprehension and for me these beautiful, sensitive creatures were doing exactly what we had done two days earlier – marking Lawrence's death in their own way.

I sat on my veranda overlooking the ocean, miles away from them, in awe of the spiritual power of these gentle giants. Why were they at my house today of all days? They would have sensed I wasn't there and yet they still came.

I understood then that it wasn't about me, it was about them.

Lawrence's ashes had long since been absorbed by the earth at Mkhulu Dam and the herd had nothing physical to touch and revere. I believe they returned to where Lawrence had lived simply to be in the same space they had once shared with him. No one had forgotten him, especially not them, and whenever I felt anxious or overwhelmed in the months that followed, I drew such strength from that visit.

They needed me but I also needed them.

12

Ubuntu

'What do we do if it's still raining tomorrow?' I asked Mabona and Winnie.

Mabona squinted up at the clouds. 'It won't.'

'Klaus and Susanne have come all the way from Denmark to have her fiftieth birthday with us in the bush and the last thing they want is to be indoors. What do *you* think, Winnie?'

'I think we should stop worrying about the weather and think about the food. I have the party menu right here.'

She held out a copy with a soft smile. She is as sweet and shy today as she was when she arrived as a timid sixteen-year-old, and she still hates being in the limelight – even when guests want to applaud her for a fantastic meal. Her love of garlic and chillies makes her lethal in the kitchen and even my hungriest ranger thinks twice about being her guinea pig when she's rustled up a new dish using either ingredient!

'French onion soup for starters,' I read out loud. 'Followed by a choice of venison, either on the barbecue or as bourguignon. What about veggies?'

'Crushed garlic potatoes, three types of beans, deep-fried aubergine slices, and corn on the cob with amarula butter. I prepared the butter yesterday.'

'Go easy on the garlic, please,' I laughed. 'How many people will be at the dinner?'

'The Simonsens are six, plus you and four other lodge guests.'

'We'll bake Susanne's favourite chocolate cake in the morning. Pity we don't have fifty candles for it,' Mabona sighed.

'She'll be relieved to hear that! Yesterday she told me how happy she was that she's escaping the fuss back home and that she wanted her fiftieth to disappear.'

'She should be so lucky! Her kids are up to something,' Mabona grinned.

The Simonsens are a warm, animal-loving Danish family who have been coming to Thula Thula since Lawrence and I built the lodge – long before anyone really knew we existed. The only reason Klaus's father, Jorgen, had discovered us was because one of his South African clients had told him about a luxury game lodge that had opened near their Richards Bay aluminium factory. Jorgen was a keen nature photographer and immediately booked a chalet with us for his next trip.

He was a handsome Viking with platinum-white hair and an easy-going way that made everyone feel they were his friend. From the first time he and Lawrence met, they liked each other – two very different men with strong, colourful characters and a passion for wildlife that turned into deep friendship. They shared the same grab-life-with-both-hands approach: don't delay, don't overthink, just get out and do what has to be done. On Jorgen's second visit, he brought Tove, his petite and gracious wife, and a few trips later they came with their children. Each year the Simonsen booking got bigger, because the kids grew up and brought their partners and then the grandchildren tagged along too. Lawrence and I always looked forward to their visits. The Simonsens understood what we were working towards and we loved how much it meant to them to be part of what we were doing.

'Is there enough champagne?' I asked Mabona.

'Always, but I don't have any that's cold.'

'We can't have her fiftieth without champagne! Please ask one of the guys to take bottles out of the storeroom and pop them in the fridge. We *must* start with champers. In fact, why don't we change the menu and . . .'

'It's too late for changes,' Winnie objected.

'*Mais non!* Susanne will love it.'

'Please leave things as they are,' she begged. 'Susanne is happy with the menu and we don't want to worry her with last-minute changes.'

'But wouldn't it be great if we rustled up something creative with champagne?'

Mabona rolled her eyes. 'Remember the last time you were creative?'

'That Camembert and Roquefort ice cream with red berry coulis was sublime.'

'Except nobody else thought so,' Mabona groaned theatrically. 'Overruled. Imagine if your champagne creation is a flop!'

That got my attention. I'll never forget how enthusiastic Jorgen and Tove were about our cuisine when we were just getting going. They said they had eaten better in the bush at Thula Thula than at any French restaurant in Copenhagen. I was so proud to get such a lovely compliment from a couple who had eaten at the best restaurants in the world.

I reluctantly agreed not to meddle with Winnie's menu, and for the rest of the day she and Mabona kept out of my way. They know how dangerous I am when I'm in a creative mood.

When I went to bed it was still raining, and every time I woke up I heard rain. Poor Susanne. The party would have to be held inside. At dawn, Jeff, my Labrador, woke me with a wet-nose kiss and I held him to me and listened. Silence. I threw open the curtains.

The sky was a blush of pink with not a cloud in sight.

By six that evening, the dining *boma* was a hive of activity and the firepit was already blazing in the middle. Two girls were lighting lanterns and candles, and Winnie was keeping a watchful eye on the men grilling the venison on the *braai*. I checked the tables. Safari-print tablecloths with crisp linen overlays. I smiled at the napkins and knew exactly who had folded them into exquisite floral shapes. Water glasses, champagne glasses, wine glasses. Everything was in order, as it always is when Mabona and Winnie are in charge.

There's something magical about eating outdoors under the stars in Africa, close to a roaring fire, cocooned by a circle of reeds. It connects the past, the present and the future, and makes you feel you're the only people on earth.

It's a time to share stories, be with those you love, and relish the closeness to Mother Nature. How I wished Lawrence could have been with us. He would have been so touched that Jorgen's daughter-in-law was celebrating her big birthday at Thula Thula. I stared out into the darkness. It was hard to believe it was my second winter without him. Where had the time gone? Sometimes it felt as if he had died in a strange other life, and other times, like that night, my loss was as raw as the day he died.

Just before dessert, Mabona stood next to the fire and sang *Thula Baba*, the haunting African lullaby that Lawrence had loved and that had inspired Thula Thula's name. The flames glowed. Her voice soared into the night. Susanne and I wiped away tears. When Mabona sings that song, you feel it in your soul.

Klaus Simonsen tapped a spoon against a glass. He reminds me so much of his father – tall, friendly and always smiling. The *boma* fell silent. Grinning broadly, Klaus and their three adult children plus a family friend stood in a row in front of Susanne.

'Are they going to sing?' I whispered.

She shrugged, eyes gleaming in anticipation.

Frederick, the eldest son, took off his sweater and turned around. The number 12½ was printed on his shirt. Her second son, Nikolaj, turned too. Another 12½. Susanne and I began to giggle. We knew what was coming before the others finished turning around.

Sara, her daughter, and the one who had teased her the most about getting older, revealed the grand finale – a huge number 50.

'Now *everyone* knows,' Susanne complained cheerfully.

Klaus tapped the glass again.

'Susanne, happy birthday!' He kissed her and gave her a card. 'This is your *second* birthday present. Please read it out to everyone.'

She took it from him, looking very confused.

'To my wonderful family,' she began. 'Thank you for the present I'm about to receive and that I know nothing about . . .' She paused with a frown. Klaus waved at her to continue. 'As you know, I turned fifty today. Well, that gave me an idea to use the number 50 in a different way. I would therefore like to ask Françoise to come and stand next to me . . .'

Laughing in delight at being included, I filled two champagne glasses and joined her, just as curious to know what Klaus was up to. He handed her a second card to read out.

'Dear Françoise . . .' she started.

Me? I looked at Klaus. Now what? He and the children beamed at me.

'This present is for you.' Susanne's voice began to shake. 'It's my small way of being part of the fantastic work you do here at Thula Thula.'

A cheque for R50,000.

I was speechless. Everyone clapped and whooped and the Zulu staff broke into elated ululation. Tears streamed down Susanne's cheeks.

'I didn't know,' she whispered.

I'm not often lost for words, but that night I couldn't speak. At a time when my life was so adrift, so scary, this beautiful family helped moor my shaky boat. I hadn't realized until that moment how lonely I was.

Ubuntu is a powerful Zulu word that means we don't exist on our own and that we are never alone because we are part of a bigger connected world of humanity. Before coming to South Africa, I lived in a society where being an individual was more valued than being part of a community. It's not like that here. In traditional Africa, 'us' is more meaningful than 'me'. *Ubuntu* means that I am who I am only because of who we all are together.

Lawrence always used to say that every contribution makes a difference because, big or small, they all come with the same goodwill and love. Whether it's a huge cheque like Susanne's or knitted blankets for orphaned animals, it's all part of humanity coming together.

Kelsey Paul's contribution is a good example. She was just sixteen when she visited Thula Thula with her family, and on her first night Thabo and Ntombi slept under her window. She barely slept a wink in excitement and was horrified the next day to learn that without 24/7 armed guards, they would be killed by poachers. She went back home to the USA, determined to spread the word that rhinos were in danger of extinction. This intrepid young girl and her mum, Jill, wrote a children's book about Thabo and Ntombi – *My Baby Rhinos* – and all proceeds go to our rhino fund. In a world where teenagers are more often than not glued to their phones, Kelsey stepped in to make a difference.

Every cent helps, every person who helps is important. It wasn't just the Simonsens' generosity that moved me so much, it was their understanding that I couldn't do it on my own.

By midnight, only Klaus, Susanne and I were left around the firepit, boots up on the stone edge for warmth. I finally found the words to thank them properly.

'It means so much to know I'm not alone,' I said quietly.

'*We're* the ones who are grateful,' Klaus said. 'Thula Thula has changed the lives of three generations in our family – two of our kids have even chosen to work with animals because of what they've seen and learned here.'

Susanne brushed curls away from her face and gazed into the fire. She's an earth mother, serene and nurturing, and just being with her is calming.

'Coming to Thula Thula and getting to know Nana has made me a better person,' she said. 'Nana has taught me that when you're a matriarch, you have to be strong and you have to do everything to keep your family together, especially when life gets tough.' She glanced at me. 'And she also taught me about hope. The herd was on the verge of being shot and look what happened – you and Lawrence came into their lives and they were given a second chance. That's hope, Françoise. Never forget that. There's always hope.'

My wise Nana was touching lives on the other side of the planet. I raised my glass, teary-eyed.

'Here's to another matriarch, Lawrence's mum, who even in her nineties keeps the Anthony clan together. Our Nana really did live up to his hopes that she would be as wise and strong a leader as his mother.'

'To courage and wisdom,' Susanne smiled, raising her glass.

'When she first arrived, we didn't know what to expect from her,' I reminisced. 'The original matriarch had been shot and she was forced to take over her role in terrifying circumstances. Can you imagine her fear and distress? Her leader killed, transported in huge noisy vehicles, an unknown terrain. And yet, right from the moment they arrived, Nana rose to the challenge and led her little family with confidence and wisdom.'

Susanne took my hand.

'You also ended up with responsibilities you were unprepared for, and were forced into a role you never thought would be yours. And you handled it like Nana, with dignity and courage. We know, we watched.'

We fell silent and listened to the orchestra of night sounds. From deep in the reserve, I sensed Nana's love and I basked in the wonder of *ubuntu*.

13

Stars are brighter in Africa

A late-night hello from a sociable rhino when you're staying in a tent is a hair-raising experience, whether it's your first time in the bush or your hundredth. Despite Thabo's years as a free rhino in the wild, he still loved human company – the downside of not being reared in a dedicated centre where contact with people is limited to carers. Fortunately the American guests Thabo visited stayed relatively calm and, with a bit of creativity, they even managed to persuade him that a midnight pyjama party wasn't on the cards.

'Our ranger had escorted us to our tent after dinner and we were just getting ready to go to bed when I heard something strange outside,' Mike told me the next morning. 'No footsteps, just breathing.'

'I've never been so scared in my life! I mean, the only thing between us and the *thing* was some fabric,' said his wife Jeanne.

'You know where we're staying, right?' Mike asked me.

I shook my head. He flung his arms in the air.

'It's the last one, right at the end, where there's *nothing* but wilderness.'

I did my best not to laugh. 'What did you think the thing was?'

'No clue. We just knew it was big and too close for comfort.'

Jeanne rolled her eyes. 'My hero.'

'When did you work out it was Thabo?'

'We didn't at first. It was full moon so the thing cast a huge shadow onto the tent and then it started to push against the canvas, as if it wanted to get in. Bloody hell. It could have been *anything*.'

'And we had no signal on our mobiles. We couldn't even phone for help if we needed it,' groaned Jeanne.

'I don't know what was worse – being clueless about what it was or knowing it was a flipping rhino. We had no idea it was Thabo himself, but we realized damn quickly it was a rhino from the shape of the horn through the fabric.'

'We were terrified the tent would tear,' Jeanne said. 'You see these things on YouTube but you never think it could happen to you.'

They were horrified and I didn't blame them. Thabo was a smart teenager in rhino years and he had worked out that tents meant his favourite two-legged creatures were inside.

'I'm so sorry,' I said. 'Hopefully after another year in the bush he won't be so tame any more, but a year is a long way off. I'm going to have to find a way to keep tents off limits from him.'

'Don't do that! He's adorable as he is,' Jeanne laughed.

'Thabo trusts people too much for his own good,' I said. 'The tamer he is, the greater the risk of him being killed.'

Because we lacked a proper rehab centre, Thabo and Ntombi had grown up at the lodge, surrounded by all of us, a big human family who doted on them. But like most kids who leave home, they loved coming back and often chose to sleep outside their old room. I think it comforted them because they knew they were safe there. It was endearing but dangerous. Wild rhinos usually run a mile from humans and that's how it should be.

'How on earth did you get him to leave?' I quizzed my still-frazzled guests.

'I banged the tent with my hairdryer and he gave a couple of very annoyed squeals then lumbered off and disappeared.'

'Not that we slept a wink after that,' Mike grumbled.

'I wouldn't let him go back to sleep in case Thabo came back, but what a night! Our kids back in Raleigh will never believe us.'

Thank heavens Thabo hadn't tried harder to join them. Two petrified humans, a curious rhino and a collapsed tent would have been catastrophic. We had done our best with Thabo and Ntombi but I knew that we could never raise more orphaned animals without a dedicated facility.

Thabo's adventure with Mike and Jeanne happened years ago, and today he and Ntombi are like any other wild animal – they don't like strangers. He has even become skittish around people he grew up with, as our lodge hostess discovered recently with almost deadly consequences.

No one is allowed to walk in the bush outside the fenced-in areas. That may seem obvious but it happens all the time in game reserves. People get complacent, especially when animals don't have a history of being aggressive. Despite the rules, our employees occasionally walk where they shouldn't, particularly if they're in a rush and don't want to wait for a 4×4 to give them a lift.

But just because animals haven't attacked, doesn't mean they won't.

One afternoon, Sindi, a vivacious Zulu woman who has been with us since she was a teenager, was outside the safety zone, walking to the main gate to meet a friend. She saw Thabo and Ntombi in the distance but wasn't the least bit concerned. She had known them since they were babies and adored them. As she approached the gate, the guard began to yell at her.

'Sindi, run! Thabo's coming for you!'

Clifford was a member of Thabo's armed protection unit and knew him better than anyone. She grinned and waved at him, thinking he was joking.

'*Baleka*, Sindi. *Baleka!*' Run, Sindi. Run!

She turned and saw Thabo hurtling towards her.

Rhinos can pick up speed surprisingly quickly – going from zero to fifty-five kilometres per hour in three seconds flat. That's not much time to get out of the way, unless you're next to a tree and you're a fast climber. Paralysed, Sindi watched Thabo come closer and closer.

'*Move!* MOVE!' Clifford yelled.

Thabo crashed into her. She flew into the air and landed on her back, flabbergasted that he had hit her. He did a U-turn and thundered towards her again, headbutting and flinging her like a rag doll. Clifford ran towards them, hoping like crazy that Thabo would recognize him.

'*Ngyacela mfana wami ungamlimazi, uSindi!*' Please, my boy, don't hurt Sindi.

Thabo snorted angrily and pounded in his direction.

Clifford dived to the ground and rolled out of the way. Thabo spun around and rammed him with his head.

'Thabo, *stop*!' Clifford bellowed.

Andrew, one of our rangers, was washing his Land Cruiser in the workshop, about a hundred metres from the gate. He heard the commotion but thought someone outside the fence was yelling at dogs. It wasn't until he heard two voices that he took notice. He ran outside, saw Thabo hammering Clifford and leapt into his 4×4 and raced towards them.

Sindi was hidden by the tall grass and he only spotted her at the last minute – he yanked the steering wheel to the left and narrowly missed running her over. Thabo was getting ready for another charge. Andrew aimed the vehicle at him and used the bull bar to push him away. It was a dangerous manoeuvre, because if Thabo had wanted to, he could have immobilized the 4×4 in a heartbeat.

Confused by this unusual aggression from a vehicle, Thabo veered off, only to turn around and target Sindi again. She curled into the foetal position, whimpering in pain. Andrew slammed into reverse and, engine screaming, drove between Thabo and her. Thabo stopped, bewildered. A second ranger heard the noise and came tearing across the veldt.

'Cover me so I can get to her!' Shandu yelled at Andrew.

Andrew revved the engine loudly, drove forwards, then slammed into reverse.

'He's charging. Get Sindi in the car!' he screamed.

Shandu scooped her up, laid her on the back seat then vaulted in next to her.

Their troubles were far from over.

Andrew eyed the gate and wondered if he could reach it

before Thabo hit them. Rhinos don't mock-charge like elephants do and two tons of rhino would have flipped the vehicle.

But Thabo swerved and missed them.

Then, as if it was just another casual day in Africa, he trotted up to Ntombi, exchanged snout snuffles with her and off they trundled, side by side, like an old married couple.

Clifford survived with massive bruises and everyone's admiration for his bravery but Sindi spent ten days in hospital with a shattered pelvis.

'*Why* would he attack me like that? What did I do to make him want to kill me? He *knows* me. I thought he was playing,' she anguished. 'If Andrew and Shandu hadn't arrived, I would be dead.'

Like everyone, she saw Thabo as the affectionate calf he'd once been, and it broke her heart that he had turned violent.

We don't know what happened to Thabo that day. Was it Sindi's bright-pink sun umbrella that set him off? Or was he protecting Ntombi because she was pregnant? For weeks, I studied her enormous belly and tried to gauge if she was bigger than before. It was impossible to tell, and as the months went by, it was clear that she wasn't.

Whatever the reason, it wasn't Thabo's fault, and in a way it was a kind of graduation for everyone. Thabo earned his I'm-a-wild-rhino badge and we all realized that our big baby had grown up and wasn't a harmless little rhino calf any more.

Being tame is not only dangerous for the animals, it's dangerous for us too.

After Clifford had yelled his warning at Sindi, she had

more than enough time to get out of Thabo's way but she didn't in a million years believe he would harm her. She had known him all his life and she loved him, and that love almost killed her.

If Thabo had been reared with limited human contact, his instinct to fear man would still be there, and we wouldn't have become used to him being so lovable around us. Of course, orphaned rhinos need twenty-four-hour care, especially in the beginning, so it's impossible to prevent them forming relationships with their guardians, but we can minimize it. The world is a treacherous place for rhinos and we *need* them to be distrustful of people. It's a fine balance between giving calves enough nurturing to thrive but not allowing them to become too tame.

The first time I wrote about my dream of opening a rhino sanctuary was in a newsletter in August 2013. Elisabeth, the German journalist who my friend Jos had introduced me to, sent it to every animal welfare organization she knew, and that's how it landed in Heli Dungler's inbox. Heli is founder and CEO of an Austrian animal welfare organization called Four Paws and the newsletter piqued his interest, so he decided to see for himself what we were doing at Thula Thula and tagged a visit to us onto a scheduled business trip to South Africa.

We showed him and his daughter what we had achieved with the herd and with Thabo and Ntombi, and I talked at length about our hopes of one day being able to help animal orphans. He asked lots of questions and told us about the projects his foundation sponsored across the globe. As far as he is concerned, no animal is too big, too small or too far away to help, whether it's saving bears on Asian bile farms or tackling the puppy trade in Europe.

They say passion is contagious and Heli's passion has that effect on everyone. He comes alive when he talks about his work and he has an amazing capacity to stay upbeat despite the horrendous suffering he has witnessed.

Out of the blue a month after his visit, I received an email from him asking me what finance we would need for a rhino sanctuary. I couldn't believe my eyes. We had talked about my hopes of creating one but he hadn't said a word about the possibility of doing a joint project together, and now there it was, in black and white, a request for me to send him a proposal to build it!

Neither Alyson nor I had any experience in writing proposals and I was very worried that ours wouldn't be up to scratch. We sat down together to figure out how to begin.

'Lawrence always handled this kind of thing,' I said blankly.

'I'm useless at it. I can't even organize my own admin, let alone do something like this,' Alyson grimaced.

'Why don't we start the proposal with an introduction to you? You're a vet nurse with all the right experience and we can use your work with Thabo and Ntombi as a case study. We'll talk about what we did right and where we think we could have done things differently.' I paused. 'We should also contact people with rhino orphan experience for advice. I'll ask around.'

I scribbled *rhino experts, wildlife vets, other orphanages* on my notepad.

'We'll need detailed quotes so we can give Four Paws exact figures for what the building work, fencing and security installations will cost,' Alyson added.

Writing the proposal was intimidating, but one of the things that I learned on the turbulent ride of coping on my own was the power of saying *I don't know*. I've realized that it's easier to admit that I don't know something than to pretend that I do. Anyway, it's the truth. Our animals had always been Lawrence's responsibility and I knew next to nothing about what was involved in looking after them.

'What else do you think we need?' I asked.

'An ambulance. We can't have a rescue centre without an emergency vehicle.'

'It'd better be a sturdy one. Look how quickly Thabo and Ntombi grew – they doubled in size every few months until Thabo could bulldoze down a door without even trying.'

'*Everything* has to be sturdy,' she agreed. 'The babies will be terrified when they first get here and probably very unpredictable, even aggressive, so their rooms, feeding areas and all the outside enclosures must be strong enough to withstand a pretty good thumping.' She gave me a concerned look. 'This is going to cost a fortune. Do you have any idea how much Four Paws wants to donate?'

'Nope. But they asked for the proposal and they have far more experience than we do so they must know what's involved moneywise.'

'It would be incredible if they said yes,' Alyson sighed, then shifted forward in her chair. 'Right. Back to work. Dreaming will get us nowhere.'

'Dreaming will get us *everywhere*,' I said softly, walking

over to the window. It was dusk and the trees were black lace silhouettes against a coral sky. 'For so long, I dreamed of having a haven on our doorstep where orphaned animals could heal from their trauma.' I turned to her. 'You know the house up on the hill near the southern fence line? That's where it should be.'

'I thought it belonged to the local chiefs?'

'It does, but they gave it to us for animal conservation and I'm sure they'll be on board to turn it into a rehabilitation centre. We could even create something much broader and use it as a base from which to teach local kids about animal welfare. Who knows? Maybe there's a budding ranger among them.' I shook my head in frustration. 'We're not short of ideas, just short of money. I guess we shouldn't get our hopes up too high. Four Paws probably has thousands of people needing their help.'

Alyson wagged her finger at me.

'Oh no you don't. You said we should dream, didn't you? I think we stand a good chance. They were really interested in what we were doing with Thabo and Ntombi when they were here.'

Alyson and I raced around getting advice, calling in architects and builders, sourcing quotes, and she wrote and rewrote the proposal more times than I can remember.

'Enough. Let's send it,' she said one morning. 'It's as ready as it's ever going to be.'

I glanced at her over my laptop. 'Sure?'

She gave me a thumbs up. I hit Send and sank back in my chair.

'I'm exhausted,' Alyson yawned.

She left to get some well-earned sleep and I stayed to tackle my neglected inbox. I finished just before midnight, locked up and walked across the lawn to my home. A tawny owl hooted nearby and a haunting reply echoed back through the stillness. A sliver of moon curved like an open palm on the horizon. I smiled to myself. Maybe it was a sign that Four Paws would say yes.

I searched the sky for the Milky Way. There it was. My star-spangled highway of dreams. Wherever I am, I look for it, and it's true what they say – stars are brighter in Africa. Even my own life shines brighter here. Moving to Africa triggered an awakening in me that changed my world, but nothing puts things into perspective as sharply as losing a partner without warning. No long illness, no hospital stay to prepare you: just a brutal overnight loss. I've never minded being on my own, but when you suddenly go from being two to being one, it shakes your existence – and will either crush you or make you stronger. For a long time after I lost him, I thought I was drowning, lurching from one crisis to the next, never feeling anything was under control, but slowly, as time passed after Lawrence's death, I was becoming more and more confident about what to do with my life.

14

How do I keep you safe?

It's been years since our beloved rhino Heidi was killed but I still have nightmares about what they did to her. Her death in 2009 was my first experience of the horror of poaching. Once you've seen what poachers do to a rhino's face, you can't unsee it. She had the sweetest nature, a serene gentleness that was so unexpected in such a huge and powerful animal. They turned her beautiful face into a gruesome mess of blood and flesh, and she was alive when they did it.

If she had died from a bullet, I might have learned to live with it. If the poachers had made sure she was dead before they hacked her face then I could have consoled myself that her death was in fact a godsend. But they didn't. They butchered her while she was a breathing, living, feeling rhino.

Our dear friend Dr Ian Player expressed it perfectly.

'Rhinos,' he said, 'have a particularly plaintive cry which once heard, is never forgotten. The screams of agony from rhinos that have had their horns chopped off while still alive should reach into the hearts of all of us.'

How right he was. There are times when I feel so overwhelmed by what is happening to animals in this world that I feel dead inside and the only way I can cope is by shutting down for a while. I disappear into my home with just my dogs for company. Their love is so pure and they help me find my grounding and remind me why I can never give up looking after our animals.

Immediately after Thabo was shot, I had taken Vusi's advice to appoint Richard and his team to guard our rhinos every single minute of the day and night. It was costly and I couldn't have afforded it without donations from friends and guests who understood the need for this ongoing beefed-up security. I slept better knowing they were protected.

I've realized that the only way to survive the poaching onslaught is to accept that I will never be able to change the world but that I can have an impact on my 4,500 hectares of it.

So when I heard about an experimental technique to protect rhinos that was being used by a couple of private game reserves near Johannesburg, I jumped at the chance to try it out at Thula Thula.

South Africans are amazingly inventive people, especially when they have their backs to the wall. Lock them in a cage and they're guaranteed to find an ingenious way out. Poaching was decimating rhinos and there was nothing to counter it – until a South African found a way to make horns unsellable *and* unusable. I thought the idea was brilliant and I immediately tracked down an organization with experience in the procedure. The woman I spoke to was very enthusiastic about how poisoning horns was the answer to saving Africa's rhinos.

'I'm not a scientist so please explain how it works,' I asked.

'We inject a cocktail of toxins and indelible dye straight into the horn using special high pressure equipment that forces the infusion to spread through the horn. You can't see the dye but X-ray machines at airports can pick it up.'

'But surely that will poison my rhinos?'

'Not at all. The horn has no direct blood vessel contact with the body so there's no risk whatsoever for the animal. It's an absolute breakthrough in protecting them. The more poisoned horns we have in South Africa, the safer our rhinos will be.'

'But how can it be legal to poison something that we know people might eat? I don't want anyone's death on my conscience, no matter how much I hate that they buy rhino horn.'

'It won't kill them, but believe me, it'll make them very sick. No one is going to want our horns! Imagine how fantastic that would be.'

It sounded too good to be true, and very expensive.

'It's about the same price as dehorning, and included in the price is the dye, micro-chipping the horns *and* we take a DNA sample for the national rhino database.'

'You're a good saleswoman,' I laughed.

'I believe it's the only thing that will save rhinos. Everything else that's out there hasn't helped. This will.'

Her company's solution certainly had a lot going for it, although it still carried the risk of having to anaesthetize the rhino.

'Have you ever had a procedure go wrong?' I asked.

She seemed to hesitate for a moment.

'It didn't really go *wrong*, because there are always risks with immobilizing large mammals. Put it this way, we've had a less than two per cent mortality rate since we've been doing this.'

Was it my imagination or had her language suddenly become more corporate? It was always the same. When questions got too close to the bone, language became detached, as if that somehow made reality easier to stomach. I knew two per cent was low but I couldn't bear anything to happen to Thabo and Ntombi.

'It's low compared to the risk of poaching,' the woman said.

She knew how to press buttons. The chances of Thabo and Ntombi being shot by poachers were a damn sight higher than the risk of dying from an anaesthetic.

'I'm just worried about my animals,' I sighed.

'We're all worried about rhinos. This technique helps keep them safe. It's quick, lasts longer than dehorning and over time, with international publicity, it will go a long way to make the world a safer place for rhinos.'

The thinking was that by making the end product unattractive to buyers, poachers would stay away from poisoned horns. This meant putting up signs along the entire length of our perimeter fence in both English and Zulu, and working hard with local newspapers and radio stations to get the message across that Thula Thula's rhino horns were 'damaged goods'.

Some game reserves had gone for the more aggressive solution of removing their rhinos' horns but I couldn't bear the thought of that. Taking away the majestic horns of these powerful creatures went against everything I was trying to do.

I thanked her for the information and immediately made arrangements with Dr Mike Toft to poison Thabo and Ntombi's horns. He knew our rhinos well and I didn't want anyone else doing it. Although the technique was still in its early experimental stages and there wasn't any scientific data to back it up, if it had a small chance of keeping my rhinos safe, I wanted to try it. Lawrence and I often made decisions based on gut feeling, and so far it had worked for us. Look at his decisions with Nana and the herd. Everyone told us that the best way to settle down a rogue herd was to leave them alone without any human contact whatsoever. Lawrence listened to his instincts and did the complete opposite. It paid off and today they were healthy and happy, and making babies at a rate that was getting me into trouble.

The big day for the horn poisoning came far too quickly and I was very relieved that both Thabo and Ntombi were near the lodge when Mike arrived with his team. It meant we wouldn't have to put them through the trauma of capture. Mike Toft saw how worried I was and took the time to explain what was going to happen.

'I'll start with Ntombi. She's right here so it'll be easy to dart her with the tranquillizer. As soon as she gets groggy and we can approach her, we'll help her drop safely to the ground and then I'll anaesthetize her. Once she's out, we'll monitor her breathing and heart rate the entire time.'

'She won't feel anything, will she?'

'Nothing at all. Once we've stabilized her, I'll drill a hole in the horn and insert a probe through which we'll pump the poison, then she gets the reversal drug and will wake up as if nothing's happened.'

'What if something goes wrong?'

'She's a healthy four-year-old, Françoise. Nothing's going to go wrong. Trust me.'

I did trust him. But this was my girl orphan and I was scared.

'Is it okay if I watch?'

'I think you should. You'll feel better when you see how straightforward it is,' he nodded.

He pushed a long dart into the back of the gun then plugged up the rifle. The body of the dart is filled with tranquillizer and it has a hypodermic needle on one end, and a fluffy red tail on the other that stabilizes the dart in flight. I shuddered. Even though I understood that the gun was specially tooled for tranquillizing procedures like this, it looked as lethal as any gun I'd seen on a poacher.

Mike lodged the gun against his shoulder and aimed. I knew it wouldn't be loud but I still blocked my ears. The dart flew through the air and landed bang in the middle of Ntombi's left flank. She took a few confused steps, then the rangers ran to her side and guided her as she crumpled to the ground. I felt stricken, as if I'd betrayed her.

The minute she dropped, Thabo bolted over to her and began sniffing her face and body. The rangers tried to push him away but I stopped them.

'Let him stay with her for a few seconds.'

He nudged her with his huge square snout then walked around her and gently rested his chin on her back, as if reassuring her that everything was going to be fine. He didn't seem the slightest bit stressed yet he clearly sensed something wasn't right, and I have no doubt that the presence of people he knew and loved made him trust the strange situation he was in.

Alyson and Siya quickly laid out some lucerne for him a few metres away and our foodie rhino lumbered over and tucked into his favourite treat. Two rangers parked their 4×4s at an angle near Ntombi's head to protect her from any further investigations from Thabo.

Her eyes were covered with a black cloth and two rolls of fabric were inserted into each ear to cocoon her from the noise of the procedure.

'Heart rate stable. Six breaths per minute,' Mike said tersely.

I forced myself to keep looking, devastated to see my big strong Ntombi out cold on the ground. When Mike picked up the drill and positioned it against her horn, I closed my eyes. It's a horn, it's keratin. I knew she wouldn't feel it but I couldn't bear to see it. The screech of the drill entering her horn made my flesh crawl.

She can't feel it, I kept thinking.

'It's not hurting her, Françoise,' Mike said.

I reluctantly watched him screw a long probe into the hole, then he switched on the high-pressure pump and bright-blue infusion entered the horn. I hated every minute of it. I knew it had to be done but it was gut-wrenching to see her surrounded by cold metal – 4×4s, infusion equipment, wires, probe – and with men crouched at her head wearing long black gloves to protect themselves against the toxic liquid they were injecting into her. It felt more like dramatic head surgery than a simple thirty-minute procedure.

We were out in the open but it was as quiet and solemn as a church.

No one spoke, and when they did, it was in low measured voices. Only the twittering and chirping of birds broke the silence. Ntombi didn't move: not a twitch, not a tremor. I could see the mighty curve of her vertebrae under her hide and ran my fingers over the scratches and scars that were testimony to her two years of freedom in the bush. For a frightening moment, I thought she had stopped breathing but then her tail flicked and the relief brought tears to my eyes.

I laid my palm on her beautiful strong back, felt her warmth against my skin.

I'm sorry we have to do this, but I don't know how else to keep you safe. I will never stop protecting you, I promised silently.

Mike shifted his attention to Thabo and once he had successfully poisoned his horn too, and both rhinos were back on their feet, he packed away his tools and medical kit and looked at me.

'I've got some good news for you,' he smiled. 'I found a solution to control the elephant population.'

'Really? No culling?' I asked.

'We're going to put the bulls on the pill!'

'That makes a nice change,' I grinned. 'For once, males will be responsible for birth control.'

He outlined his strategy to me. Twice a year, the older bulls would be darted with a special contraceptive formula that would not only control their fertility but would also help manage their periods of being in musth, when their behaviour becomes aggressive and unpredictable. The method was affordable, available and reversible.

'How does it work?'

'That's the beauty of it. It's steroid based so we're not injecting them with hormones, which means there's no risk of making them more aggressive or changing their behaviour in a long-term way.'

'No risks at all, are you sure?'

'Absolutely. If you don't count the bulls being irritated by the helicopter when we're darting them.'

'How soon can you do it?'

'We'll need to apply for permission but that shouldn't take long. Quite frankly, I think the authorities will be delighted for us to try this out.'

I felt like throwing my arms around the man. He had handed me a much-needed reprieve from the wildlife authorities. Things were looking up.

15

Never give up

Not even six weeks after sending Four Paws our proposal, an email arrived from Heli Dungler. I was excited to see it pop up on my phone and assumed he was getting in touch to ask for more information. I clicked it open.

Dear Françoise, I am happy to tell you – and of course Alyson – that Four Paws will be supporting the expansion of Thula Thula and the establishment of a rhino orphanage with the amount of 300,000 euros.

I was stunned. Had he added an extra zero by mistake? It was an enormous amount of money. Enough to refurbish the old house, construct an orphanage wing, create several outdoor enclosures, and buy medical equipment, medicine and food. I phoned Heli just to make sure.

'It isn't a typo,' he said, a smile in his voice. 'Your orphanage is going to happen.'

If anyone knew about the complexity and challenges of rescuing animals, it was him, and I could think of no better person to have as a partner in our animal sanctuary.

'We believe in dialogue with the locals,' he told me once. 'Because the only way we can achieve our goals is by working with the community. Without their commitment, we'll never achieve real change in how animals are treated.'

It's exactly what Lawrence and I had believed when he was alive. We didn't want to be an island where local people weren't included. What would the point of that be? Our vision at Thula Thula was to create something that we could *all* be proud of. Almost every member of our staff comes from within five kilometres of Thula Thula.

I felt proud, thrilled and terrified.

The responsibility was overwhelming – not only to Four Paws but to every creature we would be caring for. It was also the first time I would be doing something this big without Lawrence.

When construction started in January 2014, I kept telling myself that we had built the lodge and tented camp from scratch, and that with the help of the right people I could do it again. But it was one thing telling myself I could do anything I wanted; it was another believing it, and no amount of positive thinking could get rid of the knot in my stomach. Building a facility for poaching victims was far more daunting than building a luxury lodge for ecotourists. There was so much at stake. If the heating fails in our lodge, we might get a bad rating on TripAdvisor, but the guests won't die. Heating failure in our high-care ward would kill the vulnerable animals. There was no room for error.

'Don't forget about us,' Mabona chided me gently.

She was right. The business side of Thula Thula pays for our running costs and salaries, and it funds our conservation, so I couldn't afford to take my eye off the ball. I very quickly realized that I would never be able to manage the build *and* run the game reserve at the same time. I was already stretched to the limit – the lodge and tented camp needed my full attention, I was still learning about our animals, I was working flat out on marketing Thula Thula, and I was trying to raise funds to expand the reserve to meet the land regulations set by the wildlife authorities for the herd.

I'm not Superwoman and it just wasn't possible for me to do everything.

Common sense won and I pulled together a team of experienced people to help me with the construction and administration of the orphanage project.

I struggled to stay away though, and went there as often as I could. It had been my dream for so long and I loved seeing it come together. Alyson and the rangers were on-site every day and we brought in several wildlife consultants to guide us. They say it takes a village to raise a child, and this child, our orphanage, was the product of so many people – all with the same vision of building a safe haven for victims of poaching. Everyone wanted it to be a success.

My main focus during this time was getting to grips with our security. We were losing animals to poaching every day and I had no idea how to stop it.

Newspapers and television tend to focus on rhino and elephant poaching, but smaller game suffer as badly from poaching, and the number of wildebeest, buffalo, buck and even vultures that were being killed on game reserves in South Africa was horrific.

We have one of the largest breeding colonies of white-backed vultures in the region nesting in the majestic wild fig trees along the Nseleni River, and they were dying in droves. These powerful aerial athletes have a seven-foot wingspan and eyesight that is eight times better than human eyesight.

They aren't poached for the pot, they're killed for *muthi*, traditional medicine sold by unscrupulous 'healers'. So many of these vultures have died that the species is on the critically endangered list.

It is believed that smoking dried vulture brain or sleeping with it under your pillow gives clairvoyant powers – visions of the future. A tempting tool if you're living on the bread-line and a Lotto or horse racing jackpot stands between you and freedom from poverty. The so-called healers who sell this useless magic are scavengers preying on those who can least afford it. The white-backed vulture will become extinct if it doesn't stop. And it won't stop. How can it? Those buying the vulture *muthi* don't know better and those selling it won't give up the money they make. It was a losing battle but not one I was prepared to give up on.

By now, I had had two years of trying to manage security but was no closer to feeling that this crucial part of the reserve was under control. The man I had employed to take over from Connie as head of security had lasted six months, and I went through three more managers after that. Part of the problem was that they didn't like taking instruction from a woman, especially not a foreign one who couldn't speak their language properly. Clearly it wasn't just that and my instincts told me there was a bigger underlying issue. But what? And how could I fix it?

Fighting poaching is a brutal compromise of choices. Daily or weekly foot patrol? Guns or no guns? Do it ourselves or contract out?

If I had a bottomless pot of gold, I would have men scouring the reserve non-stop, equipped with night-vision binoculars, the best firearms, and top-level communication equipment. I would have infrared cameras set up everywhere and regular helicopter patrols. The reality was that I didn't have a blank cheque, nor Lawrence's magic money tree, and it was only thanks to our rhino fund that I was able to send my four best men for top-level anti-poaching training in the Limpopo and that I could afford to bring in ProTrack – a specialized paramilitary anti-poaching unit – to upskill the rest of our team and to deploy a full snare sweep of all 4,500 hectares of the reserve.

Day three of the snare sweep, and my mobile rang. It was Mark, head of the ProTrack task force.

'You'd better come down,' he said.

'I'm on my way.'

Twelve men stood in a semicircle, faces grim, semi-automatics at their sides. No poacher was going to get away on their watch. Twenty-two snares lay at their feet. And that was after only three days. Mark used a knife to hook up one of the wire strands and pointed to small tufts of fur.

'It's an old one but something died in it. The men found a dozen in the first three hours. You've got a big problem here.'

I nodded, nauseated at the thought of the slow deaths happening on my doorstep.

'If it's any consolation, you're in the same boat as most of the reserves we've worked with.' He scratched a map of Thula Thula in the sand and pointed to where the snares had been found, then he stabbed it with his knife. 'We've done this section already, and tomorrow we go here, here and here.'

They found a staggering sixty-three snares in total, nine

with carcasses that the poachers hadn't bothered to come back for, and one with a small deer that was still alive, but the snare was so embedded in its throat that we had to euthanize it.

ProTrack taught our rangers and guards how to spot signs of poachers – litter, cigarette butts, boot prints, broken branches. They showed them how to track poachers once they were on the reserve and how to catch them.

In an ideal world, none of this should be necessary.

A facility for orphaned animals shouldn't be necessary either.

But it's not an ideal world and poaching is here to stay. So was my determination to fight it. Having well-trained men on the ground would help keep our animals safe, and soon we would be able to look after the young victims of poaching elsewhere, right here at Thula Thula.

16

An elephant in my kitchen

I carried the pile of paperwork over to the coffee table, almost tripping over Jeff who was sprawled out in the middle of the lounge snoring his head off. Gypsy was asleep on my bed and Gin trotted behind me, hoping I would make a snack before I started work. His timing was a bit off. It was nine at night and I had already had dinner.

'The thing about you, Gin, is that you only love me for my food.'

He wagged his tail in agreement. I bent down and gave him a nuzzle. I love all Jack Russells but this one was extra special. A friend had called me a few months after Lawrence had passed away to tell me about puppies that would be put down if they didn't find homes. I was at the rescue centre within fifteen minutes and I could have taken every one of them. But I managed to control myself and chose Gin, who was the litter's runt, and his brother, a scrawny black-and-white live wire whom I named Tonic.

Gin and Tonic loved each other as puppies but as Tonic grew older, he began to bully his little brother. His alpha dog behaviour was so out of control that I was forever pulling him off Gin and didn't dare leave them alone. Eventually I was forced to send Tonic to live with my manageress at the tented camp. Not that he minded. He had a thing about chasing monkeys so was in his element.

In his first week there, he saw a monkey steal a butternut from the kitchen and chased after it. The monkey scampered up a tree and sat on a branch with its spoils, gloating down at Tonic, clearly thinking it was safe. Refusing to be outwitted by a *monkey*, Tonic leapt up and managed to scramble onto a low branch, barking furiously. The monkey got such a fright, it dropped the butternut and the two of them bolted after it with the monkey grabbing one end and Tonic getting his jaws around the other. My Jack Russell won his tug of war but the monkey never forgave him and pelted him with rock-hard amarulas whenever it saw him.

Needless to say, Gin didn't miss his bully brother one bit and loved having me and his food bowl to himself.

He nudged my leg and yapped to remind me he would like a snack and I was just about to relent when Jeff lifted his head and gave a lazy growl.

There was a sharp knock on the door. I stood still. Surprise visitors are unusual at that time of the night in the bush.

'Françoise? It's me,' a woman whispered.

I threw open the door. '*Tom?* What are you doing here? What's wrong?'

She motioned frantically for me to come outside. 'There's a baby ellie here.'

'An *elephant*?'

'She's right here, outside your house. She's tiny and terrified.'

Some of my staff love a good practical joke but Tom is more serious than that. She was a petite, shy little thing when she joined us after leaving school, and so scared of her new environment that whenever Lawrence went into the kitchen, she hid in the laundry! She faced her fears with the courage of a lioness and today she is a superb chef who is a magician at making pastries.

'It must be ET's one-week-old daughter,' I said grimly.

The calf had been seen inside the electric fence the night before, but I'd been assured that she was back with her mother and I was horrified that she clearly wasn't. I huddled the dogs into my bedroom while Tom told me what had happened.

'I heard a noise outside my room but when I looked out through the window, there was nothing. I presumed it was a bush pig or a buck and went back to bed, but then I kept hearing it,' she frowned.

Tom had grown up in rural Zululand and wasn't easily unnerved by night noises, but this was something she hadn't heard before. She took her flashlight, opened the door a fraction and shone it across the garden.

A tiny elephant stared back at her, eyes bulging in terror.

Stunned, she softly closed the door and climbed out of a back window to call me.

A baby elephant in trouble is a code-red emergency. Always. And this little one had been alone for a dangerous length of time. My tented camp manager Zelda had reported to me earlier that day that she had seen it during the night, after the incessant screeching and alarm calls of a bushbaby had woken her and made her get out of bed to investigate.

Bushbabies are part monkey, part gremlin, and when another animal invades their space they have a cry that sounds as if a thousand hyenas are attacking them. They're cute but they're drama queens, so Zelda had ignored it at first, but when it didn't stop she decided to see what the racket was about, and was astonished to see that a baby elephant had slipped under the electric perimeter fence – its single wires strung at a height aimed at keeping out the bigger elephants. The little ones can technically slip under the lowest wire, but that had never happened before.

'But where on earth was the rest of the herd?' I asked.

'Ngubane was on night duty and said he hadn't seen them, but we both know elephants don't leave a baby running around on its own and we figured they were close by. He promised to keep an eye on her until she joined up with them again so I went back to bed. Apparently after about an hour, he heard branches breaking behind Tent 1 and saw the calf run towards it.

'But did he actually *see* her with ET?'

'According to him it was too dark to see much but the noise sounded like elephants so he was sure they had come to fetch her. I've been up since six this morning and haven't seen her around camp, or any of the elephants for that matter. I'm sure there's nothing to worry about, Françoise.'

I was uneasy that no one had actually seen the calf back with the herd but elephants are fantastic mothers and would never leave a baby unattended, especially not a newborn, so I assumed that Zelda and Ngubane were right.

Which just goes to show how dangerous assumptions are, because here we were, almost a day later, and the calf was still alone. It seemed impossible. How on earth had she managed to get all the way from our tented camp to my home? We don't have lions at Thula Thula but there are plenty of animals that are dangerous to a baby elephant – hyenas, crocodiles, snakes, and even our rhinos, who are very territorial. And then there was the Nseleni River. I shuddered. What does a week-old calf know about the dangers of water?

Tom and I had to get her inside and keep her safe until we could get her back to her mother. We found her cowering behind a mulberry bush on the side of the house. Frightened eyes peered at us through the leaves. I put my hand on Tom's arm, signalled to her to wait, and walked slowly towards the calf. She watched me, paralysed, but as soon as I was in touching distance, she squealed and bolted behind the house. Tom and I ran after her and tracked her down near the cars. Tom went to the left and I went to the right, but she slipped between us and hurtled away, trumpeting in panicked shrieks.

Other staff heard the commotion and came to help. She wouldn't let us anywhere near her. I was scared stiff she would wriggle under the fence and disappear. If she ran into the reserve we would never find her, and if she got lost she wouldn't make it out alive.

I scanned the bush around the house. Where on earth was the herd? The calf was making so much noise they must have heard her by now, but there was no sign of them. I began to wonder if they had rejected her, as they had rejected baby Thula ten years earlier. It was a terrifying thought. Our rehabilitation centre was far from being finished and in no state to receive a baby elephant. What was I going to do if the calf was sick?

Well past ten o'clock, we still hadn't managed to catch her. I phoned Vusi for help. He didn't answer. I tried Promise but the phone rang and rang. I suddenly remembered both men had two days off and were only due back the next day. Now what? Tom and I might be able to get the calf into my home without them but I didn't want to risk keeping her away from ET until morning. We had to find the herd and get the calf back to them that night, but how would I do that without Vusi and Promise?

It's times like this that I feel so alone. Lawrence would have known exactly what to do. I stood in the middle of the lawn and gazed out into the blackness, willing the herd to come back and fetch their little one.

My phone rang. Vusi. Thank God. They were in Empangeni, an hour away. I explained what had happened and he didn't hesitate about coming back.

'*That's* why they were so vocal and restless when we drove past them on our way out,' he exclaimed. 'We're on our way. Keep her safe.'

Thank heavens he and Promise were close enough to drive home. Without their tracking skills, we'd never find the herd. We still had no clue why they had abandoned the calf, and I knew that if they had rejected her they wouldn't take her back. I pushed the thoughts away. I would deal with that if it happened.

Tom had in the meantime called Alyson and the two of them had managed to corner the calf in the parking area between the house and the staff rooms. She stood completely still, head down, ears drooping; just her eyes flitted anxiously at any movement or sound. I tried approaching her again and this time she didn't resist, allowing Tom and me to gently herd her into my home. Once inside she panicked again, running through my kitchen in frenzied zigzags, trumpeting in fear. Thank goodness my dogs kept quiet – as if they knew that any noise from them would make it worse for her.

I kept talking to her, telling her she was safe and that we would get her back to her mum that night. Food would calm her, but I had nothing in my kitchen for her. No formula, no bottles. Alyson called Mike Toft who confirmed that the priority was to get her to drink.

'If you don't have soya milk, use cow's milk until you can get some. It'll probably give her diarrhoea but it's better to get *something* into her than nothing at all.'

Next challenge – how to feed her without anything even resembling a bottle. There are no emergency night pharmacies in the bush! Alyson had the brainwave of adapting latex gloves. She used a needle to pierce the tiniest of holes into the glove thumb and we started up a very efficient feeding line.

Tom warmed the milk. I held the doctored glove open. She filled it. I tied it closed. Alyson did the feeding.

We never usually insert fingers into a baby animal's mouth. The risk of passing on bacteria and germs is too high, but an elephant calf's sucking reflex is strong and we were worried the latex might break so Alyson carefully put two fingers into her mouth and placed the makeshift teat on top. She drank straight away. We were so excited and relieved. She gulped down the first glove-bottle and nudged Alyson's hands for more! The calf was in such a rush to eat, she spilled milk everywhere – on the floor, over her face and all over Alyson. I had to give Alyson one of my shirts to wear when hers became drenched in milk.

I couldn't get baby Thula out of my mind. Had the herd

really rejected this little calf too? She *looked* so healthy. Her legs were strong and she had proved that she could outrun all of us. She was drinking up a storm, looking at us with grateful, trusting eyes. Was there something wrong with her that I couldn't see? Nature knows about things like this, as I had learned with baby Thula, but I couldn't bear to have another calf die in my home.

She drank four gloves of milk.

Thirst quenched, she began to inspect us with great interest, surfing her inquisitive trunk all over us, sniffing our faces and bodies, poking it under our hair and armpits. We tried to avoid too much physical contact with her because I was worried ET might reject her if she smelled us on her, but my little house guest pooh-poohed our efforts and demanded love, pushing her soft forehead against me as she would against her mother. How could I refuse? I pressed back gently, reassuring her that the rangers were scouring the reserve for her mum.

She dozed off, like babies do when their tummies are full and they feel secure. I sat next to her on the kitchen floor with my legs up against her in case she woke and felt frightened.

We were in constant radio contact with Vusi, who had hauled every ranger out of bed to search for the herd. I was flummoxed that the elephants weren't close by. We know how well they communicate but they didn't seem to be looking for the calf or even know she was with me, and yet Vusi had said that the herd had been visibly stressed that morning. What was going on?

I examined every part of her and found nothing wrong. No

open wounds, no swellings, no obvious deformities. She was a perfect little elephant. If the herd hadn't rejected her for health reasons, where were they? Why weren't they at the fence, trumpeting to have her back? It didn't make sense.

Long after midnight, the radio crackled.

'We found them!' Vusi said. 'And they're not too far away, near the pipeline.'

Only half an hour away. There are miles of wilderness on our reserve, so thirty minutes wasn't far. It was fantastic news. Now for the real test. What if ET ignored her? Or worse, became violent? Our ET has a temper if she feels threatened and I'd also heard of cases of baby elephants being trampled to death when they have been rejected by the herd.

'We're on our way back. I'll bring the truck to your door and we'll load her up and take her home,' Vusi said.

Alyson and Tom prepared another glove-bottle in case our sleeping beauty panicked when we woke her up. We needn't have worried. She wasn't the slightest bit bothered to find herself in my kitchen and was more interested in my brown suede sofa than in the anxious stand-in mums around her. I think she found the soft fabric comforting, because she rested her tiny trunk on top of the armrest and nestled her mouth against the edge with half-closed sleepy eyes. I crouched next to her and hugged her.

'You'll be with your mummy soon,' I promised.

We heard the rattle of the *bakkie* on the dirt track, followed by two quick hoots. Vusi had arrived. Alyson fed the calf and Tom and I carried blankets to the truck to soften the ride for her. Siya jumped down to help us. I nodded at Vusi in approval. Siya was an eagle-eyed tracker and an excellent choice to help him locate the herd. He became our head ranger in 2017, and is calm and earnest with the impeccable manners of a gentleman, even when he's under enormous pressure.

'What's the plan?' I asked Vusi.

'We'll release her close to the herd and stick around as long as it takes to make sure she joins up with them.'

He made it sound so easy. Approaching a herd with one of their babies would be a dangerous operation in broad daylight, but in the dark it was bordering on madness.

'How does the herd seem?' I asked.

'Tense and skittish. The females are secreting from their temporal glands,' Siya said.

I felt bewildered by the herd. They were clearly stressed, yet hadn't come to fetch the calf. All the signs pointed to rejection.

Tom had appointed herself the calf's foster mum and insisted on joining the rangers, as did Alyson. I wasn't at all happy about them being exposed to this level of danger but they weren't taking no for an answer. These plucky young women were true champions of the bush – all they cared about was helping the baby. How could I stop them?

The men lifted the calf onto the truck, her trunk wriggling wildly at all the interesting new smells. Vusi took the wheel and the others clambered onto the back with the calf. They did their best to persuade her to lie down, but no, siesta time was over and she was on an exciting adventure. She even gave a couple of happy trumpets for good measure. It looked like she was having the time of her life. And that for a little one-week-old calf. If she survived, she was going to be a remarkable elephant one day.

I waved them off with dread in my heart. *Please take her back, ET.* I'm not superstitious but I crossed my fingers and blew a kiss to the sky, refusing to believe this little one had been abandoned like baby Thula.

The rangers divided into two groups. One team would go with Siya to monitor the elephants and the other would stay with Vusi to help get the calf off the truck. The idea was to get as close to the herd as was safe, offload the baby and drive away as fast as the 4×4 could go, then monitor the reunion from a safe distance.

That was the plan. It had two serious problems.

One, the herd was already highly agitated and if they thought the rangers had stolen the calf, they would attack. No question about it. The herd trusted us but rule number one in the bush is never to forget that the animals are wild.

Two, we didn't know how the herd would react to the calf. If they didn't want her back, we had no way of protecting her.

It was a typical summer's night in Zululand – hot, muggy and humid. I couldn't sit still, and instead set about trying to bring order back into my kitchen. It was a lonely job, made harder by the dogs who were going berserk at the smells of the interloper that had been in their home. I couldn't stop thinking about Lawrence. It felt as if he had left with Vusi and the rangers and would be coming back in a few hours to tell me what had happened.

Jeff, Gin and Gypsy ran around, panting and sniffing every corner of my kitchen, staring at me with big eyes as if to say, *what happened here?* I gave them each a bone and they forgave me immediately and munched noisily, growling and eyeing each other. I wished I could have distracted myself as easily.

The herd had in the meantime started to head south, and Vusi had driven to a clearing that they were likely to traverse. Siya trailed them, radioing Vusi with their progress.

'They're still heading south. Stand by.'

The rangers, along with Alyson and Tom, were on red alert. They knew the danger but nobody backed out. Sensing the tension, the calf lay down and began to suckle her blanket for comfort.

'Expect visual on the herd in five,' Siya radioed.

'Time to offload the calf. Go, guys!' Vusi said.

They lowered her off the back of the truck and formed a ring around her to stop her from running off. The last thing they needed was her disappearing on another bush escapade. The clatter of breaking trees became louder. The herd was close.

The team leapt back onto the truck and banged the cab roof.

'Drive!' they yelled at Vusi.

The calf trumpeted in bewilderment as her saviours drove off and wobbled after them. This was bad. Very bad.

Vusi stopped, beckoned for the second Land Cruiser to take Alyson and Tom to safety, then he and Promise reversed back to the calf. Promise jumped off and crouched next to her, eyes scanning the darkness for the elephants. Cloud cover blocked out any moonlight and the night was shadowless. They could hear the elephants but not see them.

The calf huddled against Promise. Who could blame her? She was only a week old, it was pitch-black and she didn't know her mother was coming to get her. Or maybe she knew and feared she wouldn't be taken back.

The herd had caught scent of the baby and thundered closer. Vusi and Promise didn't know how ET would react. They waited, bracing themselves.

The herd broke cover and pounded towards them – Frankie, ET and Mabula in the lead. Vusi pushed the gears into first, Promise gritted his teeth and stayed with the calf.

She saw her mother but wouldn't leave Promise.

The herd pounded closer. Vusi and Promise didn't budge. ET skidded to a standstill, the length of a Land Cruiser away, her ears pinned back, breath ragged. Promise edged back. ET glared at him. He took another step, stopped. They stared at each other. The herd flocked behind her, silent.

His eyes dropped to the calf: *she's all yours.*

ET's trunk curled over her daughter and pulled her under her belly.

Promise waited, willing the calf to start suckling. The baby stood still, watching him.

'Time to go,' Vusi said in a low voice.

Promise shuffled backwards, terrified the calf would follow. Vusi started the engine. ET trumpeted loudly and pushed her daughter into the middle of the herd. A tangle of trunks excitedly welcomed her. Promise vaulted over the door and into the vehicle and the two men sped off.

Thanks to their skill and nerves of steel, our runaway was reunited with her family.

So far so good. They hadn't rejected her, but we weren't

out of the woods. Not by a long shot. We couldn't relax until we had seen her suckle.

At first light, Promise and Alyson left to check on the calf's status. They found the herd in a clearing near Mkhulu Dam but they scattered as soon as the vehicle approached.

'Any sign of the baby?' I radioed.

'Negative,' Promise replied. 'The herd's not happy about us being here. We'd better give them some space and try again in a few hours.'

I groaned in despair. If they hadn't spotted the baby while the herd was in plain sight then where on earth was she? Had they killed her? Gypsy nudged my leg, her soulful black eyes filled with tenderness. I lifted her onto my lap and held her to me.

'Let's hope she's okay,' I whispered.

At 8.30 a.m., I dispatched every 4×4 on the reserve to search for the baby. Vusi decided to head back to the dam with Siya. His instincts were spot on, because the entire herd was there, as if waiting for him.

'Herd's here. No baby,' Vusi radioed.

'Stay safe,' I urged.

He manoeuvred closer, radio against his mouth, binoculars trained on the herd.

'I've got eyes!' he said hoarsely.

'*Eish*, she's suckling,' I heard Siya say.

I named the calf Tom in honour of my gentle chef, whose presence of mind in investigating a strange noise had saved the little one's life. We monitored baby Tom for weeks to make sure she didn't wander off again, but ET had obviously grounded her daredevil daughter because every time the rangers saw ET, baby Tom was right there at her mother's side.

At last we relaxed.

I have witnessed amazing phenomena in my years at Thula Thula and the miraculous way baby Tom found her way to me is something I have no answers for. She was only a week old, so how did she end up at my home? How did she know she would be safe with me?

My chef Tom and many of my Zulu staff believe Lawrence's spirit is still with us, watching over his animal and human family like he did when he was alive, and they believe he guided the baby to me.

I believe it's a combination of things. I too sense Lawrence's presence at Thula Thula and his influence still touches us every day, and I also feel that our elephants share knowledge amongst themselves. After years of living so close to them and observing their behaviour, I have seen their extraordinary ability to communicate.

Maybe ET walked past my house with her baby during the first few days of her life, and maybe she told her daughter the story of how Lawrence and I had rescued her fourteen years earlier, and maybe, just maybe, little Tom remembered and knew that my home was the safest place for her to go.

17

Follow your dreams, they know the way

We unofficially opened the doors to our orphanage at the end of 2014, almost a year to the day after receiving funding from Four Paws. I would have loved to have made more of a fuss but we hadn't yet received final clearance from the authorities, and without proper permits we weren't allowed to take in animals.

The morning before Christmas, I drove up to check on the building. Work had pretty much finished for the year and everyone had left for the summer shutdown. Gypsy was curled up on the passenger seat next to me, panting in the heat. It was thirty-nine degrees at 8 a.m. Despite the heat, the air was heavy with humidity. This was the tropics and a storm was brewing. Eerie portholes of blue sky gleamed through thick black clouds. A few fat drops splattered on my dusty windscreen. Good. I hoped it would turn into a downpour.

When we first bought the reserve and built the lodge, I never understood Lawrence's fixation with rain. I always saw it as a nuisance, because game drives aren't much fun for guests in a downpour, but my first real experience of a drought changed this very European outlook.

Summer is usually our rainy season in KwaZulu-Natal, but that particular year it had been steaming hot and hadn't rained for months. The dams dried up and the sun scorched the veldt and killed off the grass, leaving nothing for our wildlife to eat or drink. Animals belonging to local villagers were skin and bones. Neighbouring reserves began to consider culling as a last-ditch attempt to save at least some of their game. The earth was so arid that clouds of dust hovered everywhere.

There is no such thing as piped water in rural areas and we're all entirely dependent on boreholes or municipal water deliveries. Disaster struck when the government official responsible for coordinating water deliveries disappeared on holiday without making alternative arrangements. From one day to the next, Buchanana, the pastoral hamlet where the families of most of our employees live, had no water. The people are so poor that buying bottled water was an unthinkable luxury. We had a borehole and emergency water storage facilities at Thula Thula but they had nothing. Coming from Paris, it was a huge shock to see people I knew and loved panicking about something as basic as water.

I went with Vusi to meet with the village elders. Children played in the dirt outside the sturdy brick meeting room and the sun baked on the tin roof. It was hotter inside than out.

'If we don't get water soon, we won't be able to control the people's anger,' Mr Khumalo warned.

'How much do you have left?' I asked.

His thumb and forefinger formed a circle. I glanced at Vusi. This was catastrophic.

'We'll give you what we can,' I promised.

'I'll bring some down myself with the truck,' Vusi said.

'I'll phone the municipality. They can't *all* be on holiday,' I said.

I spent the rest of the afternoon trying to find an official who would take responsibility for delivering water to the village. My calls rang unanswered, my messages weren't returned. No one was contactable.

The villagers rioted, burning tyres, blockading roads. Our guests couldn't get in or out. We shared whatever water we had. In desperation, I phoned the newspapers and it was only when images of the villagers' plight went viral that someone sat up and took notice. Within two hours, a convoy of seven trucks of water arrived: barely enough for a few days, but it was a start.

I never looked at rain the same way again. Without water, life stops.

I stretched my arm through my car window and watched the plump raindrops bounce off my palm. Those first drops after a dry spell always seem heavier and rounder. They look as if they're falling slowly, taking their time to come to earth after the long wait. Thunder rumbled and the wind swirled dust around my car – signs that more rain clouds would be rolling in. I started my car again. Getting stuck in a storm wasn't how I planned to spend my morning.

There was nobody at the orphanage and it was bucketing down by the time I went inside. The clatter of rain on the corrugated tin roof crashed through the empty rooms. Lawrence was always as exuberant as a kid when we achieved something new and he would have been so proud. I tried to look at the construction through his eyes. He had been much better than me at picking out problems.

'Take off those rose-tinted glasses,' I could hear him say.

I gazed at the infrared lamps and wondered which little creature would be the first to lie under their life-saving warmth. We had space for up to twenty orphans but I hoped it would never come to that. Twenty orphans meant twenty dead mothers and that was too horrific to contemplate.

Bricks and mortar are only one part of an emergency facility like ours. Its heartbeat and soul are the people who give up their lives to care for the animals, and I couldn't have asked for a more dedicated team.

Alyson had been part of the Thula Thula family for years and it was reassuring for me to have someone there whom I trusted and liked so much. The first thing you notice about her is her smile, quickly followed by her belly laugh. And believe me, you need laughter to do the work our animal carers do. Looking after distressed and injured creatures takes guts and grit. Not only was Alyson a capable veterinary nurse, she also had a natural instinct for animal psychology, and it was thanks to her that Thabo overcame the trauma of being shot. Her experience with him was invaluable once we started to receive orphans. Interpreting animal behaviour and understanding them usually requires years of experience but it can also quite simply be a gift. Alyson sensed when animals were down or scared and always knew exactly what to do to lift their spirits.

'Thabo loves having his face stroked. I never knew how affectionate rhinos could be until I started looking after them. They look tough on the outside but they're so vulnerable and needy on the inside,' Alyson said.

The second person to join the orphanage team was Axel, a

tousle-haired, easy-going young man from France. His qualifications were a degree in animal behaviour and a very big heart. The animals adored him and so did everyone who worked with him. He was unflappable – unusual for a Frenchman! – and he had a knack of soothing even the most frightened creature.

Megan was the third team member, a fresh-faced young British girl who knew with a conviction beyond her years that caring for animals was what she wanted to do with her life. She arrived with an animal management diploma from England and rhino-calf nursing experience from another rhino facility.

Alyson, Axel and Megan enjoyed working together and you felt it the minute you walked in. A home-like happy atmosphere is good for the animals. Top-level wildlife vets are indispensable for the medical side, but a warm cocoon where orphans feel safe and secure is just as important.

The months that followed were strange. The orphanage was ready. Paperwork done. Permits issued. Team on standby. We were in a strange no man's land of waiting for tragedy to happen. Our caregivers lived in a bittersweet state of readiness, excited to be almost operational but also very aware that their first rhino calf would have suffered terribly before getting to them. They used the time to add the last finishing touches to the orphanage – building wallow pools, planting grass and even decorating the 'nursery' with stencilled paw prints.

The call came through early one morning in April 2015.

'The Zululand Rhino Reserve anti-poaching unit found the

carcass of a poached female but there's no sign of her calf. If they find him, can you take him?' Mike Toft asked.

'Absolutely, bring him as soon as you can. How old is he?'

'About six months. The rangers are out looking for him. No one knows if he's dead or alive. The carcass is about two days old, so he's been out there for a while. I'll get back to you as soon as I know more.'

Six months was very young, but just old enough to survive a few days on his own – as long as the rangers managed to find him before the lions did. The carers kicked into gear to get the ICU room ready for him – scrubbing floors and walls with disinfectant, laying out a clean mattress and blankets, sterilizing bottles and teats, checking food and medical supplies.

We heard nothing the next day. Or the next. The clock was ticking for this little chap. At last, on Good Friday, after four days of being alone, the calf was sighted with another female rhino and her infant.

'That's why we couldn't find it. We didn't realize the cow had *two* calves with her. They're the same age and look identical,' reported Jake, the reserve manager.

We were over the moon. It's unusual behaviour for a rhino female to look after a calf that isn't her own and we all hoped the gods were smiling on him at last. If she allowed him to stay with her, he had a chance of surviving. The orphanage was ready for him but top prize was for him not to need us at all.

'When the poachers attacked the mother, the calf must have run off with the other female,' the manager explained.

Age plays a big role in how a rhino calf copes with losing

its mother. A newborn calf stays close to its mother's carcass, no matter how terrified it is, and poachers won't hesitate to shoot it if it gets in their way. Older calves have a more developed survival instinct and will run off if threatened.

Running away saved this calf's life because he already had a tiny horn and at $90,000 per kilo, the poachers would have killed him for every gram they could get.

He was named *Ithuba*, meaning 'chance' in Zulu, because he had dodged poachers and predators for over a week and now just needed luck to stay on his side and give him a second chance at happiness – either in the wild with his adopted rhino mother or safely with us at the orphanage.

'Do you think the rhino cow will look after him if she has her own calf?' I asked.

'That's the big question. We have no idea how it'll play out but the rangers will stay with him day and night.'

'Is he old enough to survive without his mother's milk?'

'He could, but it's far from ideal at his age, although quite frankly, getting milk isn't his biggest problem right now. The adult female that he's with is the problem. If she doesn't let him stay with her, she'll chase him off or kill him.'

Rhinos aren't as generous with their love as elephants are. In an elephant herd, it's unthinkable to reject an orphan unless there's something seriously wrong with it, and even then, every adult female will try to help it survive before they walk away.

Jake phoned with an update at the end of the day. The cow was turning aggressive. Little Ithuba could smell her milk, could see the other calf drinking from his mother, but he wasn't allowed anywhere near either of them. How he must have longed for the comfort of her teats, but the rhino cow was only interested in her own calf.

I tossed and turned the whole night. At six the next morning Jake called.

'The calf's in danger. We're going in to rescue him.'

'Bring him, we're ready. When will you get here?'

'Don't know. It's going to be bloody dangerous. The two calves look identical and we're struggling to tell them apart. If we take the wrong one, the cow will kill the orphan. We're going to handle it from the ground to avoid stressing her with a helicopter.'

The situation deteriorated dangerously. As soon as the 4×4 went anywhere near Ithuba, all three rhinos scattered and disappeared into the dense bush. The rangers didn't catch him that day or the next. He lost condition and began to struggle to keep up with the female and her baby. If he was separated from them during the night, he wouldn't last until morning.

'She attacked him!' the rangers radioed. 'She threw him in the air. He's injured and the cow and calf have run off.'

With the angry rhino female out of the way, the rangers caught the terrified calf at last. Eight days after losing his mother, Ithuba arrived at the orphanage.

The ranger bringing him drove the pickup truck and trailer as close to the new clinic building as possible. Easier said than done. Access to the high-care arrival room hadn't been properly thought out. Trucks need space to manipulate large trailers and doing it in a confined area wasted time – a luxury we didn't have.

'I need him inside!' shouted the vet who had travelled with him.

'I can't get closer,' the ranger yelled back.

'Open the back of the trailer,' Vusi instructed. 'There are enough of us to get him out safely.'

'I'll get boards so we can channel him to the door,' Axel said.

It was chaos and I had a sickening flashback to the night our herd arrived and we hadn't been able to offload them quickly enough. A baby rhino is easier to control than seven elephants, but the arrival of an injured calf should be handled as serenely and efficiently as possible, and this was anything but. How could we have botched up something so important?

At last Ithuba was inside, heavily sedated with a cloth protecting his eyes. He looked tiny lying on his blanket in the emergency room and I doubted he would survive. The vet searched for a vein and inserted a drip to rehydrate him.

'He's not in good shape,' he murmured.

There were festering wounds on his groin where the female had gored him and his skin was covered in infected tick bites. The vet cleaned him and administered a hefty dose of antibiotics. Everyone spoke in hushed tones.

That first night, Ithuba slept peacefully, due no doubt to exhaustion and the effects of being sedated, because the second night was hell. It was as if he was going through all the trauma of the past week – his mother's murder, being gored by a female he thought he could trust, transported in a clanging trailer, and then finding himself in a strange room with humans who looked like the ones who had killed his mother. His high-pitched squeals of terror pierced every corner of the orphanage.

Feeding him was impossible. He was too big and too stressed for the carers to safely go into his room to give him his bottle, but he was too scared to go near the bottle they held through the barrier for him. It was a terrible catch-22 situation. He needed to eat but he had to overcome his fear of humans first.

The team took it in turns to try to persuade him to take a bottle, but his fear overruled his hunger and he cowered away from them.

In that respect, newborn calves are easier to look after, as they're still so trusting. Ithuba was six months old and he knew how dangerous humans could be; just the sight of his carers sent him careering around his room in panic. Two hundred kilos of agitated rhino can do a lot of damage to a pair of human legs. He was making it impossible to be given what he needed most – cuddles and food.

'Don't give up. He'll get used to you. Start by sitting next to his barrier so he realizes you won't hurt him. No sudden movements, no loud voices. Take it slowly,' advised the vet.

No one gave up on him. Axel jiggled a bottle of milk between the bars of the barrier.

'Come, *boytjie*. You need to eat,' he murmured.

Ithuba watched him, fear in his eyes.

Axel squeezed the bottle teat and splattered some milk on the ground. Ithuba didn't move but his nose twitched hungrily. Axel tantalized him with a few more drops. Ithuba took a step forward. Axel held the bottle still, teat facing forward.

Ithuba gave a hungry little squeak and shuffled a few steps closer, ready to bolt. The bottle was just out of his reach.

'A few more steps,' Axel encouraged gently.

Ithuba stared at him, ventured closer. Axel stretched forward and nuzzled the milk-drenched teat against Ithuba's lips. His mouth opened and he latched. His eyes fluttered closed and he drank and drank.

What a milestone. He finished that bottle and, an hour later, guzzled down a second one. Once a calf knows you are its source of food, trust follows quickly. I saw him tug on the teat, saw the milk level drop, and knew his chances of survival were good.

Then colic struck. And nightmares.

'He began to shiver and jerk about in his sleep, squealing in terror. It was terrible. I think he was reliving what had happened to his mother. I didn't know how to console him,' groaned Axel. 'I didn't want to wake him in case that made it worse so I just sat at the barrier and talked to him. He eventually woke up and he was so scared and confused that he was spinning around his room in panic, peeing all over the place and flinging himself up against the wall like he wanted to climb out.'

'Thabo and Ntombi were such healthy little thugs compared to him,' Alyson sighed unhappily.

'What Ithuba's going through isn't unusual given the trauma he experienced,' the vet assured us. 'People think post-traumatic stress is only experienced by humans but we see it in elephant poaching victims and military dogs too. I know that doesn't take away how hard it is for you, but it does give us a better handle on how to treat him. One thing's sure – his emotional recovery is going to be far more complicated than his physical recovery.'

It's heartbreakingly hard to comfort traumatized animals, especially when they first arrive. They don't understand what has happened and they're terrified of everything. You need an endless supply of courage and love to help them. Our carers gave so much to Ithuba, holding nothing back. I envied their fearlessness. After losing little Thula and then Lawrence, my heart was locked away and I was still too numb to love so boldly.

'What else can we do to help him?'

'Routine and love. His carers will become his family, and when he starts to feel safe, he'll begin to heal,' the vet replied.

'At least with Thabo and Ntombi, I knew if I rubbed their faces, it would calm them, but Ithuba won't even let us near him,' Alyson said.

'Let's see if going out of his room into the *boma* will help,' one of our rhino consultants suggested. 'If it's warm tomorrow, open the barrier and let him explore. It might distract him, and having some outdoor activity will do him good.'

Ithuba's room opened out onto a contained area with trees for shade and lots of toys to help keep him stimulated. In the bush, he would learn new skills through interactions with other rhino, so we had to recreate what he was missing, not only to stop him from getting bored and becoming destructive, but also for his own healthy development.

The next morning, the autumn sun poured warmth into the *boma*. Axel opened Ithuba's gate as soon as he had finished his bottle. He trotted to the threshold, nose high to catch new scents, ears twitching and turning towards the new bush sounds, but he didn't venture further. Our boy wasn't rushing into anything new! Two days of timid inspection followed, then he suddenly headed straight for a tyre lying close to his open door. He had obviously been eyeing it for days and the compulsion to investigate it overcame his fear.

He sniffed it with great interest then gave a confident head-butt and tossed it over his head. He was so surprised! But then it landed with such a thump that he bolted back to his room. One step forward, two steps back.

Animals are drawn to gentle spirits, and the first human being Ithuba learned to trust was Axel. No matter how stressed or how agitated Ithuba was, Axel never got flustered. He stayed calm, talked quietly to Ithuba and bathed him in love. I don't know how he did it. I'm a bag of jelly when an animal is sick or distressed. Slowly Ithuba understood that Axel was never going to hurt him as other human beings had hurt his mother.

I'll never forget the day Alyson and I saw him trotting happily next to Axel. He kept bumping his rump into Axel's leg, as if to reassure himself that he wasn't alone any more. Trust is so precious when you look after these little orphans.

Alyson joined them in the *boma* a few days later to teach him to trust more than one carer. She stayed out of his way at first, near the fence, to give him space and let him feel in control. He stared at her from the shelter of Axel's legs, then inquisitiveness won and he ambled over to her for a sniff, constantly looking over his shoulder to make sure Axel was nearby. Another huge step. Curiosity is vital at that age and it was exciting to see him display normal calf behaviour.

You can never tell which toys human children will love

most, and it's the same for rhino calves. Ithuba always homed in on anything made out of tyre, including his food bowl which was a home-made tyre contraption. He tipped it over, threw out the food, flung it about until it started rolling, then he ran after it until he managed to balance it on his head and preened and strutted about like a dressage horse.

Axel once went home to France to sort out his visa and on his return, he snuck into Ithuba's *boma* and started rolling a tyre when he wasn't there. Ithuba heard the familiar noise and came galloping in from the neighbouring *boma*, skidding to an astonished stop when he saw Axel. Pure joy followed at being reunited with his favourite human.

When you work closely with rhino calves, you learn to know when they're happy, sad or angry. It's in the way they walk or run. It's whether they play half-heartedly or with gusto. Ithuba's carers knew exactly how he was feeling and there was always one of them close by to comfort or play with him.

If a loud noise frightened him, he bolted to mum Alyson. Axel, on the other hand, was his surrogate big brother – with all the teasing, guidance and protection of an older sibling. Both of them were worried that he was still showing signs of trauma.

'He really suffers in his sleep,' fretted Axel.

'And he still has panic attacks during the day,' Alyson said. 'He'll be playing happily, clambering all over me, then he'll suddenly squeal in fright, latch onto a corner of my sleeve and suckle it like a baby sucks its thumb. I don't know what sets it off. We were playing and he seemed so happy.'

'He's making good progress,' the vet reassured them. 'He's

putting on weight, passing healthy stools and loves to play. Post-traumatic stress takes time but he'll get there.'

Luckily time was on our side and there wasn't a minute that Ithuba didn't have the safety blanket of Alyson or Axel close by. Slowly his nightmares became less frequent, his insecurity faded and his appetite exploded. By the time he was nine months old, he had doubled his weight and turned into a happy little rhino tank!

With size came confidence and he gave himself the job of Quality Control Inspector and proceeded to expose every construction weakness in the orphanage with great zeal – usually smashing his way through to prove his point. By the time the Ithuba-QC test had been performed on every door, lock and barrier, no rhino calf was ever going to break out.

Which was just as well, because his days of being the orphanage's only calf were fast coming to an end.

18

Ellie

'He's a desperately ill two-week-old elephant. Can you take him?'

'Did you say elephant?'

'Yip.'

We didn't have a permit for elephant calves but we didn't hesitate. The calf was at death's door and we were the closest emergency facility. Alyson and Axel raced off to the Bona-manzi Game Reserve and returned five hours later with a very sick little elephant. My heart lurched when I saw him. He was identical to baby Thula, a tiny pink newborn covered in soft baby fuzz.

'Blood pressure low. Breath erratic,' Mike Toft said tersely.

His herd had rejected him – a bad sign.

'He has an umbilical hernia with abscesses and a life-threatening infection,' Mike continued. 'Plus he's dangerously underweight.'

'Can we save him?' I asked, dreading the answer.

'Doubt it. Usually this kind of thing is fatal.'

I stared at him. 'Options?'

'Euthanasia,' he replied flatly. 'Or intensive round-the-clock nursing with a one per cent chance of survival. He has a deadly bacterial infection that's feeding directly into his blood supply. It's bad, really bad. If we take him on, the next few days are going to be hell, and he may not make it.'

'I'm up for it,' Megan said.

'Us too,' Axel and Alyson echoed. 'We have to try.'

Trying is an understatement. Between them, wildlife specialists across the country, our vet, and a whole bunch of angels, that little calf survived the night. He was named, quite simply, Ellie.

Alyson, Megan and Axel dived into a punishing schedule of feeds, three-hourly shifts, and constant monitoring of his blood pressure, temperature, breathing and heart rate. He had a human herd around him who smothered him in love. The slightest change caused elation or panic. Every breath was celebrated. Every change in temperature caused alarm. It was a frantic treadmill of cleaning, feeding, nursing and loving.

The team were stretched to the limit. Thabo and Ntombi still needed Alyson, and little Ithuba couldn't do without big brother Axel. Extra volunteers were called in. Megan's mother flew out from England to help.

Ellie survived twenty-four hours. Then another. Three days later, he was still with us. His temperature stabilized but he was still not feeding properly. Everyone was black and blue from trying to teach him how to drink from a bottle.

'He's going to make it,' Megan said firmly, dark rings under her eyes.

The team weren't the only ones watching over him. Our herd paid him a visit too.

The orphanage is in the north-western part of the game reserve and the herd don't typically go near the building, and yet the day after Ellie was admitted, they arrived. No one really took notice at first but then they returned the next day, and the next.

'That's three days in a row they've been here,' Megan frowned. 'I wonder if they know we have a baby elephant?'

They must have, because they visited every single day for weeks, quietly milling about and grazing. Nana and Frankie would stand side by side and gaze at the orphanage, gentle wardens keeping watch over their own kind. They hadn't shown any interest when Ithuba had arrived but were there soon after Ellie was admitted. Were they keeping tabs on him? Did they sense how ill he was? Did they send him telepathic messages of support? We'll never know, but their presence was reassuring and we took it as a sign that we had done the right thing by rescuing him.

Feeds were just becoming less of a struggle when, from one bottle to the next, diarrhoea and colic struck. We couldn't work out why. The washing machine ran day and night to keep his soiled blankets clean and hygienic. His room was scrubbed and disinfected non-stop. He squirmed and cried in pain. His carers rubbed his tummy and lay next to him. His temperature sky-rocketed and he became dangerously dehydrated.

Diarrhoea can kill. We were petrified we would lose him.

Back on the drip he went. We flew in special milk from Zimbabwe. We tried the milk formula from the Sheldrick Orphanage. Electrolytes and steroids were fed intravenously. He got sicker and sicker. Sleep-deprived and despairing, nobody gave up. Least of all him. He was such a little fighter.

At the eleventh hour, a mixture of over-cooked rice, coconut milk, desiccated coconut and special proteins and minerals did the trick. We discovered later that he was severely intolerant to milk. I don't know who fought harder for his life, little Ellie himself or Team Ellie. He began to respond. His diarrhoea eased.

Nights were the hardest. Ellie was too distressed to sleep. Dead tired, barely able to stand, he wouldn't close his eyes. He only slept if Megan was with him, so she took over his bedtime shift and curled up with him on his mattress, snuggled under his favourite Donald Duck fleece blanket, until he dropped off. She lay dead still, listening to the steady rhythm of his breath and his quiet snores, her arms and legs cramping, but not daring to move. Around 11 p.m. she carefully untangled herself to slip off to her own room while someone else did the night shift, and by 6 a.m. she was back in his room to be there when he woke up.

The team poured love into him and he gave it back with trunk-tip caresses and happy rumbles. He didn't speak 'human' but his eyes said it all.

'He makes such deep eye contact with me and I know he's saying, *thank you for helping me*,' Megan sighed happily. 'He knows we're saving his life and he loves us as much as we love him.'

His condition improved and he went from being at death's door to critical, and soon the vet proclaimed him stable. The little thing was as excited as we were that he was getting better. What a relief to see him bouncing next to Megan, his busybody trunk scooting chaotically all over her as he did his best to control the fascinating object growing out of his face.

Week four arrived and we couldn't believe he had pulled through.

'He's fallen in love with Megs,' Alyson said to me. 'Watch . . .'

Megan went into his room and was greeted by an explosion of excited rumbles. Ellie waddled up to her and trustingly lifted his head for his bottle. She nuzzled his forehead and slid the teat into his mouth. He latched straight away, then his trunk curled up and nestled over her mouth. Megan shot us a look of pure joy.

'Her breath comforts him,' Alyson whispered. 'It's the only way he'll drink.'

Inter-species communication isn't about a common language. It's about reading cues and signals that have nothing to do with words. Ellie's soulful eyes followed Megan wherever she went. He was calmer in her presence. He drank more milk. He showed his joy with rumbles, and later, when he found his voice, excited squeaky trumpets. He sensed he was safe with her, and once that first precious bit of trust was established, she and the team had something to build on. Just as Ithuba needed Axel, Ellie needed Megan.

Once Ellie was healthy enough, he loved nothing more than a wrestling match before breakfast. Megan would pretend to be a baby elephant and scamper around the room on all fours while he chased her. The winner was the one who climbed on top of the other first. As soon as he cottoned on to the 'rules', his competitive streak surfaced. Megan is a slender slip of a girl, a fraction of his weight, and he would push and bump her until she 'fell', then he would scramble onto her and claim his prize by hanging his trunk and front legs over her back. *I won! I won!* He was a very grumpy loser. If Megan pretended to win by putting *her* chest and arms over *his* back, he sulked until he won another game.

Exercise and sun are crucial for calves and it does them the world of good to go outside. We do our best to replicate their life in the wild, so every room has its own outdoor enclosure that can be shut off for a new arrival or interlinked with other enclosures for the little ones to mingle as they would in their natural habitat.

In the beginning, we kept Ellie and Ithuba apart but we gave them separate turns in the same *boma* so they could get used to each other's scent without actually seeing each other. We had no idea how a baby elephant and a young rhino would react to being together.

When Ellie had been doing well for a while, his carers felt the time was right for him to meet Ithuba. They opened his door but kept the metal barrier in place so the two of them could see and sniff each other without being in the same *boma* together. Not yet. We weren't taking any chances. Elephant calves are emotionally fragile and the last thing we needed was for Ellie to get the fright of his life and go into a downward spiral health-wise.

As soon as the door opened, Ellie shot to the barrier, expecting to be let out. He pressed his head against the bars, bewildered that he couldn't go into the *boma*.

Ithuba seemed to ignore Ellie but his ears immediately rotated towards the noise of the opening door. Rhinos have superb hearing and a powerful sense of smell to make up for their weak eyesight, so Ithuba knew very well that something interesting was happening. Curiosity eventually got the better of him and he peered over his shoulder at Ellie. He couldn't really see much with those bad eyes of his, but he could *smell* him and even though it was a familiar scent, he stuck close to Axel and didn't want to explore further.

Ellie, on the other hand, was *very* interested. He could see and smell Ithuba and his little trunk worked overtime to catch Ithuba's scent.

We held our breath.

With Axel as his bodyguard to fight off any rhino bogey-men, Ithuba nervously approached Ellie's room.

Ellie swirled his trunk up in greeting.

Ithuba squealed and darted behind Axel.

'It's fine, you big baby,' Axel laughed. 'He's only a few weeks old. Man up, little one.'

Ithuba tried, he really did, but he was terrified.

Ellie didn't know what the fuss was about and kept his forehead against the metal bars as his trunk hoovered up Ithuba's smell.

The next day, we opened the barriers again. This time, Ithuba didn't run off when Ellie slipped his trunk through the bars to smell him, but when it whirled too close to his face, his courage failed and he skedaddled off into the neigh-bouring *boma*. No bravery medal for this little rhino calf!

Ithuba was bigger than Ellie but he was clearly frightened of the strange creature with its hyperactive trunk, so we con-tinued to keep them apart, which was a pity because Ellie seemed to like the idea of some rhino company.

Ellie's easy-going reaction to Ithuba was very encouraging,

but did it mean he had really turned the corner? Megan wasn't so sure.

'He still seems lethargic and there are moments when he's so withdrawn and seems really down,' she said helplessly.

Enter Duma, a German shepherd dog who had been trained from the tender age of seven weeks to help find rhino calves missing after their mothers had been killed by poachers. He then had a brief career hop as an airport sniffer dog, but his handler there quickly realized that he was miserable operating within the concrete walls of an urban environment and that he was hankering after his old life in the bush. Given that he had grown up surrounded by baby rhinos, our orphanage was the perfect landing spot for him.

Exactly six weeks after Ellie arrived, Duma joined Team Ellie. Gypsy was as thrilled as I was and the first time they met, she skipped up to him, stretched her little neck to sniff his nose, then the two of them bounded across the lawn together – my tiny black furball dwarfed by her lion-like new best friend.

Ellie had shown such interest in Ithuba that we were looking forward to introducing him to Duma. Their first meeting at the barrier was a jumble of inquisitive trunk, sniffing snout and wagging tail. Duma restrained his excitement for about two seconds before leaping up against the bars. Ellie calmly took a few steps back, his little trunk moving constantly. It was fascinating to see him use his trunk to figure out what the intriguing apparition of lolling tongue and love-struck eyes was on the other side of the bars. He was enchanted and not the slightest bit frightened.

'Not bad for an elephant calf that has never seen a dog before,' said Megan proudly.

'What a brave little thing. When will they be allowed in the same *boma*?' I asked.

'We'll do what we did with Ithuba,' said the vet. 'Let them get used to each other with a barrier between them and then they can meet.'

For the next few days, Duma bounded up to his new friend at the barrier and they caught up on things that baby elephants and German shepherds talk about. The day for their first real play date came too soon for mum Megan.

'Duma is so boisterous. What if he's too rough with Ellie and scares him?'

'If it was Ithuba and Duma meeting for the first time, I'd agree, but your Ellie is a little warrior. *You're* the one who's scared,' teased one of the volunteers.

Duma was in the middle of a digging frenzy, sand flying everywhere, when Megan led Ellie towards him. Ellie was wary but intrigued. Duma's head shot up.

'Uh-oh,' Megan said, but to her credit, she kept walking towards him with Ellie.

Duma bucked and reared at the sight of his buddy, found his yellow ball, and dropped it at Ellie's feet – *let's play!*

Ellie's ears flapped out, his body shook and wriggled, and he whipped his trunk about like a lasso.

'He's going to charge,' Megan giggled.

Duma was definitely up for a game of chicken. They raced onto the sand pile from different directions, trunk and tail waving wildly. Duma ducked under Ellie's belly and escaped. Ellie whizzed around and lumbered after him.

They ran, they chased, they hurtled up and down the sand pile.

You didn't have to be an elephant psychologist to see that gentle Duma had helped Ellie find his mojo.

19

And then there were seven

Megan wrapped the scrawny rhino in a blanket and held him against her to warm him. He was covered in blood and carcass fluid but she ignored the stomach-churning stink. His eyes widened at the slightest sound. It was the middle of winter and he had travelled a long way to get to us.

For six days, he had stood by his mother's poached body, desperately tugging at her decaying teats while vultures tore at her flesh. He was so hungry, he gorged on mud from a nearby waterhole.

How do you even start to console a little creature like that?

Dr Mike Toft raced across KwaZulu-Natal to come to his aid. His gloved fingers massaged the calf's ear, searched for a vein, inserted an intravenous needle and hooked up a drip. Electrolytes, nutrients, glucose and antibiotics poured into him. Mike rubbed and probed the calf's distended belly.

'Rock hard. We have to get the mud out of him. Fast.'

Megan stayed with him the entire night. He ran round and round in circles, crying non-stop, too terrified to sleep, desperate to find his mother.

'I didn't stop talking to him,' she said. 'I told him what had happened to him, that he was safe with us, that there was another baby rhino just like him called Ithuba and that I was sure they would be friends.' She shrugged self-consciously. 'I always talk to them as if they understand.'

'Of course they do. Lawrence did the same,' I said gently.

'He eventually realized that I wouldn't hurt him and came up to me and stood silently at my knees as if pondering what to do next. He looked so lost. I longed to take him in my arms to comfort him but I didn't dare move in case I frightened him. Then he collapsed at my feet and fell asleep. I was thrilled that he felt safe enough to do that and covered him in a blanket and stayed on the ground with him in case he woke up and didn't know where he was.'

By noon the next day, he hadn't passed any faeces. He was listless and skittish and not interested in eating.

'If the blockage in his hindgut isn't sorted out soon, we have to operate,' Mike warned. 'But it'll be a last resort. He's too weak for surgery and I'm worried about his tick-bite abscesses. Keep trying with small amounts of formula. See if you can persuade him to walk about. Movement might help loosen his bowels.'

It took three tough days of passing hard balls of clay before he managed to get rid of all the mud he had eaten. The change in him was instantaneous. Now he couldn't stop eating and indignantly headbutted his carers if he was hungry and his bottle wasn't ready. What a breakthrough. There's nothing more rewarding than seeing a little calf put on weight again after he's been too sick to eat.

We named our number-three orphan *Impi*, meaning 'warrior' in Zulu, because he fought so hard to live. He had the sweetest nature and the same gentle, silent way of getting someone's attention as Gypsy. One morning, Megan was on her hands and knees giving the floor in his room a good scrub when she felt two little eyes boring into her and looked up. He gazed at her for a long time then shuffled closer and nestled his chin on her shoulder.

'He wasn't that heavy in the beginning so I just kept cleaning and he waddled along with me but the dopier he got, the heavier his head was!' she grinned.

Some calves are boisterous and belligerent, but not Impi. He was a tender little creature who was afraid of everything. Like Ithuba, he suffered from post-traumatic stress disorder, and any unfamiliar sounds – even a bird's squawk – would send him fleeing for cover, squealing in panic. Nights were a terrible struggle for him. No matter how exhausted he was, he didn't feel safe enough to lie down until a volunteer started reading her book to him and he quietly nestled on the hay next to her, burrowed his head into her legs and fell into the deepest sleep.

Ithuba wasn't happy about losing his pampered role as the only rhino at the orphanage and was particularly jealous when he realized that Impi was in his old room. He bumped and charged the barrier to get in and was so relentless that he knocked the sliding gate right off its rail. It was only the sound of Axel rolling his favourite tyre behind him that pulled him out of his bad mood.

The team were by now on an exhausting schedule of looking after Ithuba, Ellie and Impi, and we couldn't believe it when another rhino calf arrived.

Baby Thando was found trapped in mud in a neighbouring reserve. He was stuck neck-deep and couldn't move. To make matters worse, his mother had disappeared. It was pure luck that he was discovered before he became completely submerged and died.

Severe drought dries up waterholes and turns them into dangerous sludge that traps small creatures in a vice-like grip. One of the most tragic things I ever witnessed was an emaciated baby giraffe struggling to free itself from mud while its deeply stressed mother paced nearby. The giraffe calf fought hard to get out but became so glued in the mud that he couldn't move. Rescue was impossible and a ranger was forced to euthanize it. Its frightened calls and that gunshot will stay with me forever.

I was so grateful Thando had been found in time. The rangers were divided into two groups. One group searched for the mother while the other tried to free him from the mud. It took five men to pull the calf out and there were whoops of delight when they saw he was strong enough to stand.

The ideal procedure in situations like this is to release the calf back to its mother. It was still quite early in the day, so it was decided to set him free with a guard monitoring and protecting him from predators in the hope he would find her. In the meantime, no cost was spared to look for the mother – a helicopter was dispatched, rangers searched on foot and every available 4×4 scoured the reserve for her.

Back at the orphanage, the carers spun into action in case he wasn't reunited with his mother. A room was cleaned out and disinfected, bottles and teats were readied, drips were laid out and pots of water pre-boiled to have cool sterile water on standby when he arrived.

Meanwhile night was now falling and Thando was still

alone in the reserve. It was too risky to leave him and the decision was made to bring him to us.

Guardian angels were watching over that little calf, because he hadn't spent too long in the mud and so arrived at the orphanage in excellent condition and not nearly as frightened as Ithuba had been. We never discovered what happened to his mother. Perhaps she had realized that she couldn't save him, or maybe predators had interrupted her vigil and forced her to abandon him. We'll never know.

Right from the word go, the difference in trauma behaviour between Thando and the other two calves was startling. Thando hadn't witnessed his mother being hacked to death, nor had he been out in the wilderness on his own for nights on end. He obviously wasn't happy when he woke up in a strange room surrounded by humans, but he was more stroppy than petrified.

Like Impi, Thando had eaten a lot of mud and his stomach was swollen and painful. Shana, an emergency volunteer, tried to give him his bottle.

'He won't drink,' she despaired.

It turned out that Thando hated anything near his face, and even if really hungry, he shrank away from a bottle. Creative solutions are alive and well in the bush and soon Thando was happily slurping up his milk formula from a bright-red cat litter tray. He gained weight and very quickly became one of the orphanage's most laid-back little rhinos.

The first time he went into his *boma*, he trotted straight up to the fence to say hello to Ithuba next door. They snuffled each other through the poles with such familiarity, as if they knew each other. They had come from the same reserve but

Ithuba had already arrived at Thula Thula by the time Thando was born, so they couldn't have met before, and yet right from the word go there was a really strong connection between them. Did they have family members in common? Were they exchanging gossip about rhinos they both knew? Who knows how rhinos talk, but looking at them during that first meeting, it seemed they recognized something about each other. There was no territorial huffing and neither was the least bit skittish about being with another male calf. We know so little about the amazing capacity of animals to communicate with one another.

Within five months, we had four orphans, each with their own personality and quirks.

Ithuba was sturdy, confident, loved attention and was always up for a game of chase-the-tyre with anyone who had the energy to keep up with him. Once Thando settled down, he overcame his dislike of strangers and turned into a very curious rhino calf. He would look up at newcomers with a puzzled expression that seemed to say, *hello, I haven't seen you here before!* Impi, on the other hand, was shy and lovable, easily frightened and hated being left alone. And Ellie was the most mischievous of the bunch – a lovable, naughty and smart little elephant.

The carers were rushed off their feet. Sleep was interrupted. Food was gulped down. Burnout was close. A roster was set up to spread the workload and to make sure mistakes didn't happen. Two teams were created – Team Rhino and Team Ellie, dedicating at least three people to each orphan. Changing carers regularly not only ensured there was time for them to get some rest but it also meant the calves wouldn't get overly attached to any single person.

It was tough to implement. Orphans need love to flourish and they often bonded more deeply with one specific carer, no matter how hard we tried to stop it from happening. Ellie struggled to fall asleep without Megan, and Ithuba was happiest with Axel. Besides, with four little ones clamouring for love, a schedule was hard to stick to. The team grabbed sleep when and where they could. No one complained. They swapped information about their charges between yawns and often didn't bother with their own beds, collapsing next to one of the orphans instead.

'It's time for Impi and Thando to meet,' the team was advised. 'Neither is infectious any more and it will be good for them to have each other for company.'

'What about poor Ithuba? He's been on his own for ages,' protested Axel.

'He's much older than them and too big to play with them. He won't have a clue how strong he is and we can't take the risk that he'll hurt them by mistake. He'll have to wait until they're a bit bigger or until a rhino calf that's closer to his size arrives.'

Both Impi and Thando had explored the *bomas* often on their own and adored being outside. One overcast summer's afternoon, the doors and barriers to their rooms were left open at feeding time. The carers hovered out of sight but nearby. There was no danger to either calf but like any worried parent with a new play date, they were on tenterhooks.

Thando ignored his open door and finished lapping up his milk.

Impi walked out of his room immediately, nostrils flared and ears flicking, then he scampered over to 'his' mud wallow and dived in.

Thando heard the commotion and ran outside with a magnificent milk moustache.

In an unusually bolshie move for this timid little rhino, Impi sprang up and headed for Thando as if charging him, mud flying off him as he ran. Thando didn't blink. Baffled by this non-reaction, Impi skidded to a halt. They stared at each other. Thando calmly licked away the last milk remnants from his mouth, then trundled up to Impi and squeaked hello. Impi huffed and scampered off.

By dusk, and after a few hours of uncertain rhino posturing and strutting, the team left the door to the high-care room open and Thando and Impi jostled each other to get inside, more interested in grabbing the cosiest spot under the infrared lamps than in being territorial with each other. After more bumping and squealing, they flopped down on the mattress, stumpy little feet intertwined, and best friends were born.

Rhino calves usually have a huge warm mother to comfort them, so it was wonderful to see these two take comfort from each other, cuddling up together, playing in the mud pool, chasing each other around the *boma* and practising their charging techniques. Thando was the chunkier of the two and could be very pushy with Impi, but our little Buddha-natured calf wasn't the least bit bothered at being bossed about by his new friend.

At this stage, the game reserve, our security, the two lodges and my staff of fifty were taking up every spare minute of my life. If I could have doubled the hours in my day, I still wouldn't have fitted everything in. The orphanage was growing faster than I had dreamed possible, so during the course of 2015 I handed over all operations to an external management team. Anything to do with administration – from supplies to handling donation funds – was controlled by the Durban branch of an animal welfare organization Lawrence had created, while all health and medical matters became the responsibility of a Johannesburg-based wildlife rehabilitation consultant. It was such a relief and seemed an excellent solution to ensure that the orphanage would be supervised by committed people with more time and expertise than me. I trusted them completely and had no reason whatsoever to doubt that this partnership would work, especially as the day-to-day running of the facility wouldn't change at all – our hand-picked gang of carers continued with the toughest part of looking after the orphans. They were the ones who were there 24/7 and who gave and gave, even when they had nothing left to give.

I stayed on as director and also held on to the responsibility of raising funds, because without donations the orphanage couldn't survive. I am constantly confronted by the brutality of poaching and it's hard not to lose faith in mankind, but I also meet so many beautiful people and organizations who remind me not to give up hope because they care so deeply for animals and do everything they can to help keep facilities like ours alive.

One morning, I received an out-of-the-blue call from Reha Hutin, president of *30 Million d'Amis*, an animal charity based in France.

'We'd like to help,' she said. 'We have 15,000 euros to donate but it must be for a specific project. What do you need most?'

The timing couldn't have been better. We had realized that the orphanage needed a more specialized ward for newborns and very fragile orphans. It had to be an independent smaller building where the temperature could be properly controlled in both winter and summer, where food and medical supplies could be on hand and where handlers could sleep. A lot to ask for, but all of it was necessary if we were going to keep extremely sick animals alive.

'A neonatal unit,' I said without hesitation. 'We have an old water reservoir right next to the existing orphanage that could be converted.'

'Send me a proposal and let's get it done,' she replied.

It was one of those days that made me believe in fairy godmothers. Work started that month and construction was almost finished in November when Nandi, our first black rhino, arrived.

The difference between black and white rhinos has nothing to do with colour. They're both grey, have armour-thick skin, two horns, strong, stocky bodies and short but very powerful legs. From behind they're identical, and it's only when you look at them front on that you can tell them apart – their mouths and lips have completely different shapes. A white rhino has a flattened mouth with square lips, whereas the black rhino's mouth ends in a pointed upper lip – which makes them look almost as if they're pouting! The rhino uses this muscular finger-like lip to hold and twist leaves and twigs from bushes and trees.

Black and white rhinos have very different natures. White rhinos are typically quite even-tempered and less easily frightened, while black rhinos are shyer and as a result, more skittish. Everyone knows that if you come across a black rhino on foot, you scale the closest tree – unless you're brave enough to stand dead still, which I definitely wouldn't be!

One of the first things I learned from Lawrence was that a group of rhinos is called a *crash of rhinos*. It made me quite nervous at the time because it sounded rather aggressive, but since then I've realized that it suits these powerhouses of solid muscle really well. Interestingly, white rhinos love the company of their crash, while black rhinos tend to be loners.

Nandi was an extremely important rescue because black rhinos are at higher risk of extinction than white ones. In fact, they're on the most serious endangered list of all, and according to the World Wildlife Organization there are as few as 5,500 left in the world – versus 20,000 white rhinos.

Finding little Nandi had been nothing short of a miracle. The anti-poaching unit at a local reserve had come across the carcass of a female black rhino that had been shot in the left flank and the head. Her horn was gone and all around her body were tiny tracks and nuggets of calf faeces. The men sent out an SOS call for help straight away.

Nine rangers and guards followed the calf's spoor on foot. By four that afternoon, it still hadn't been found. At only two months, its chances of survival were zero. Black rhino calves are smaller and more vulnerable than white rhino calves and the reserve was known for its big lion pride. The calf was so little, even a hyena could have attacked it.

'The carcass is already two days old, so if the calf is still alive, it won't last the night,' the reserve's head ranger said. 'We need a chopper.'

A helicopter was dispatched in record time, and just as the sun slipped below the horizon and the sky blazed orange, the calf was spotted under a tree.

A very weak and dehydrated little rhino became the neonatal unit's first patient. Nandi was tiny but what she lacked in size, she made up for in feistiness – charging everyone in sight. The carers took turns to be with her, exchanging tips with each other on how to avoid being battered.

When these little creatures display aggressive behaviour, it's generally because they're frightened, and once they're in an eating routine and have learnt to trust their carers, they settle down quickly and show their true natures. Alyson soon won her over and Nandi proved to be a real cuddle bug. The two of them would fall asleep together under layers of cosy blankets.

What would we do without blankets! We need hundreds of them. They keep the orphans warm but they have so many other benefits too.

Underweight calves struggle to control their own body temperature and a cold calf very quickly runs the risk of falling sick, so blankets are a simple and effective way of keeping them warm. It's not only warmth that's important; sleeping on soft bedding is comforting for the calves and helps prevent hay or dirt from contaminating any open wounds. It's also much easier to inspect an animal's faecal and urine output on a blanket than on straw – an important part of monitoring their health. Needless to say, the washing machines run non-stop at the orphanage to keep blankets clean and hygienic!

Nandi loved her blanket – a bright crocheted one in rainbow colours that she dragged around with her, especially at dusk. The dark frightened her and the best way to make her feel safe was to tuck her blanket tightly around her. If it slid off, she squealed until her carer woke up and tucked her back in again. What a little princess!

The flood of orphaned rhinos didn't stop with Nandi, and within weeks two more emergency cases were brought in. Both would have died if they hadn't come to us.

The first orphan, Storm, was a sickly black rhino who had been found alone, probably rejected by his mother. He suffered from the worst worm infection the vet had ever seen and nobody knew how he came to have such a life-threatening overload of parasites. It was so bad that he was regurgitating them, and within days of arriving he got pneumonia from regurgitation that ended up in his lungs. He lost a lot of weight and yet had a swollen pot belly. The team eventually worked out that he wasn't able to process food properly. He had no appetite and we almost lost him three times. It was such a frantic time, and knowing he was a black rhino added to the trauma and stress of fighting for his survival.

The second little rescue, Gugu, was a healthy white rhino in beautiful condition. So good, in fact, that she wanted nothing to do with the carers. She wasn't looking for comfort, hated the milk she was given, and preferred to drink from a bucket – as long as it meant no one came close to her.

She wasn't keen on humans but instantly recognized her own kind and when she first saw Impi and Thando, she broke out into high-pitched calls of delight. Soon the carers opened the barriers and the three of them squealed and sniffed each other in excitement. It was wonderful to see them form their own rhino crash so naturally. Emotionally, it makes such a difference for orphaned calves to have each other for comfort and play.

Poor Ithuba was so frustrated that he couldn't join them, but it wasn't all bad news for him, because the minute Gugu laid eyes on him, we lost her. She fell in love with her strapping boy neighbour and they would spend hours walking next to each other on either side of the fence.

By Christmas, the orphanage had only been going for a year and we had taken in six rhino calves, one baby elephant, and a part-dog, part-nursemaid German shepherd. Apart from young Storm, who was still struggling to eat and process food healthily, they were all thriving. Even Ellie, our baby elephant, was loving life with Duma as her playmate – and elephants are notoriously tough to save.

At the stroke of midnight at the end of 2015, I couldn't believe I had survived another year. We had achieved so much, but emotionally it had been really tough. The greatest blow for me was that the orphanage's partnership with the outside management team wasn't working. At first, I had tried to brush off the problems as being personality clashes between strong-willed people, but sitting on my veranda at the cusp of the new year with Gypsy, Gin and Jeff milling about, I had to face the heart-wrenching reality that I was being pushed away from my own orphanage.

It had started slowly with strange complaints, such as the time I received an annoyed phone call from the admin manager to say that my anti-poaching guard had driven too close to the orphanage and that the noise of his quad bike had disturbed the calves – only to be told by my rangers later in the week that a diesel-powered strimmer was being used right next to the orphans' rooms.

Disagreements began to escalate about donations and security. I can flare up when I'm frustrated or tired – I'm French, after all – but I hate conflict and will usually do anything to keep the peace, so I shrugged it off and told myself that all that mattered was that the animals were thriving under the dedicated care of the team on the ground, with whom I still had an excellent relationship.

In situations like this, I always look for the positive, and the orphanage really had achieved so much. Lawrence would have been thrilled by our success.

'It's not just six calves that we saved,' I could hear him say. 'It's *their* children and *their* children's children. We're talking *dozens*, Frankie.'

He loved statistics like that.

Another ongoing worry for me at the time was that most of our poaching victims were from game reserves very close to Thula Thula, much too close for my liking, and I lived in constant dread that Thabo and Ntombi would be next, especially during the Christmas and year-end period. I don't know why but it's an especially dangerous time for poaching.

By then, horn infusion as an effective defence against poaching had received so much conflicting media exposure that it was useless for our rhinos.

There were many different schools of thought. Firstly, there was no scientific proof that the 'poison' really did make the end user sick, so there was bad press about the fact that the entire strategy bordered on being smoke and mirrors. Secondly, it was bounced about that if a poisoned horn *didn't* make someone disastrously ill then there was a risk of creating an added allure of 'what doesn't kill you, makes you stronger'. There was also talk that the poison didn't seep into the rest of the horn but stayed where it was injected, effectively leaving the bulk of the horn uncontaminated.

Many felt that the fear factor was worth trading on, but there was increasing belief that basing rhino safety on a bluff would create a false sense of security, and even more importantly, it didn't fight the real reasons behind the demand for rhino horn.

It had been such a bold and unusual idea, but when poachers targeted rhinos with poisoned horns at Sabi Sabi, a private game reserve next to the Kruger National Park, I realized they didn't care if horns were toxic or not, and that Thabo and Ntombi were in as much danger today as they had been before we had tried to make their horns unsellable.

I started 2016 with a knot in my stomach about the orphanage and with the knowledge that I would have to find a new way to keep Thabo and Ntombi safe.

But how? They already had round-the-clock armed security but that hadn't always helped in other reserves. Should I have their horns cut off? I couldn't bear the thought. To me, a rhino wasn't a rhino without its horn, and yet I also knew that if it would save their lives, I wouldn't hesitate.

For the time being, I decided to trust our on-the-ground security and wait to see what neighbouring reserves did. If they dehorned their rhinos, I would too. I would never run the risk of our rhinos being the only ones in the region with horns.

I hoped it would never come to that, but in my heart I knew it would.

20

Silent killers

The emergency call crackled over the radio just after lunch.

'Code red! Baby elephant in trouble!'

Vusi ran to the office and grabbed the handset.

'Vusi here! What's up?'

'Marula's baby has a snare on his face.'

'Copy that. What's the location?'

'Last sighting at Mkhulu Dam. We're trying to get closer to see how bad it is but the herd won't let us. They're skittish and on the move.'

'Stand by for assistance. Over.'

Code red means *down tools, get to main house now*. Whatever the reason for the alert, it's urgent. Within minutes, the first rangers arrived at the rendezvous point, ready for action. Vusi quickly briefed them.

'Guys, it's serious. Siya radioed in a calf with a snare. He couldn't get close enough so we need eyes on the ground. Split into pairs, grab a 4×4 and let's locate the baby before nightfall. Bring binocs. I'll take the pickup truck and meet up with Siya and Shandu. Go, go, go!'

The men raced off and began to criss-cross the reserve. Even though the elephants were last seen up north, the herd was spooked and could be anywhere. Calves need to feed every few hours to survive and this little one wasn't even ten days old. It was a life-or-death crisis. But I had faith in my rangers. They know the bush inside out and can spot animal tracks in almost any conditions.

Snares are the silent killers of the bush. All it takes is some wire and a slip-knot. The poacher strings up a noose where an animal is likely to pass – usually hanging at head level from a tree – and as soon as an unsuspecting neck or trunk passes through the loop, it pulls closed. The more the creature struggles, the more the snare tightens. Death is slow and cruel, and the animal rarely escapes. They may be able to yank the snare free from what it's attached to, but that only makes it worse because the animal goes into hiding and we have less chance of finding it to help it. Thank heavens this calf had managed to stay with the herd.

Snares are cheap, easy to set up and dreadfully effective. The first thing our anti-poaching unit does every morning is scour the reserve for them. We've gone through periods when they dismantled up to ten snares a day. Lawrence and I always used to say that you can't interfere with nature, but sometimes you have to, *especially* when an animal is injured because of humans – as with snares.

Our rhino Ntombi had a chunk of ear wrenched off by a snare. Both ET's daughter and granddaughter have had close calls with snares. Her daughter had a snare wrapped around her foot that became so embedded that she could have lost it to infection, and her granddaughter Susanna had a snare around her ear. Luckily a sharp-eyed ranger noticed that the ear was bent back at an unnatural angle and we were able to remove the wire. Both cases required daring interventions involving a helicopter, darting, and adrenalin-pumping activity on the ground by the vet and rangers to separate the injured elephant from the herd. The first calf's foot was saved but Susanna lost part of her ear.

Not so long ago, an old male giraffe ended up with a snare on his leg. What a nightmare. Saving baby elephants from snares is tough enough as it is, but removing snares from giraffes is even tougher because sedating them is such a complex procedure. You can't just immobilize a giraffe. Its long legs and neck and its heavy head carry the risk of life-threatening injuries should the giraffe fall badly.

The procedure is done in three stages.

First, the animal is mildly tranquillized so that it is docile and dopey enough to allow the rangers to approach safely.

Next, ropes are lassoed over its neck and around its legs.

Lastly, it is properly anaesthetized and its fall is carefully managed so that it lands without injury.

Even when the giraffe is down, the process is very different from that with elephants, and far more people-intensive. Two groups of strong men are needed to keep both the vet and the animal safe. One group ensures the head and neck stay flat on the ground, while the other is in charge of the legs. A giraffe's neck is immensely powerful – as I learned from Lawrence on my first visit – and once the animal is able to lift its head, it very quickly gains the momentum to stand and can be back on its feet within seconds: a potentially lethal situation in the middle of a snare-removal procedure.

So much trauma is caused by heartless poachers and their snares.

I understand that there are desperate people who genuinely

need to eat, but if they are going to kill an animal, why can't they choose a more humane way? Poachers killing for food typically break in through our perimeter barrier at night, string up a whole lot of snares and slip out again. A few days later, they're back to pick up the animals they've trapped. Once they've taken as many as they can carry, they disappear again without bothering to disable the remaining snares. Any captured animal they leave behind dies a slow death. Where is their conscience? The cruelty destroys me.

There are two types of poachers – those killing for the pot and those killing for profit.

The latter type is hell-bent on money and doesn't give a damn about animals or endangered species, and he won't hesitate to shoot the men and women who risk their lives to protect them. His focus is financial gain and he knows he'll be well paid for practically every part of the animal – skin, horns, tusks and meat. And he'll get an even higher price if the body parts are bought for the more sinister, bad *muthi*, the dark side of traditional medicine.

Muthi means both tree and medicine in Zulu, and involves plant-based remedies used for traditional African healing. English-speaking South Africans often write it without the h – *muti* – because this is how it is pronounced.

As with many ancient cultures, there can be good and bad applications of traditional healing methods. Genuine herbal medicines are administered by experienced and wise healers, while less-than-honest witch doctors use a type of black magic to exploit superstition and ignorance.

Muthi is more common in rural areas, but there are plenty

of urbanites who would never admit to believing it works yet wouldn't dare write it off completely, just in case it does.

Historically, only *inyangas* used these herbal remedies, whilst *sangomas* tended to throw bones and consult with the ancestors, but times have changed, roles have blurred and nowadays both types of traditional healer regularly use both methods, and the word *sangoma* has become the most common way to describe them.

You don't wake up and decide to be a *sangoma*. It's a calling, usually involving your ancestors and an older, experienced *sangoma*. In rural Zululand, the ancestors play an important role in mind, body and soul matters, and it is the *sangoma* who is the intermediary between the living and the dead. *Sangomas* true to their calling are deeply spiritual and would never use bad *muthi*. They know that this would risk the wrath of the ancestors.

I love how traditional ways blend into life in South Africa today. The *sangomas* are legally recognized like other practitioners of alternative medicine, and the result is a rich tapestry of ancient wisdom and modern living.

Years ago, I once asked a *sangoma* to help me solve a problem at the lodge.

Soon after we opened, petty theft became a problem. Nothing serious, just very frustrating and annoying. I asked the *sangoma* to bless the lodge and to do what she could to stop the theft. My educated Zulu staff laughed at me but I waved away their scepticism and believed it would work. We live in deep rural Zululand and it made sense to me to ask for help in this way.

The *sangoma* arrived at night, a regal yet humble Zulu

woman in her late seventies. She was barefoot, dressed in traditional red and black finery, and she wore a magnificent beaded headpiece, framing dark eyes that looked deep into my soul and bathed me in kindness. I felt as if I had known her forever.

She moved around the lodge, going from room to room, softly chanting mysterious words of prayer, a gentle meditation to the universal forces of good. When she completed her rounds, I asked her to bless my own home too.

'Of course,' she smiled, as if she had known I would ask.

Before she left, the same sceptics who had teased me asked her to bless their rooms too! Her presence lingered for a long time afterwards, leaving an air of such peace wherever she had passed.

Best of all, our petty theft problems came to an end the same day.

Unfortunately, for every honest and well-meaning *sangoma*, there's a charlatan out there who doesn't care what his potions are used for, and there are people prepared to dole out enormous amounts of money for his services. The power of this malevolent *muthi* can be so persuasive that those who believe they've received a death curse will actually die.

This bad *muthi* has a terrible impact on us because it often requires animal parts – and in extreme cases, human parts. Poachers don't care what happens to the animals they kill. Money is money.

All this was going through my mind while I was waiting to hear from Vusi about the elephant calf. These babies are so curious and use their trunks to explore and touch everything they see, and a piece of wire glinting in the sun would be a tantalizing object to investigate. Once that little trunk is in the snare, the slip-knot tightens and only a strong pair of cutters can save it.

I felt sick at the thought of his suffering and his mother's distress. Marula would be trying to help but probably making things worse as the wire dug deeper and deeper into her son's face.

Frankie would be right there, next to them both, guarding her daughter and grandson, but powerless to do anything. Her instincts would be prompting her to hide the injured baby and keep him safe from predators. How on earth would our vet get close enough to save him? She would never allow him to approach.

The rangers kept me informed as the hours flew by. The herd had disappeared. At five o'clock, my phone rang.

'No sight of them,' Vusi said.

'Keep looking. We can't give up.'

Time was running out. We didn't know how long the snare had been around the calf's face and another night without food could be fatal.

Just before nightfall, Siya and Shandu radioed Vusi to say they had located the herd.

'They're near the fence line but won't let us close.'

'Stand by. I'm on my way,' Vusi replied.

He raced across the reserve in his Toyota pickup truck and as he swung around the corner he saw the herd. He drove as close to them as he dared, signalled to the rangers on the other side of the clearing to stay where they were, then he killed his engine and trained the binoculars on the elephants.

Frankie raised her trunk and swivelled it in his direction. Vusi radioed the rangers.

'Don't move. Let's see what she does.'

He waited to see how Frankie would react to his presence, keeping his hand on the ignition in case she charged. She had an injured grandson to protect and that made her unpredictable. She watched him quietly, the herd tightly clustered behind her. She stood still and seemed relaxed. Her ears weren't flapping and her tail was limp. Marula and the baby were nowhere to be seen.

Slowly Frankie began to walk towards Vusi. The herd followed.

He scanned them through the binoculars. Still no sign of the calf. He kept the 4×4 in gear, ready to fly off. The elephants would be on tenterhooks and wary of him. They knew him from his visits with Lawrence but wild animals protecting their injured young can be lethal. If Frankie led a charge, he would be mincemeat.

He weighed up his options, eyes never leaving the approaching hulks. His truck was on a track that ran parallel to the open veldt and would be relatively easy to navigate at speed. He decided to wait.

He lowered his binoculars and frowned in confusion.

Why were they coming towards him?

He radioed a second instruction to Siya and Shandu to stay back. It was a risky call but if he didn't get a proper look at the baby, he wouldn't know how to help.

Frankie stopped a few metres away from him. The others stopped at exactly the same time. Vusi sensed no anger, no aggression. Frankie fixed him with her expressive amber eyes and from within the herd Marula appeared, her calf sheltered under her massive body.

Stunned, Vusi picked up his mobile phone and took photos for the vet. The better prepared Mike could be, the more chance they had of a successful rescue.

Marula's trunk curled over her baby's body and gently tugged him out from under her and pushed him towards Vusi. Frankie, wise, brave matriarch that she was, had worked out that the only way the calf would survive was with human intervention and she chose Lawrence's right-hand man to help.

Vusi swapped his mobile for binoculars to properly assess the wound. Not good. The snare was gripped around the calf's face and trunk, narrowly missing one eye. The baby couldn't open his mouth at all. Marula stood serene and un-afraid, her trunk tip caressing her son's forehead. The baby didn't respond to her touch. A bad sign. Starvation and dehy-dration were beginning to take their toll. Frankie hovered near the pair, their trusted sentinel.

Vusi started the engine. He'd seen enough.

The only solution was a dicey exercise that would involve separating the calf from his mother and the herd. That alone would require a helicopter and several 4×4s. Once isolated, he would have to be sedated, treated, and released again – while his mother and every single adult female would be desperate to get back to protect it. Yes, Frankie knew they could help, but in the bush, instinct rules and her inborn drive would be to keep humans away from the dying calf.

The setting sun was slipping away and streaks of vermilion layered the horizon behind the darkening figures of the elephants. It was 6.40 p.m. Within half an hour, it would be pitch-black. Vusi called me with an update.

'It's not good, Françoise. The wire's over his trunk and mouth. He can't suckle.'

'Mike Toft's on standby. He's organized a helicopter and will be here by daybreak.' I paused, afraid to ask my question. 'Will the baby make it?'

'*Angazi.*' I don't know.

My heart squeezed with fear. Every hour the snare prevented the baby from suckling, he was a step closer to death. I sat on my veranda that night with an ochre full moon hovering overhead. I hoped it was a good omen. We had done this kind of rescue many times and I knew we could do it again. I poured love towards the calf.

'Stay alive until morning, *mon bébé*,' I murmured.

During the night, I heard trumpeting. The herd was agitated and distressed but it reassured me – it meant they were staying close by and not going into hiding.

Dr Mike Toft was as good as his word and at dawn the *tak-tak-tak* of a helicopter crashed through the silence. The weather report had threatened a storm, but thank heavens they were wrong. The skies were cloudless and there wasn't a breath of wind in the air. The pilot landed near the house in a tornado of noise and dust.

'They're still in the same area,' Vusi reported.

'And the baby?' asked Mike.

'We've seen the herd. No sign of the baby. Head for the fence line past the airstrip and Siya and Shandu will direct you from there. I'll follow in my truck.'

The chopper soared off. Vusi followed on the ground with

his team. Every available man and vehicle was on hand to help isolate the calf from his mother. Lawrence would have been right there in the thick of things. Nothing frightened him, especially not if one of his beloved elephants needed help.

I didn't have his gung-ho fearlessness to join in, and to be honest, I found it too hard emotionally. I was terrified. What if the baby hadn't survived the night? What if something went wrong with the procedure? I don't have nerves of steel.

The 4×4s took up position on the dirt tracks and the helicopter flew in low and swung dangerously close to the herd. The pilot was a fearless genius. Off the elephants thundered with Frankie in front, head swivelling constantly, eyeing the chopper above and the vehicles on either side of her.

Vusi radioed me.

'The calf's alive! He's weak and can't keep up with the herd.'

'That's a good thing, isn't it?'

'Very. He'll be easier to dart. I'll call you when it's over.'

It's awful to use a helicopter to force the elephants to scatter but it's the only way to safely reach an animal needing medical care. The vet took aim and darted the calf with a sedative. Within seconds, the medicine kicked in and the calf sank to the ground.

The helicopter dropped Mike off near the fallen baby then shot back into the sky to keep the herd at a safe distance. The 4×4s kept vigil too, in case Marula managed to come back for her child.

The calf was tiny and malnourished with down-like fluff covering the baby folds of his skin. He had landed beautifully on his belly. Perfect for removing the rusted wire from his face.

Vusi snipped the snare in several places and he and Mike eased each piece free, then Mike flushed out the wounds and applied a thick coat of antiseptic salve. He checked the calf's vitals and gave everyone in the waiting 4×4s a broad grin and a thumbs up.

'He's going to make it!' he shouted.

Vusi radioed the helicopter pilot.

'We're done and about to head back. Give us five.'

Mike injected the revival drug into the calf and sprinted to the vehicle with Vusi. They sped off and joined up with Siya and Shandu, a good hundred metres away. No one wanted to be anywhere near the calf when the herd returned. They trained their binoculars on him. He was already struggling to his feet, searching for his mother.

On cue, Marula broke through the bush, dark streaks from her stress glands blackening her cheeks. The calf wobbled unsteadily towards her. She tenderly explored his face with her trunk. Freed from the snare, his trunk curled up against her belly and his little mouth searched hungrily for her teat.

There was silence in the vehicles as the four men watched him suckle.

That day, in our long-standing tradition of naming baby elephants after the person who helped save them, I christened the calf Vusi, and I was so proud of the team that I put a few bottles of champagne on ice and invited everyone for celebratory drinks at 6.30 that evening at the lodge. What could have been a really tough rescue operation had gone so smoothly that it had taken less than half an hour. That was partly thanks to Mike Toft and my courageous rangers but also thanks to the beautiful faith the herd had in us. I felt so honoured that they had entrusted their injured baby to us. Everyone, humans and elephants, had worked together to save him.

My house on Thula Thula is about two kilometres from where we were having the champagne celebration so I only left at 6.25 p.m. to go there. Who should be at the entrance of the lodge to meet me?

The entire herd!

I couldn't believe my eyes. When elephants go through such trauma – helicopter, panic stampeding, forced to abandon their calf – they can disappear for weeks on end. Not this time. They were all there, every single one of them, and they stayed with us for hours, so serene, moving silently along the lodge fence. Who knows for sure what they were thinking? But they were looking at us and glowing with warmth and love. There was no doubt in my mind that they had come to say thank you.

21

Only when the well dries do we know the value of water

Ellie had learnt to open doors. Not the one from his room, which was secured by both a door and a barrier, but the one to the kitchen. Our clever little elephant had put two and two together and figured out where his food came from *and* how to twist open the door handle with his trunk. I don't know what it is with our elephant calves and kitchens but they always seem to find their way there!

His inventiveness was an encouraging sign of how well he was. When baby elephants are sick, they sleep a lot and just want love and food in their bellies, but when they're happy and full of energy, they can get up to as much mischief as a human toddler.

Fifteen years earlier, when Lawrence's beloved elephant Mnumzane was still a youngster, he once saw Lawrence put bags into our storeroom and realized they were full of food. He waited for Lawrence to drive off then smashed the window with his trunk and broke away part of the wall.

That was the easy part – knocking a hole in a wall is nothing for an elephant his size. The next trick was opening the bags. No problem. He lifted out one fifty-kilogram bag at a time, dropped it at his feet and stomped on it, creating an explosion of flour that turned him into a gigantic ghost with startled black eyes.

Ellie was as smart as Mnumzane and also loved food, so it didn't surprise me in the least that he had worked out how to break into the kitchen. It was a full-time job keeping the little rascal entertained and making sure he stayed out of trouble. Thank heavens he had Duma to burn off some of his energy! One of their favourite toys was a big silver Pilates ball that Ellie would chase, dribble and back-kick away from Duma with ball control that David Beckham would be proud of.

Given how sick and tiny Ellie was when he first arrived, I still couldn't believe what a healthy, bouncy elephant he had turned into. He did everything with relish. When he ran, his trunk and his tail, and all the bits in-between, jiggled in glee. He had so much *joie de vivre*, as the French would say – joy of life. Sometimes he would zigzag about in the garden making such happy high-pitched trumpets that Axel and Megan would run after him, terrified the herd would hear and want to investigate. But they never did. Somehow they knew that once he was better, the orphanage was the safest place for him to be.

Ellie was crazy about water. Switch on the sprinkler and he would dash into the spray, trunk flying high to catch the water. We bought him his own bright-blue paddling pool. He wasn't too sure about it at first and watched in astonishment as it filled up with water, then he approached it cautiously and ran his trunk all around the sides of it, even pushing it as far underneath as he could. When the water reached halfway, he dipped his trunk in.

The penny dropped. *Water!*

He lurched forward to get inside, blundering against the pool. The plastic sides bulged without giving way. He raised his leg but couldn't get it high enough. Frustrated, he lowered his head over the edge, bent low, bum high, and keeled over.

His first dive-bomb.

Up he got, out he scrambled, off he ran, around he spun, back he hurtled, in he dived, feet thrashing in the air. The only reason he got out was to plunge back in again.

I wasn't there when he discovered his paddling pool, but every milestone our orphans reached was always so exciting that I heard within minutes via the bush telegraph. Our herd also loves a good water romp and it was beautiful that Ellie was displaying similar water antics. When a traumatized young animal behaves the way he should without ever having seen his own kind, it means he stands a good chance of being a normal wild animal. I never take such an important step for granted and whenever it happens, I feel the same joy, relief and sense of achievement.

One of my most uplifting experiences with our herd was when a downpour ended a really bad drought. Weather has become so unpredictable that we can't rely on summer rains any more and my greatest fear is that one day, water shortages will become as big a problem for us as poaching.

The orphanage is particularly dependent on water. We need water to keep the orphans' rooms hygienic and sterile. We need it to wash blankets. We need it to top up drinking troughs and mud wallows, and to cool down the young animals when it's hot. During a drought, there are days when the carers don't bath or shower so there will be enough water left over for the orphans.

You don't realize how dependent you are on water until there is none.

That particular summer, in 2016, the Nseleni River was unusually dry and our dams were so dangerously low that our hippo family – Romeo, Juliet and baby Chump – had moved from their favourite spot at Mkhulu Dam to Mine Dam, the only dam that still had enough water to cover them. I was worried sick it would dry up too.

Hippo means *water horse* in Greek and it's a perfect description because they do everything in water except eat. They can spend up to sixteen hours a day in it, so not surprisingly, they're good swimmers, even graceful ones. While they can't breathe underwater, they can hold their breath for as long as five minutes, and because they're so heavy, they're able to walk along the bottom of a lake as easily as walking on land.

Water is such a natural habitat for hippos that the minute a baby is born, it knows to swim to the surface, take a gulp or two of air, then head back under again to suckle, closing its ears and nostrils against the water.

I went to sleep that night panicking about their dam and woke to the wonderful sound of rain in the middle of the night. I cuddled Gypsy and listened to it battering my thatched roof and clattering on the terrace. I love the sound and smell of new rain.

It poured for forty-eight glorious hours.

Dust turned to mud. The air smelled clean and green. The Nseleni River flowed. Our dams and waterholes glistened.

The world felt softer. Nature replenished herself, as she always does.

By the third morning, the violent cloudbursts had turned to soft drizzle and I went outside to savour the hazy mist of floating droplets.

Right in front of me, just on the other side of the fence, was the herd.

Frankie first, followed by Nana and her daughter Nandi, then the youngsters and babies, with the big boys Gobisa and Mandla following at their own leisurely pace. Every single member of the herd was heading towards the pool of rain-water that had formed near the house during the storm. Mabula began to dig up the ground with his powerful tusks, churning and stirring the sand into mud. The little ones, Natal and Themba, copied him but didn't realize they didn't have tusks like their uncle and ended up with the kind of thick mud packs beauty salons charge fortunes for.

The entire herd tumbled about in utter abandon, flinging sludge over themselves in magnificent arcs. Again and again they made eye contact with me, as if wanting me to know how happy they were. They had 4,500 hectares of mud pools to choose from and they came to the one outside my home.

I pulled my purple dressing gown tightly around me, deeply moved by their joy and so grateful to them for sharing this moment with me.

Nana sat on her massive rear, trunk high, spraying mud all over herself. I noticed that her breasts were still full of milk – clearly her son Lolo had not yet had his morning suckle. Although he was four years old and had been eating vegetation for a while already, he still suckled regularly and would continue to do so until he weaned himself, or until Nana pushed him away. But at that moment, food was the last thing on his little mind and he hurtled after Natal and Themba and piled on top of them in a joyous goulash of muddy elephants.

Every time I watched Ellie play in his paddling pool, I marvelled at the similarities between him and the herd's babies and I felt so sad that he didn't have elephant playmates of his own. Thank heavens for Duma, who outdid himself as stand-in elephant friend and raced around Ellie's paddling pond, pawing the sides and barking his heart out in excitement.

One morning Ellie didn't finish his bottle. At first we thought the heat had affected his appetite but he drank even less from his next bottle and when he rejected his third bottle, we called the vet.

'His temperature is 38.4 degrees. That's high,' he said grimly.

Elephants have similar body temperatures to humans and if a calf as vulnerable as Ellie has a temperature spike, it's serious. To make matters worse, Ellie's blood proteins were dangerously low. The vet hooked up a drip to feed and hydrate him. We kept him inside to protect him from the sun. Duma sensed his buddy was sick and stayed close by, patrolling non-stop, licking his face and trying to persuade him to get up with nose nudges. Ellie barely reacted, lethargically twitching his trunk when Duma dropped his favourite dinosaur toy in front of him. His eyes lost their sparkle. His temperature didn't stabilize. He shifted about in pain.

I couldn't believe we were reliving the baby Thula nightmare. Like Thula, Ellie had been doing really well and everyone had been confident that he had turned the corner. The vet thought he was fighting an infection but didn't know what had caused it. These little creatures are so vulnerable. We work so hard to save them and then out of the blue, they fall ill and we have no idea how to help them.

'It could be that pockets of his old infection are still in his body and have flared up,' the vet speculated. 'I'll pump him with antibiotics and nutrients.'

'Please say he'll get better,' Megan pleaded.

He looked at her, unwilling to answer.

'Let's just focus on the fact that he's a much stronger and healthier little calf than when he first came here,' he said quietly.

Day four and Ellie wasn't any better. He hadn't even stabilized. We still kept our hopes up. He had survived once, he would survive twice. Megan was beside herself and didn't leave him for a minute, stroking his baby face.

'You can't die, my Ellie. You've got things to do, a life to lead. You're going to be a magnificent tusker like Mabula with a herd of your own.'

He looked back at her with sunken eyes. Diarrhoea struck. The vet battled to keep him hydrated. Nothing helped. Ellie couldn't move without pain. Megan covered him in blankets and lay on his mattress with him. Duma slept near his head.

Our Ellie took his last breath cocooned in love by his human and doggie family.

He had fought valiantly to get better but the infection was

too strong and he gently surrendered to his fate, missing his six-month birthday by just a few days.

Everyone was inconsolable. But there were hungry rhino mouths to feed and no time to grieve. The carers kept going. The void Ellie left was unbearable. We kept expecting him to come bounding around the corner whenever the hosepipe was switched on. His paddling pool was packed away. Duma spent days lying on his grey friend's bed.

Ellie was laid to rest on a balmy summer's day with his favourite blankie, his green dinosaur and the silver Pilates ball he had shared with Duma. Cotton wool clouds floated overhead and the leaves whispered hymns in the breeze. He lies in peace in an old riverbed, protected from vultures and scavengers, and his spirit mingles with other brave spirits buried at Thula Thula.

22

Rather a live rhino without a horn than a dead rhino without one

'Siya to base. Do you copy?'

'Roger that. Go ahead,' replied Christiaan, manager of our tented camp.

'Drone sighting over Mkhulu Dam.'

'What the *hell*? Maintain line of sight. On my way. Over and out.'

Christiaan grabbed his rifle, called Vusi to join him and the two of them bolted to the Land Cruiser. On the way, they called me.

'Françoise, there's a drone over the reserve.'

I froze. There's only one reason a drone flies over Thula Thula and that's to locate our rhinos.

'Do we know where Thabo and Ntombi are?' I asked quietly.

'Richard is with them. He's armed and prepped for trouble. I've called backup.'

'Good. And the drone?'

'We'll shoot the damn thing.'

Twenty minutes of rutted dirt tracks later, and Christiaan and Vusi joined Siya on the hill overlooking Mkhulu Dam.

'It flew off the minute I radioed you,' Siya reported tersely.

Christiaan slammed his fist on the vehicle in frustration. He is a man of the bush through and through, even having changed careers, swapping his pilot's uniform for khakis. He has a better bullshit detector than I'll ever have – a good man to have on your side when interrogating poachers.

'Damn it! They're on our frequency. This isn't the first bloody time this has happened.'

We had long suspected that our radio frequency was being accessed, probably by a disgruntled ex-employee, but changing frequency regularly in the bush is complicated and without concrete proof we were powerless to do anything about it.

I felt sick with fear. The reserve had never been breached before by anything as high-tech as a drone. Poaching was fast becoming so well financed and organized that I despaired of ever being able to keep Thabo and Ntombi safe.

'We'd better increase boots on the ground for a while,' Christiaan said.

I nodded bleakly. That afternoon, eight extra men arrived from the private security firm we used in emergencies.

'They're doing a perimeter check before nightfall,' reported Christiaan. 'Then they'll fan out across the reserve with our own guys to look for signs of poachers.'

They found nothing. The fence hadn't been breached. There were no remains of furtively packed away camps. It was good news but it didn't mean Thabo and Ntombi were safe. Today's reprieve is tomorrow's poaching opportunity. You can never take your foot off the pedal.

Two days later, Christiaan dropped a copy of the *Zululand Observer* on my desk.

Poacher Wounded in Shootout. I scanned the first paragraph. Three rhinos killed at a neighbouring reserve.

'Cops received a tip-off but they arrived just as the poachers were making their getaway,' he said. 'They went after them and nailed one guy. The other got away.'

The police had pursued the poachers' Isuzu truck on the R22 heading down to Durban. I grimaced. It was a bad enough road as it was. Throw in a high-speed chase with poachers who didn't give a damn about their own lives, let alone anyone else's, and it could have ended in a catastrophic pile-up with innocent people killed. I shook out the paper and kept reading. The police had fired at the truck, hit a tyre, and the vehicle had veered off the road into a ditch. One man disappeared on foot, the other was shot and caught. A 9-mm pistol and a .303 hunting rifle without serial numbers were found in the back of the truck, along with ammunition and two bloodied axes.

'And the horns?' I frowned.

'The cops think they were in a second car.'

'This is close, Christiaan. Much too close.'

'Must be the same crew that sent the drone. Keep reading. It gets worse. One of the rhinos they killed had been dehorned a couple of months ago.'

I stared at him, aghast. It takes three years for a horn to grow back. The rhino had been slaughtered for little more than a stub.

'They risked their lives for next to nothing,' I said.

'They must have thought it was worth it.'

We digested the horror of the attack.

'I'm calling Mike Toft and we're going to dehorn Thabo and Ntombi,' I said.

As fast as that, I made one of the toughest decisions of my life.

What choice did I have? It's a war out there and I didn't know what else to do any more. A rhino's horn is Mother Nature in all its glory and when I look at our rhinos, I see prehistory, power and dignity. Poachers see dollars.

I had had such high hopes for the infusion procedure but it had failed. I'm glad I tried but I had to move on, accept it hadn't worked, and find a safer solution for Thabo and Ntombi.

There are only 25,500 rhinos left in our world and they are being wiped out. Rhinos have no natural predators other than man, and beyond using their horns for territorial scraps amongst themselves or to protect their young, they can fortunately live without them.

White rhinos have a small horn and a second very long one that they use to dig up mud for their wallows. They dig, make mud, lie down, dig some more, roll about. When the mud dries up, they churn it up some more. It's useful but not crucial to their survival.

Black rhinos on the other hand, have two long horns that they also use to churn up mud, but I've seen our two orphans, Nandi and Storm, manoeuvre a branch between their horns, give a sharp twist and break the branch to get to the leaves. Again, the horns are useful but not life-and-death necessary.

With my stomach in a knot, I called Mike Toft.

'You're doing the right thing, Françoise,' he reassured me.

'I've dehorned over two hundred rhinos in recent months and it's the only way to keep them safe.'

'But did you hear what happened this week? One of the rhinos poached had been dehorned not so long ago.'

'I saw the headlines. The strange thing is that the reserve had made arrangements with me to dehorn the other two next month.'

It took me a moment to join the dots. 'You think the poachers had inside information?'

'Who knows, Françoise? Who knows.'

We all work so hard to protect our rhinos but access to information about them is impossible to control. Inside a game reserve, anyone from housekeeping to rangers could be the source of a leak, and outside the reserve, anyone from clerk to government official could be 'persuaded'. The rhino information chain has more holes than a sieve.

'Look, dehorning isn't a guarantee of safety,' Mike continued. 'But it's better than having Thabo and Ntombi walking around with a few million rand on their faces. If we dehorn them, we *know* they'll be alive the next day. If we don't, there's a chance they won't be.'

'How soon can you do it?'

'It'll take me a few weeks to do all the paperwork. What about the end of July?'

I wrote *Thabo and Ntombi* in my diary, unable to write the word *dehorning*.

'Anything you need from us?' I asked.

'Some of your guys in case they don't fall properly once I've darted them. I'll need their muscle to move them into the right position.' He paused. 'And you'd better arrange extra security for the horns.'

I put down the phone, overcome by sadness. There was no going back.

Dehorning is a tightly controlled procedure and is taken very seriously. Wildlife officials have to be informed, a permit issued. An Ezemvelo wildlife monitor must be present. The horn is weighed, marked, microchipped and every bit of it, even the smallest shaving, is gathered up. I immediately made arrangements for top-level security transportation of the horns. I didn't want horns worth R10 million at Thula Thula for a moment longer than necessary. The best place for them was a high-security vault that was nowhere near us.

Two weeks flew past and D-Day arrived with a winter chill in the air and icy shreds of cloud overhead. Thabo and Ntombi had been watched over 24/7 for the entire period.

'They're on the airstrip,' reported Richard, one of their armed guards.

Airstrip is an extravagant word for a narrow strip of flat, grassy bushland. Perfect for landing small aircraft and for darting two rhinos. Having them so accessible meant we could dart them from the ground. Helicopter darting is extremely stressful, not only for the animals being darted, but for any other animal in the vicinity of the terrible racket that the rotor blades make.

I have always been present at every procedure carried out on Thabo and Ntombi, but this one was the hardest of all. I still couldn't believe it had come to this.

We drove up to the airstrip in a dusty procession of 4×4s. Ntombi looked up but Thabo kept grazing, indifferent to the clatter of approaching vehicles. Still so trusting. I felt the same terrible pang of betrayal as I did when I had put them through the horn infusion, but this was worse, far worse. They were about to lose the very part of them that made them rhinos. If I could have stopped Mike there and then, I would have.

He lodged the gun against his shoulder and fired off two darts in quick succession. Thabo and Ntombi began to teeter within minutes. Vusi, Christiaan, Promise, Siya and Andrew leapt out of the Land Cruiser and ran towards them to control their fall. I sat dead still, hating every minute of what I was seeing.

'They're down,' shouted Vusi.

'Looking good, guys,' said Mike. 'I'll bring the 4×4 closer.'

He stopped the vehicle next to Thabo, and he and his assistants flew into action. Thabo and Ntombi's eyes were covered, ears plugged, heart rates monitored.

'Jenny, you take Ntombi. Martin, you're with Thabo. Six breaths a minute. If it drops below, I want to know.'

Their confidence eased my anguish. Mike positioned a visor over his eyes, slid on industrial earmuffs and gloves then revved up a bright-orange Husqvarna chainsaw. The shriek of the machine gave me gooseflesh. The blade plunged into Thabo's horn. I know it doesn't hurt but it looks like it should. The blade sliced deeper and white horn shavings flew everywhere. A black tarpaulin caught every scrap that fell. Nothing could be left behind; the horn is so valuable that thugs would come just for the shavings.

The chainsaw fell silent. Thabo's horn lay on the ground.

I gritted my teeth, gulped back tears. Mike caught my eye

and gave a sympathetic nod. He knew how hard this was for me. One of our anti-poaching men wiped his eyes, devastated by the mutilation of the rhinos he had protected for so long.

Mike trimmed away the last bits of horn with a smaller chainsaw and finally, an angle grinder. *Short back and sides*, was his description. It's a new technique he developed to leave behind as little as possible. The old method left up to a kilogram of horn – too much, too risky.

Mike carried the equipment over to Ntombi while his assistant rubbed purple Mercurochrome on Thabo's horn base to sterilize it, then added special oil to stop the stump from cracking.

I plucked up the courage to go closer and watch Mike operate on Ntombi. The noise was shattering and I was shocked at how quickly the horn was cut off – although I shouldn't have been. Horn is just keratin. It looks rock-hard but it's no harder than a tree trunk.

The horns were put into a Checkers supermarket packet and placed on the back seat of the Land Cruiser. Mike injected the reversal drugs, and minutes later two groggy rhinos tottered down the airstrip, none the worse for the dehorning. It had been tougher for us than for them. As soon as we were confident that the rhinos had recovered from the anaesthetic, we weighed and marked the horns and headed to the lodge to unload ten million rands' worth of keratin to the security company responsible for their transportation.

Five 4×4s, ten men and their K9 unit were waiting for us at the lodge. The men stood next to their vehicles, alert, grim-faced, armed to the teeth and wearing full camouflage with bulletproof jackets. They knew the risks. I handed over my supermarket packet to Larry Erasmus, head of the company, and they were gone, the horns securely protected in a reinforced Land Cruiser in the middle of their military-style convoy.

The transfer took less than three minutes but it was all I needed to realize how weak our own guards were. For the first time I saw what real security looked like, and I wanted it for Thula Thula. The Security-4U men were hardcore professionals who meant business. My guards were amateurs by comparison. No wonder our radios were going mad every day with sightings of animals killed by poachers. No wonder I hadn't been able to protect our wildlife, even with twenty-three full-time guards.

It may sound like a big team but once you factor in annual holidays, bank holidays, sick leave, shift breaks, and the unpredictability of managing a group of Rambos-in-the-making who didn't want to report to a woman, even indirectly, it wasn't enough to keep our animals safe.

It was time for an upgrade.

Within six weeks, Larry Erasmus and I reached an agreement for Security-4U to take over Thula Thula's security. All I kept in house was a small anti-poaching unit of four guards, reporting directly to Christiaan, to ensure Thabo and Ntombi's 24/7 protection. Everything else related to security became Larry's responsibility. It was such a weight off my shoulders and my only regret was that I hadn't done it sooner.

The next challenge was letting our guards know about the changes. Yet another manager had in the meantime resigned so it was up to me to talk to them. I had never had direct contact with them so they knew something was up. We set up chairs outside the main office building for the meeting.

I stood in front of them and tried to hide my nerves. They slouched in their chairs, shirts unbuttoned, boots unlaced, picking their teeth with twigs. What a contrast to the seven men from Security-4U who were standing behind me.

'*Sanibonani*,' I greeted them in Zulu.

'*Sawubona*,' some murmured back.

The majority didn't speak English – another drawback – but Vusi was there to translate for me.

'I'm here today to talk about changes that will be coming soon,' I said.

The tension ratcheted up a notch. I took a deep breath.

'It's been four years since Lawrence passed away and I've realized that I can't manage security on my own. I don't know enough about it to do the best for you and for the animals you protect. My plan is to outsource all security matters to a company that knows what it's doing.' I glanced behind me at Larry and his business partner. 'Mr Erasmus and Mr Mathabela have been in the security business for well over twenty years and they are better equipped than me to provide you with training, firearms and knowledge to protect our wildlife.'

The men shifted in their seats and began to talk amongst themselves. I didn't know what they were saying, but they weren't happy. Some of the men had been with us for a long time and I tried to put their minds at rest that they weren't being fired.

'As long as you meet their standards, Security-4U will employ you.'

'We were doing fine without them,' someone shouted from the back.

'We can do better,' I said quietly. 'We're losing too many animals to poaching and it's got to stop but I can't do it on my own, especially not now that your boss has left.'

'*You* be our boss,' a man in the second row snapped.

'I can't. I know about marketing, hospitality and finance, but I know nothing about security and I need help. Look at me, I can't even speak Zulu to you.' I nodded at Vusi. 'And I can't ask Vusi to be there every time we want to talk to each other. That's not the right way to work together. There are twenty-three of you, and many of you I'm only meeting for the first time today. It's better for you to have a boss who knows you, who you can talk to in your own language and who can give you the assistance and training you need.'

'Are our jobs guaranteed?' asked Njabulo, one of the few guards I knew.

'Mr Erasmus and Mr Mathabela have assured me that they will take on everyone who meets their criteria.'

There was a lot of head-shaking and muttering. Our guards must have realized from looking at Larry and Musa's men that their days of not being accountable to anyone were over. I didn't give up and kept trying to persuade them that it was for the best.

'We're a game reserve that's committed to conservation, and making our security more professional will help keep our animals safe. Please think about everything I've said and let's meet again in a few days to talk about any questions you might have,' I said.

The second meeting was just as fraught with anger and

tension. No matter what I said, they didn't see the need for change. The move to Security-4U was scheduled for the end of August so I called one last meeting with the guards to see if I could convince them that the changes would be good for everyone, them included.

We met in front of the workshop, with Vusi helping again as translator. I had spent half the night preparing what I wanted to say and had a letter for them which outlined what was going to happen, confirming in writing that they could all apply for employment at Security-4U. Naively, I wasn't as anxious this time, still believing that they would see the value of what I was doing. Larry and his men stood behind me, as they had done at each meeting. I went over what I had said in the previous meetings.

'Please remember, the idea is that you will now work for Security-4U,' I emphasized. 'When we're done today, Mr Erasmus will make arrangements to start the interview process as quickly as possible.'

I stared at the stony faces in front of me, feeling helpless and frustrated that they weren't taking me seriously. They simply weren't interested in listening to a blonde French-woman who in their opinion was just trying to get rid of them.

My dogs are always with me wherever I go, and they were running around as they usually do. Gypsy trotted along the front row of men and stopped to sniff a pair of boots. The man kicked her. She yelped in pain and scuttled behind me, tail between her legs. Dumbstruck, I stared at the man. He glared back at me, rage in his eyes. Larry and Musa's men slid their hands to their guns and closed in around me. The mood tightened. Hostility crackled. Without Larry and his men behind me, I don't know what would have happened. Not everyone was against me but we were a hair's breadth away from things turning ugly. I swallowed hard.

'You are employed to keep animals safe and this is how you treat a defenceless dog?' My voice was firm but I was a wreck inside. 'You have shown your true colours and there is no place at Thula Thula for you. I'm now handing the rest of you over to your new boss.'

It wasn't only because Gypsy had been kicked that I was so devastated. It was the violence I had seen in the man's eyes. Nobody had ever looked at me with such hatred. I knew not all of the men were like him, because there had been a few very shocked expressions, but it was a turning point for me. The best thing I could do for Thula Thula was to leave anything to do with security to the professionals.

The takeover kicked into place immediately.

Many of the men applied for jobs with Security-4U and each one had to follow a stringent interview process that started with fingerprinting, polygraph tests, and checking their qualifications, rifle-handling skills and police records.

That's how I learned to my horror that seven of my guards had criminal records and weren't even allowed to handle weapons.

The bombshells didn't stop, because on digging deeper into our weapon permits, I discovered that they were either wrong or out of date, so not only was it illegal for some of the guards to use weapons, but many of the weapons themselves weren't legal. It was a nightmare. Especially for me, because I hated anything to do with guns.

In the early days of Thula Thula, Lawrence had been concerned about security and decided I needed to own a gun.

'Lolo, I don't want one,' I protested.

'Crime's on the rise and we live in the middle of nowhere. You need one,' he insisted.

I reluctantly went with a friend for shooting lessons in order to obtain a gun licence. I think the man teaching us was more frightened than we were, particularly the day we had to handle a massive bazooka-type weapon that spits out hundreds of bullets a minute.

'We don't want to shoot guns like this,' I objected, barely able to lift the darn thing.

'If you want your licence, you have to.'

I don't know how we managed but we were awarded our gun licences and I became officially armed and dangerous – and not happy about it at all.

The gun Lawrence had given me was a little thing that was supposed to fit in my handbag. It was a nuisance. I would grab it instead of my mobile phone and it felt like it weighed a ton. I forgot everything I learned at the shooting range and couldn't even remember how to load or unload it, but Lawrence loved it and he often popped it in his pocket when he was going out into the game reserve. I don't know what he thought he could shoot with such a small gun but he took it with him anyway. When he didn't have it on him, he badgered me to carry it around with me.

'This is ridiculous. No one wants to harm me,' I said.

'You never know,' he warned.

'Nonsense,' I sniffed. 'Keep it. I don't want it.'

One morning, we headed off to Durban airport to catch a

flight to attend an event in Johannesburg, where we were guests of honour and Lawrence was going to be presented with an award for rescuing the animals in Baghdad Zoo. I'm now a bush girl through and through but I still love the occasional city fling and I was dressed up like a Christmas tree for my outing to South Africa's glittering capital.

Lawrence's hand luggage went through the X-ray tunnel and because I had put it onto the conveyor belt, the security man asked me to open it.

Inside was my gun. I turned to Lawrence in horror. His eyes widened in surprise.

'Oh, shit. I forgot to lock it up in the safe before we left.'

'I need backup! Now!' shouted the security man into his radio.

'That won't be necessary,' I laughed, reaching for the gun.

'Step away from the bag!' he yelled.

Lawrence yanked me away. 'Do as he says.'

'What were you *thinking*?' I muttered to him.

Two armed airport policemen ran up to us and escorted us away.

'We can't miss our flight,' I pleaded.

'Your flight's the least of your worries today, lady.'

I bit back a retort and smiled calmly.

'Whose bag is this?' he barked.

'Mine,' replied Lawrence. 'But it's an honest mistake. I didn't mean to bring the gun with me.'

The policeman slid a form across the table to him. 'Fill it in.'

I looked at my watch.

'Would it be at all possible to get us onto another flight?' I asked.

The men ignored me.

'Gun licence?' they asked Lawrence.

'I don't have it. It's not mine. It's hers,' he replied.

The policemen turned to me as if noticing me for the first time.

'It's *his* gun. I never use it,' I smiled.

They turned back to Lawrence. 'Whose name is it in?'

He paused. I could see he was tempted to lie, but by now I understood we were in trouble and I didn't want to make it worse when we had a flight to catch and a party to go to. We had to get the red tape over as quickly as possible.

'It's mine but he uses it. I really don't like guns,' I said.

'*Where* is the licence?'

'At home. We didn't mean to bring the gun.'

One of them stood up. 'We're booking you right now.'

'Can we call a lawyer for advice?' Lawrence asked politely.

'Sure,' they shrugged.

Lawrence called a lawyer, a *criminal* lawyer. I had gone from guest of honour to detainee in a flash. The lawyer advised me not to say anything when I was interrogated.

That didn't go down well at all.

'No comment,' I repeated.

They looked at me, nodded at each other, then one of them flicked his hand at Lawrence.

'You can catch your flight.' He jabbed a finger at me. 'We'll keep her.'

'I think I'll stay,' he said quickly.

They put me into a police van and locked me in a holding

cell, taking away my scarf in case of who knows what. In that filthy little cell, I would have needed a lot of imagination to find a way to kill myself. No hooks on the ceiling, not even bars on the window.

'Please could I have a glass of water?' I asked.

They laughed at me. It was Friday and they didn't give a damn. I started to feel really frightened. The closer we got to the end of the day, the higher the risk of being locked up for the night. Three long hours later, my lawyer arrived, a huge bald guy who looked more like a mafioso than my legal saviour.

'Don't say anything,' he advised. 'Let me do the talking.'

That hasn't exactly worked well for me so far, I felt like saying.

He came back after ten minutes with the news that I would be spending the weekend in jail. I panicked, cried, begged the police to let me go. Jail was not how I envisaged spending my weekend.

The lawyer left and Lawrence did his best to persuade the station commander to free me. I pleaded with him too, apologizing again and again. And I *was* sorry. So was Lawrence. Very sorry.

The police must have taken pity on me, or maybe they understood what had happened and took pity on Lawrence, because once the paperwork was done, they let me go. Just like that. After all their bullying and scare tactics, they freed me without another word.

We even managed to get onto the last flight to Johannesburg that night.

A few weeks later I appeared in court, accused of aviation

terrorism and failing to safeguard a firearm with ammunition. By then, we had a new lawyer and I got off with a warning from the judge, and a promise from Lawrence never to bring up the subject of guns again.

After what had happened at the airport all those years ago, then being faced with such hostility from my guards *and* discovering that most of our firearms were illegal, I never wanted anything to do with guns or security.

For the first time since Lawrence died, I began to feel that all the fires had been put out and I could focus on our herd, Thabo and Ntombi, the orphanage and growing Lawrence's legacy.

23

The hippo who hated water

When Lawrence and I first dreamed of building a wildlife rehabilitation sanctuary at Thula Thula, it was because poaching was a growing problem and we wanted to help, but nothing prepared me for the harrowing arrival of orphan after orphan.

Charlie was a sick little hippo calf found on his own close to Mzingazi Lake near Richards Bay, about fifty kilometres from Thula Thula.

'I was taking a shortcut along the footpath next to the lake to go to the clinic at Mandlazini when I heard something running at me in the reeds,' said Ngema, a local man. 'I thought I was being robbed and couldn't believe my eyes when I saw a baby hippo.'

Everyone knows that you don't come between a hippo mother and her baby, so Ngema frantically looked around for an escape route and was about to bolt up the closest tree when the little hippo ran up to him and rubbed his nose against his legs.

'Maybe he thought I was his mum, because he followed me like a little duck. How could I leave him? I didn't have a clue what to do but I had the emergency phone number for the area's wildlife guy on my mobile and I knew he would.'

'I was there within half an hour, and thank goodness he got hold of me because the calf wouldn't have survived the night,' reported Frans, the wildlife officer.

The men searched everywhere for the mother, constantly on the alert that she might come charging out of the bush at them, but there wasn't a hippo nor hippo tracks in sight. They broadened their search to the other side of the lake. They contacted neighbouring properties. Nobody had seen her. The sun was sinking on the Zululand horizon and the men debated what to do about the calf.

'The lake is a hotspot for meat poaching,' Frans said. 'No way were we going to leave that little thing on his own. We parked our 4×4 close by to keep an eye on him but believe me, we were bloody terrified. If his mother had seen us near him, she would have rammed us and pushed the whole damn car into the lake. But heck, man, by then the baby had adopted us and we were pretty much responsible for him.'

'*And* you were a bit in love with him,' grinned Ngema.

A team of rangers arrived to take over the vigil but Frans and Ngema were as reluctant to leave the hippo calf as he was to let them leave, staying glued to their legs and squealing in panic if he couldn't see them. The rangers insisted they let them take over.

'We're armed, you guys aren't. It's safer if we stay with him.'

A southwester howled throughout the night and the calf sheltered between the wheels of the 4×4. It was so bitterly cold that the rangers worried the calf wouldn't make it. At first light, they radioed through their decision.

'No sign of the mother. We're bringing him in. Over and out.'

His mother was never found, despite an extensive hunt for her.

'Hippo mums hide their newborns in the beginning to protect them from being killed by territorial males, but they always stay nearby and are excellent mothers,' frowned Frans. 'In all my years in conservation, I've never come across an abandoned hippo calf before.'

A few hours later, Charlie arrived at the orphanage. He hated being separated from his rescuers and tried to make himself invisible to us by turning his back and pointing his bum in our direction. *I can't see you, so you can't see me.*

A locum vet from Richards Bay checked him over and my heart sank when I heard the diagnosis. *Patent urachus.* I didn't know what it was, only that it sounded like a death sentence. He was so round and tubby, it was hard to believe how sick he was.

'There's urine dribbling from his navel and he might need surgery, but if he's lucky, it might just be a developmental issue that he'll grow out of.'

I took it as good news. When animals are that small and vulnerable, you hold on to every scrap of hope.

'His biggest risk is navel infection. The area is directly connected to his bloodstream so any infection will spread quickly and he'll be too weak to fight it off,' explained the vet. 'Let's hope antibiotics do their bit and nature does the rest.'

Charlie was fed a special formula that came as close as

possible to what he would get from his mother – a mixture of full-cream milk, egg yolks, minerals and vitamins.

The first time he was given his bottle, he licked the teat but couldn't figure out how to get to the rest of the milk and squeaked in frustration. He half nibbled, half slurped the teat but didn't realize he should suck. His carer slipped on a sterile glove, covered her fingers with milk and inserted them in his mouth. He sucked hungrily. She gave an excited thumbs up.

'His sucking reflex is weak, but it's a start,' she grinned.

'Keep trying,' urged the vet.

She drenched her fingers with milk again, positioned the teat between them and inserted this little bundle into Charlie's mouth. It took over an hour of painstaking struggle, but he finished his first bottle. Three hours later, he wouldn't latch onto the second bottle. Axel was on shift and patiently sat with him, dribbling warm milk into his mouth until he worked out that he had to curl his tongue around the teat and close his lips and suck. He grunted in pleasure and drank the bottle dry.

Charlie was easily frightened and very skittish but eventually it sank in that there were cuddles and milk on tap and he began to trust his new home.

Two weeks of food, love and meds later, and Charlie was on the mend. His navel closed up without surgery and soon he was eating almost as much as Ithuba and quickly became the orphanage's resident clown.

He was round and smooth and looked like a portly Michelin baby. It was astonishing how fast he could pump his stumpy legs, darting about with his jaws stretched wide, looking for something or someone to chomp. He could open his mouth twice as wide as his head and he used it to explore his terrain, his room, his toys and his humans. His gummy bites didn't hurt, but once his teeth pushed through, his mouth would be his weapon. It's not for nothing that hippos are Africa's most dangerous creature and responsible for more human deaths than any other large animal. Looking at our gawky little hippo, it was hard to imagine he would ever be that lethal.

The carers were just catching their breath when an alert reached us about a newborn white rhino that was too small to feed. Her mother hadn't been able to provide enough nutrition *in utero* and the little thing was so tiny at birth that she couldn't reach her mother's teats. She would starve if we didn't intervene.

The team grabbed their emergency kits and raced along 220 kilometres of bad roads to fetch her. On the way back, they stopped at a garage to check on her. She was struggling to breathe and her heart rate had dropped dangerously.

'I don't like this one bit,' muttered the vet. 'How much longer to the orphanage?'

'A good hour.'

'She won't make it. I'm going to put her on a new drip right now.'

There was no time to waste. The back of the Land Cruiser became a makeshift ICU and the calf was given life-saving nutrients and liquids. Unbeknown to the team, members of the Zulu royal family witnessed their desperate attempts to save her life, and as they were packing up to leave, a black-suited bodyguard approached them. He listened to their explanation and passed on the information to the royal party. Five minutes later, he was back.

'Queen Zwelithini would like to bless the calf,' he announced gravely.

And that is how a sick little rhino received a royal blessing and was named Makhosi by the queen of the Zulus. Our rhino princess arrived at the orphanage just after sunset and was placed in the same neonatal room as Charlie, with just a barrier separating them. They were both under a week old, our youngest orphans by far, and so miserable that we hoped that having another warm body nearby would help cheer them up. Charlie had never seen a rhino in his life before and stared through the bars at the strange creature running helter-skelter in the room next to his.

By 3 a.m., Makhosi was near collapse but too frightened to sleep, and poor Charlie hadn't slept a wink either, so the team decided to drop the barrier between them.

Amazingly, Makhosi scampered straight up to Charlie. He swayed his head from side to side in greeting and reached his snout towards her. They exchanged interested noisy snuffles. Makhosi lowered her head and Charlie opened his jaws and gently chomped her ears. She stood still, as if being caressed. Charlie calmed her and made her feel safe.

Their carers moved Makhosi's mattress next to his but she didn't want separate beds! She climbed onto his mattress, nuzzled up against him and fell fast asleep. Such a bond, such tenderness, developed between our scared little rhino and lonely hippo. They comforted each other, went everywhere together, cuddled up when it was cold, and if one woke and cried to be fed, the other demanded a bottle too.

We can learn so much from the sweet acceptance that animals of different species have for one another. Here were two animal orphans who had never seen anything like the other before, but it didn't matter. They were delighted to be roommates and helped each other adjust to a scary and unfamiliar environment.

Makhosi was the weaker of the two. She hadn't benefited from her mother's colostrum, the all-important first milk, and had a bad start with painful colic, but being with Charlie soothed her and made it much easier for the carers to feed her and treat her stomach cramps. She was a tiny tot with the gumption of a fully grown rhino and she became very good at dishing out bruises if she didn't get fed quickly enough.

At this stage, Thando, Gugu and Impi were between ten and twelve months old, and big and sturdy enough for the much older Ithuba to safely join them at last. No more watching enviously through the fence any more! What a bunch of happy hooligans they were together. Ithuba loved being the biggest and the others happily let him be the big brother in their newly formed rhino crash.

Their enclosure was next to Charlie and Makhosi, and little Makhosi was at the fence separating the two *bomas* every day, squeezing her nose between the poles to 'chat' with the rhino gang on the other side. Charlie adored Makhosi but he never joined her when she was bonding with her friends next door. It was as if his rhino neighbours didn't exist.

Maybe he thought Makhosi was a hippo like him. Who knows?

Charlie's teeth started to cut through; his gums became swollen and sore and he lost his appetite and chewed on everything in sight, covering his mattress, humans and Makhosi in dribble. Nurse Makhosi ignored his grumpiness and comforted him with gentle nudges, sleeping up against him with her snout touching his as they snored the night away.

Once his incisors were fully grown, he went from being a toothless baby to a young calf with a full set of perfect milk teeth. It was as if he knew he should be proud of them, because he ran around showing them off with his mouth wide open. How I wished we could teach him to keep his jaws closed. Hippos aren't as endangered as elephants but that day is coming, because ivory hunters are increasingly targeting them for their teeth, which are smaller and easier to hide than elephant tusks. In this crazy world, no ivory-bearing animal is safe any more and one day, our boy hippo will also be at risk.

I never stop worrying about the poaching danger our animals are in, and I am always grateful for the animals we've managed to save so far. There's nothing more rewarding than seeing new orphans play and knowing they're happy.

Our nine orphans had very distinct personalities and quirks, but one thing they all shared was a love of water.

Ellie had adored frolicking in his paddling pool and the rhino calves relished a good mud bath. Charlie was in his element under the garden sprinkler and was always the first to run outside if it rained, so I was looking forward to seeing him be a proper little hippo in water. If he was still living in the wild, he would have spent more time underwater than on land, so it was important to get him swimming. Once his navel was healed, we gave him a big green paddling pool that was deep enough for him to be partly submerged.

Charlie watched Axel fill it with water, curious but wary. We assumed the noise of blowing it up had spooked him. Makhosi was very intrigued and ran up to it, dipping her mouth in for a drink. Charlie saw what she was doing but didn't follow her.

'He'll go in tomorrow,' said Mireille, a German wildlife photographer who was volunteering at the orphanage.

The next day, Makhosi and Charlie spent the entire afternoon chasing each other and playing with a thick rope hanging from a tree in their *boma*. Makhosi would charge it with great gusto for such a tiny creature and Charlie would chomp at the knot and try to yank it down. They could do that for hours, Makhosi banging it with her head to get it swinging and Charlie trying to catch it with his huge mouth.

They ignored the new paddling pool completely.

'He's a flipping hippo! *Why* won't he swim?' muttered Axel.

'Maybe he doesn't know what to do,' joked Sandy, a young American volunteer.

Axel didn't need prompting and leapt into the pool, thrashing about in his best hippo-having-fun impersonation. It half worked. Charlie scampered over for a closer look but he only had eyes for his favourite human and didn't even sniff the water.

'Perhaps he thinks it's too deep?' suggested Mireille.

Water was siphoned out until only the bottom of the pool was covered.

Charlie wouldn't go in. A sprinkler was set up so water cascaded into the pool, in the hope that he could be tricked into following the water flow. He bolted around under the swirling spray, trying to catch the drops in his mouth, tripping over his own feet in excitement – but he avoided the pool.

'How on earth will he survive as an adult without water?' I fretted.

'He's only six weeks old so it's early days,' the vet said.

'What if he *never* likes water?'

'Of course he will. He probably hates the colour green,' shrugged Sandy.

It was worth a try. Ellie's old pool was hauled out of storage, patched up and inflated.

'Here you go, Charlie. A *blue* pool with Disney characters all over it!'

No luck. Charlie chose his rope toy and play-biting Makhosi's bottom over the paddling pool. We phoned several wildlife centres for advice but no one had come across a hippo that didn't like water. We wondered if he was frightened of it because he had been abandoned near a lake. Whatever the reason, we had to help him get over his fear, as he wouldn't survive as an adult without water.

'At least he likes rain and the sprinkler,' the vet said. 'Give it time.'

Out of the blue, our little clown lost his appetite and his carers immediately raised the alarm.

'He's missed two bottles,' reported Sandy.

I never get used to the speed at which these babies fall ill and we've learned not to hesitate to get medical help for them, no matter what the cost. The vet rushed over during a bank holiday weekend.

'His temperature is high, his chest is congested and his breath is wheezy,' he reported.

Bacterial pneumonia was diagnosed and Charlie was put on an intensive course of antibiotics. Makhosi was bewildered that he wouldn't play with her and ran circles around him to persuade him to chase her. He watched listlessly, not even lifting his head. You can tell so much about an animal from the way he interacts with those he loves and the fact that not even Makhosi was getting a reaction from him was extremely worrying.

Ellie's death a few months earlier was still very raw and we were all on tenterhooks.

On the third day of antibiotics, Charlie seemed to be feeling better. He still had a fever but at least he drank something – not much, but half a bottle was better than nothing. Axel opened the door to the *boma* and persuaded him to go for a walk.

'Come along, mister. Makhosi is waiting for you.'

Charlie lumbered after Axel, head low, looking decidedly down in the dumps. Makhosi and Duma hopped about like excited goats to see their friend. Charlie stretched open his mouth in a half-hearted hello, then trundled over to Ellie's paddling pool and walked right in!

'I couldn't believe my eyes,' said Axel. 'The sun had evaporated most of the water but there was enough left to cover his feet.'

Charlie stood in the pool for a good ten minutes. He didn't lie down and didn't move much but at least he was in the pool. It was such a surprise. Was it because he still had a fever and went into the water to cool down? Did primeval instincts to lower his body temperature overrule his fear? It didn't matter. Charlie the hippo was standing in water. Axel switched on the hosepipe and gently sprayed him. He shook his head in delight, snorting happily.

Within a week, he was his old self again, eating up a storm and putting on the weight he had lost. We tried to tempt him with a bigger paddling pool but he only wanted Ellie's old blue one. He eventually plucked up the courage to lie down in it but only if the water was very shallow. Even when he outgrew his pool and had to hang his head over the side to fit in, he refused to upgrade to a more luxurious option. Charlie was perfectly content to wallow in his tiny bit of water.

It was thanks to Makhosi that he took the next step. She was lolling about in her mud wallow and he must have realized that she was having fun and that mud couldn't be dangerous, because one morning, without any hesitation, he just walked in and joined her!

It was more rhino than hippo behaviour but who cared? It was another mini milestone.

Now we just had to coax him into enjoying being more submerged. The bigger green pool was brought out again and filled with a couple of centimetres of water – just a fraction deeper than his blue pool but quite a bit wider. Charlie wasn't interested.

A blistering hot day was the turning point. He finally figured out that sloshing about in the green pool was going to cool him down more than Makhosi's mud wallow or his little blue pool. Nature is amazing. Somewhere in his make-up, his instincts kicked in and he knew that having more of his body submerged was better for him on a hot day. His carers surreptitiously slid in the hosepipe and added more water to the green pool.

Charlie loved it. The hippo who hated water had become a proper little hippo at last.

24

Love in the bush

I never judge people or animals by their appearance and prefer to look into their eyes to see who they are. It was how Lawrence understood that Nana had accepted Thula Thula as her new home.

'I saw it in her eyes,' he said.

'But yesterday she was still so angry,' I frowned.

'She's different today.' He stared out into the bush, gathering his thoughts. 'She *looked* at me, Françoise. Really *looked* at me and something happened between us. I can tell you now, that girl won't try to escape again.'

Of course Nana couldn't understand what Lawrence was saying when he explained over and over that she and her herd were safe with us, but I believe she picked up the gentleness in his voice and saw in his eyes that he wasn't dangerous.

Who needs words when eyes can do the talking?

Take Frankie and me. One look from her and I know I'm irritating her. Ever since our run-in on the quad bike all those years ago, she's been huffy with me – as if she still holds it against me for giving her such a fright. She has a headmistressy way of scowling at me that makes me wish I was invisible.

One morning, my dogs got me into such trouble with her.

The herd was at the fence and I was in the garden watching them with Jeff, Gin and Gypsy at my feet. They know how to behave when our elephants visit so I never worry they'll do something silly.

The 'fence' is simply a few rows of electrified strands that Lawrence strung up around the main house compound. It's a couple of metres high and has a powerful enough voltage to send a hefty no-entry message to the elephants, but dogs and humans can slip underneath without any risk of being zapped.

Frankie and Gobisa were standing slightly apart from the rest of the herd, trunks intertwined and foreheads touching as if sharing secrets. I love seeing them together. It's a lonely job being matriarch and I'm so happy for her that she has Gobisa as a mate.

He is devoted to her, to the point of disregarding bush etiquette that dictates he step aside when other bulls come into musth so mating can take place. Not Gobisa. And it's caused quite a few skirmishes with the testosterone-fuelled youngsters if they swagger too close to her, but he stands his ground and bulldozes them away.

Two calves scampered past the lovebirds and chased after each other in amongst the towering pillars of the herd. I recognized one of them as Tonic, Nana's grandson. He was born on the same day a python killed Tonic, my monkey-chasing Jack Russell, and to keep his memory alive, I named the new calf after him.

When the babies reached Nana, Tonic skidded to a halt and slipped under her belly for a morning suckle. She let him drink his fill, trunk tip caressing his face. He was her daughter

Induna's firstborn, but as Induna had been too young to produce her own milk, Nana happily helped feed him. Luckily for Tonic his grandmother was still feeding her own son and so had milk enough to share.

The way our elephants help each other inspires me and I've learnt so much from them over the years. They coexist in a harmonious, natural way with endless respect and love for one another, living by simple rules where egos are secondary for the good of all. Yes, the bulls have occasional power struggles, but there's none of the jockeying for personal gain that is the rot of so many governments. How I wish our planet was run by elephants! Politics wouldn't exist and it would be a much safer and happier place.

Baby Tonic was still in the middle of his feed when I saw Siya and Khaya drive up on the other side of the herd on a dirt track that runs parallel to my garden. They waved and switched off their engine to enjoy the elephants with me. The dogs recognized the 4×4 and jumped up and down in excitement, yapping boisterously.

'It's just Siya and Khaya,' I shushed.

But Gin has a mind of his own and shot across the lawn, ducked under the electric fence and bolted through the herd like a mini missile.

'Gin, *heel*!'

He ignored me, fixated on Siya and Khaya and oblivious to any danger. Frankie saw the bolt of flying fur and trumpeted indignantly. I held my hands on my head and yelled at Gin to come back. Frankie charged after him, picking up speed as she went. Siya jumped out of the 4×4 but couldn't do anything without risking his own life.

Jeff paced up and down, sensing Gin was in trouble. They have a love–hate relationship and I latched onto his collar in case he decided that, today of all days, he liked Gin enough to try and save him.

'Gin, *stop!*' shouted Siya, gesticulating him away with his hands.

Frankie was a metre from Gin. One stomp and he would be crushed. Only then did he notice the grey mountain closing in on him. He yelped in fright, spun on his back paws, and flew back under the wires, barely touching the ground. Frankie stormed after him, pulling up just short of the fence, and lasered me with an angry glare.

'I'm sorry,' I said helplessly.

She shot me a you-should-know-better look over her shoulder and sashayed back to Gobisa. I hugged Gin to me and he licked my face, as happy as me that he had escaped.

'How am I *ever* going to get back into her good books now?' I muttered.

Not long after that, I was in Durban for a fundraiser with some friends. It ended at six in the evening and we were starving but hadn't booked a restaurant, so someone suggested going to a nearby pub for dinner.

'Count me out,' I laughed. 'That place is way too noisy for a bush girl. We can't talk in there! I haven't seen any of you in ages, let's go home instead and I'll rustle up something for us.'

'Who goes to a pub to *talk*?' grinned Michelle.

'Come on, Frankie,' urged another friend. 'It'll do you

good to see how the rest of the world lives when they're not working.'

I reluctantly gave in, grimacing theatrically at the music blaring from the speakers above the pub's door. Michelle hooked her arm through mine and propelled me inside. A silver-haired man was sitting with his back to us at the bar and turned as we walked up.

'Hello,' he smiled.

I looked into the kindest eyes, felt a little flustered and wondered if we had met before. Perhaps he had been a guest at Thula Thula. My friends assumed I knew him and clustered around. Someone ordered a bottle of Alto Rouge with five glasses. South Africa is a village like that. People make friends easily and have a natural way of chatting to anyone they meet. A far cry from the stand-offish reserve of Parisians.

'I'm Clément,' said the man.

'Your name sounds French,' said Michelle.

'Sort of French, I suppose. I'm Mauritian but I was born here.' He looked at me. 'You're definitely French.'

'*C'est vrai.* I've been here forever and still can't lose my accent!'

'And believe me, it gets worse the longer she lives here,' Michelle teased.

He lived and worked in Durban but although he had heard about Thula Thula, he confessed sheepishly that he hadn't read *The Elephant Whisperer*.

'I'll send you a copy,' I promised.

An hour later, I glanced at my watch and wondered if my friends would allow me to escape.

'Is the noise in here also getting on your nerves?' asked

Clément. 'I'm house-sitting at my sister's just around the corner, why don't I cook up a Mauritian curry for all of us?'

I was delighted to get away from the pub and we bundled into our cars and followed him to a tranquil all-white beach house. We sat on the deck and listened to the waves crashing on the rocks while mouth-watering garlic, cumin and chilli smells drifted out from the kitchen.

Clément and I sat next to each other over dinner and chatted about everything under the sun. He told me where to buy the best crayfish in Durban and I gave him my secret recipe for a foolproof *crème brûlée*. I learned that he also came from a big family and had four sisters, a brother and three grandchildren.

There wasn't a breath of wind, and at midnight we watched the moon rise over the horizon and turn the sea into a glistening pool of amber. We talked so late that the others gave up on us and went home. I didn't even notice. By the time I drove home, I felt as if I'd known him for years. A week later, we met again for a proper date. He arrived with roses and those gentle eyes, and before I knew what was happening, I was falling in love.

What a surprise. I thought I had done such a good job of locking my heart away! Never in a million years did I think I would have another chance at love. After I lost Lawrence, I threw myself into work. At first, it was to bury my grief but then it just became a bad habit. There was always so much to do that I barely had enough time for myself, let alone a new *us*.

I found balance in my life again with Clément. We love cooking, the bush, the ocean and being at home. He understands how important Thula Thula's human and animal families are to me, even when they keep me away from him.

When my mother turned ninety-two, Clément and I flew to France so they could meet. My parents were married for sixty-seven years and lived a very normal life, like my brothers and sister do. They're all doctors, have stable families and sane lives. I'm the black sheep – going off to different countries, giving up a good career to live in Africa, and not even coming home after being widowed in my fifties.

I was nervous about the introduction because my mum was a very traditional French matriarch. Respect and courtesy were important to her and she belonged to a generation who valued restraint. She rarely showed her feelings, certainly not to someone she barely knew.

And Clément is the complete opposite. He is as easy-going and friendly as she was reserved and formal. His roots are Mauritian but he was born in South Africa and he speaks French in a haphazard jumble of *franglais* – part French, part English. But as no one in my family speaks a word of English, at least I knew he would be able to communicate with them.

'Maman, this is Clément,' I said. 'Clément, my mum.'

He kissed her hand. *'Enchanté.'*

She was charmed.

'Françoise m'a beaucoup parlé de toi,' he said. Françoise has told me a lot about you.

I froze. He had used the familiar form of you – *toi* – as all Mauritians do.

She was a little less charmed.

Unaware of his faux pas, he chatted away, asking her about

her collection of antique teaspoons and wolfing down a second helping of her *tarte tatin* with oohs and ahs and pleas for the recipe.

She thawed a little after that and a whole lot more the next day, because she spent most of the afternoon cooking and I knew it was for him. Like me, she fed people she loved. And when she asked him to help her chop onions, I knew we had her blessing.

Such genuine warmth developed between them in a very short space of time that when we left she hugged us both in a rare show of affection. Six weeks later, she passed away quietly in her sleep and I often wonder if she felt free to go because she knew I wasn't alone any more.

Just before she died, I had been looking forward to a visit from Susanne Simonsen and her sister. We had talked over the past two years about doing something to honour her late father-in-law Jorgen, whose discovery of Thula Thula had introduced three generations of their family to the bush and instilled in them all a deep commitment to wildlife conservation. We decided her trip would be the ideal occasion to hold a small ceremony at which we would hang a plaque at the orphanage in his name. Their most recent donation had paid for extra-sturdy barriers to stop our little rhino thugs from escaping, so it was the perfect time to celebrate the meaningful impact of their generosity. Giving her father-in-law this simple recognition meant so much to Susanne, as he had deeply influenced her own life.

When I phoned to tell her about my mother and that I was devastated to miss the ceremony, she was her usual gracious self.

'We'll be fine. Go to your family,' she urged. 'Promise and Christiaan will celebrate with me.'

I rushed off to France for the funeral, struggling to come to terms with the fact that I had lost my mum so soon after seeing her. I was gone for ten days and it was only upon my return that my assistant Jojo sat me down and told me what a disaster the event had turned out to be.

'Christiaan and I went up to the orphanage before the others so we could prepare a couple of things,' she said grimly.

When they got there, a very embarrassed Axel told them they weren't allowed to put up the plaque.

'You're joking, right?' laughed Christiaan.

He wasn't, unfortunately. The orphanage's Durban-based admin manager had phoned through an explicit instruction to prevent the ceremony from taking place.

I stared at Jojo in horror. My dear friends had been caught bang-smack in the middle of the petty human politics that I had tried so hard to protect them from. All Susanne had wanted to do was honour her father-in-law with a plaque, and then be allowed to take some photos that would help spread the word about Thula Thula's conservation projects through their wildlife foundation network.

'What happened then?' I asked.

'Promise and Siya arrived with the Simonsens and . . .' She fell silent. 'It was *so* awkward. I tried to make it better by suggesting to Susanne that we find a spot at Mkhulu Dam for the plaque but she wouldn't hear of it.'

'It doesn't belong in the middle of the bush and *especially* not at Thula Thula's most sacred place,' Susanne had protested vehemently.

If I had been there, I doubt that the instruction to stop the plaque from going up would have been given in the first place. It was a shockingly heartless thing to do while I was 10,000 kilometres away, burying my mother.

To his credit, Axel showed the Simonsens the new barriers and gamely participated in the photographs. He did his best to handle the very uncomfortable situation imposed on him by his boss.

Susanne then had the difficult task of going home to Denmark and reporting to her husband and brother-in-law that their father had not been honoured in the way they had hoped. At that stage, she didn't know about the management difficulties that I was experiencing at the orphanage, and being the gentle and considerate person she is, she let it be and didn't even raise the subject with me afterwards. In a way her kindness made me even more upset that the partners to whom I had entrusted the orphanage could have cold-shouldered the family who had helped us so much.

'If the Simonsens can move on then so should you,' advised Clément.

He was such a calming, steady support during that awful period and all I could do was continually remind myself that the animals at the orphanage came first.

Very few people knew about the conflict I was going through with the outside management team and I preferred it that way. It was distressing to talk about and seemed so petty in the bigger scheme of things, going against everything Lawrence and I had dreamed of – which was to create some-

The construction of the Thula Thula orphanage with Promise and Andre, one of our game rangers.

Our amazing head game ranger, Siya.

Axel and Megan with Ithuba in his *boma*.

Baby Ellie loved his paddling pool.

Duma and Nandi, our baby black rhino, playing football together.

Thabo saying hello to our game ranger Khaya.

Baby Charlie – the hippo who was scared of water – standing bravely in his paddling pool with his friend Makhosi.

When the drought broke at last, the herd came to mud pools at my house to celebrate the rains with me.

Our rhino orphans playing together in the mud.

Dehorning Thabo and Ntombi was the only way I could keep them safe. It was one of the most difficult decisions I have ever made. Dr Mike Toft (*far right*) anaesthetized them before cutting off their horns.

The Thula Thula anti-poaching team – this professional outfit is what we need to keep our animals safe.

Vusi holding the snare that had been wrapped around the
trunk and mouth of Marula's baby.

We were relieved to see Susanna suckling so soon after
losing the tip of her trunk in a snare injury.

Me with Clément and Katja.

Gobisa, the herd's oldest bull, taking it upon himself to check out my new mate.

A new beginning with the Thula Thula Wildlife Rehabilitation Centre.

Kenya, our newly arrived baby kudu, who was one of the first rescues at the new rehab centre.

Kayleigh with Bruce, a rescue dog turned bodyguard for staff at the rehab centre.

Me with my beloved doggies, Gypsy and Gin. They are such an important part of my life and I am so grateful to have them constantly by my side.

thing that went beyond Thula Thula, where anyone who loved animals could find a way to help and be involved in wildlife conservation.

Although Lawrence had been gone for many years by then, I was unsure how people would react to me having met someone. I don't know why I fretted so much, because everyone was thrilled for me, and I was so touched when Lawrence's mother Regina invited us both to join the Anthony clan for her ninetieth birthday celebrations.

But Clément still had to pass the scrutiny of my dogs and I was very curious about how they would react. Gin loves everyone, so he was a pushover, but my Labrador, Jeff, was almost ten years old and had become very possessive of me. The day they met, he was fast asleep on the kitchen floor. I tiptoed past him and shot Clément a warning look.

'Be careful. He's grumpy and doesn't like strangers.'

Jeff heard my voice and lifted his head, looked at me, looked at Clément, registered I was with someone he didn't know, then thumped his tail twice and went back to his old man's siesta.

'Two down, one to go,' Clément grinned.

Gypsy is my most discerning dog. She's smart and has an excellent nose for trouble, so if she didn't like him, it would be a bad sign. Clément had brought a bag of bones but she isn't easily fooled and would have seen right through his tactic if she hadn't fallen head over heels for him first. Not that he was her priority. She snatched up her bone and disappeared outside without a backward glance.

'That's a bit of a non-reaction!' I laughed.

'She'll come back later and say thanks,' he smiled.

He was right, she did, and now there are five of us fighting for space on the sofa.

Even Gobisa gave his stamp of approval.

One weekend, Clément drove up to Thula Thula to spend a few days with me and persuaded me to abandon my in-tray and go along with him on a game drive, which was quite a feat because I rarely went on drives any more.

My nervousness around the herd developed slowly and without me really being aware that I was coming up with excuses to avoid going into the bush – usually work-related excuses, because who could argue with that? I loved being with our elephants from the safety of my home but I always felt unsure and worried if I was on foot or in a car, and after Lawrence died, my anxiety became worse.

I reluctantly followed Clément into the Land Cruiser and made sure I sat in the middle of the seat, with him on one side of me and a guest on the other. I sat bolt upright and did my best to hide my nerves.

We hadn't had rain for weeks and the Zululand hills looked like a painting – layers and layers of golden savannah against a deep-blue sky. No artist paints as vividly as Mother Nature.

Our ranger Andrew radioed Siya for the location of the last sighting of the herd.

'We saw them heading south,' he reported.

'Rain must be coming at last,' Andrew said to us.

The sky was clear and cloudless and rain didn't seem possible but our elephants are never wrong. We don't need a weather station in the bush, we watch our animals. If a cold front is coming, the herd take shelter in the south of the reserve, where there are more trees and there's less chance of them losing their footing going down wet and muddy hills.

Rain in our Zululand paradise is often regarded by locals as a blessing. I smiled to myself. These rain blessings couldn't be coming at a better time. Two of our rhino orphans, Ithuba and Thando, had 'graduated' and gone back to the reserve they had come from, and the next two, Impi and Gugu, were also close to going home. With all the people problems at the orphanage, I hadn't been present when Ithuba and Thando had left, but I had heard from the reserve that they were settling in well. I would have given anything to have been present for these important milestones, but by then, it was just less painful for me to stay away. It was tough, though, really tough, to be excluded. What kept me going was that getting these little creatures back to the wild was why we had built the orphanage in the first place.

I was jolted back to the present with the vehicle bumping across the veldt as Andrew did a U-turn, and not even fifteen minutes later, we saw the herd about 500 metres ahead and coming towards us along the dirt track.

Andrew stopped the 4×4 near a magnificent acacia tree.

'They'll be munching on it within minutes,' he predicted.

Acacias are queens of the African wilderness; tall, tenacious survivors of droughts that hide their spear-sharp thorns within gracious leafy canopies. Our elephants love them.

My heart thudded as they ambled towards us, slow and steady. Frankie and Nana were in the lead, the other mums behind them with their little ones holding onto their tails, and trailing much further back were the bulls: Mabula, Gobisa and our gentle giant Mandla. Frankie stopped on cue

under the acacia tree and broke off a branch, nimbly manoeu-
vring it into her mouth with her trunk. This was a sign to the
rest of the herd that it was time for a snack. Nandi walked
protectively on Nana's blind side and led her mother to a tree
without thorns.

With both matriarchs distracted, our youngest elephant
Themba decided to charge us, slinging his trunk in the air like
a lasso. But like all kids, he hadn't yet realized that mothers
– and aunts – have eyes in the back of their heads. Frankie
spun around, mouth sprouting leaves, and rumbled a warning
at him to behave. I kept my eyes riveted on her, terrified she
would realize I was in the 4×4.

Themba stopped dead in his tracks, stared warily at her,
then flew off like a bullet in the opposite direction towards
Mandla. Baby elephants love to charge and this little one was
bubbling over with mischief and energy.

Mandla may be six tons of intimidating bull, but inside he's
a marshmallow and the best uncle a calf could wish for. He
slowly lowered his head and Themba crashed into a wall of
muscle and skull and toppled over. Mandla coiled his trunk
around him and gently helped him up.

'That's how Themba will learn who to pick his battles
with,' smiled Andrew.

The herd milled about, nibbling on trees and grass with not
a care in the world. I felt such a rush of love for them and
their Zen-like way of being, and at the same time I felt confused that I had allowed myself to become so anxious around
them. They show me how happy they are every day, and yet
over the years I had slowly stopped spending this kind of
close-up time with them.

As for Frankie – she was either ignoring me or she hadn't even picked up that I was there!

Suddenly Gobisa stopped and jerked his head towards us. His trunk shot up and rotated in our direction, picking up the scent of everyone in the 4×4. Then he strode towards us. I gritted my teeth and watched Frankie like a hawk. Clément took my hand and smiled at me. He knows the bush and wasn't the least bit concerned.

'He's just popping in to say hello,' Andrew murmured. 'Stay calm, keep still and make sure your phones and flashes are off.'

Gobisa walked straight up to Clément and stopped in front of him. We held our breath. He gazed down at him, huge body blocking the sky. Clément looked up, hand tightening over mine. They stared at each other. Gobisa leaned his massive forehead against the Land Cruiser's canopy, his tusk prodding Clément's side. The vehicle shifted and creaked under the weight.

'I only saw peace in those hazelnut eyes,' Clément said to me afterwards.

I watched in amazement as Gobisa floated his trunk over him. An elephant can yank an oak tree out of the ground but it can also caress with infinite tenderness. His trunk fluttered over Clément's chest, moved to his face, explored his cheeks, nose, hair.

'He looked at me the whole time as if expecting something from me. I didn't know what he wanted so I just kept looking back at him. He was serene and his eyes were kind. I could see the furrows cleaving his skin, the veins on his ears. But I didn't want to be a hero and touch him back. I'm not the one who talks to elephants,' he smiled wryly.

Andrew started up the Land Cruiser and Gobisa stepped back. The engine purred patiently while we waited for him to leave but he continued to quietly study Clément before stepping up to him again, touching him one last time with his trunk, then sauntering off to join the rest of the herd.

I gripped Clément's hand, stunned, filled with the deepest calm.

Who knows why Gobisa homed in on Clément like that, but my Zulu rangers say that as the herd's oldest bull, he was checking out my new mate. If eyes are the windows to the soul then I know he left reassured that I was with someone who made me happy and who would never come between me and them.

25

Nowhere is safe

Lightning blitzed white through my bedroom. Thunder cracked like gunshots. The storm was close, very close, and it had been hammering for hours. I stroked Gypsy to reassure her and registered that my phone was ringing.

I groped for it and checked who was calling at 2 a.m. in the morning. Unknown number. I dropped the mobile on my bedside table and fell back on the pillows.

It rang again. One wrong number is possible, two unlikely. 'Hello?' I mumbled.

'The orphanage has been hit. They shot two rhinos and attacked the volunteers.'

It was the orphanage's wildlife consultant calling from Johannesburg. I sat bolt upright. *Hit. Shot. Attacked.* I couldn't process the words. I called my assistant Kim. No answer. I tried Vusi. No answer. Between sleep, the storm and the time of night, no one heard their phones. I pulled on khakis and a jersey, ran to the cottage nearest mine and banged on my general manager's door. She had only been with us for a few weeks and I was about to discover that, over and above being a strong and capable woman, she had steady nerves and a clear head in a crisis.

'Lynda! It's me! Open up!' I shivered in the rain, waiting

for her to let me in. 'Poachers at the orphanage. I'll never manage the roads in this weather. We need your 4×4.'

She saw the horror on my face, asked no questions. 'Give me five minutes.'

The rain smacked hard as hail as we sprinted to her car. We crept along the dirt track at a snail's pace, struggling to see, not speaking, hearts hammering. There were four volunteers helping Axel, animal-mad girls who had travelled a long way to care for our calves. I couldn't get my thoughts straight. What would we find? Had they been hurt, or worse, killed? Slashing a rhino's face for its horn is barbaric, and the men who do it are dangerous beyond anything these trusting youngsters would understand. Even if they did everything the men told them to do, one wrong move or word and an agitated lunatic could pull a trigger. The journey took forever. Slowly, painfully slowly, we struggled through the downpour until we drove up the orphanage's long driveway.

Our anti-poaching rhino guards were the first people I saw. One of them ran outside to meet us.

'What were you thinking driving here on your own?' he burst out. 'The attackers could still be in the reserve! Quick. Get under cover.'

I stared at him. It hadn't crossed my mind that going there without a guard was dangerous.

'Is anyone hurt?' I asked.

He nodded, grim-faced, and took us inside. The police were already there, scouring the orphanage for anything the poachers might have left behind.

I found the girls huddled together in the office, distraught and disorientated. I hugged them, held them tight, so relieved they were alive. Young Caitlin had only been with us for a few hours, her dream of working with orphaned animals now a savage nightmare.

The rain battered on the corrugated iron roof. We could hardly hear each other speak. The girls talked through tears and sobs. Everyone was paralysed. No one knew what to do. Who to phone. How to get help. I realized Larry from Security-4U should be on-site.

'Has someone called Larry Erasmus?' I asked numbly.

They didn't know. I was a robot on automatic, barely functioning. I fumbled for my phone. Larry answered immediately, already on his way.

'The guard escaped and got hold of me. How bad is it?' he shouted over the thunder.

'Worse than bad. Where are you?'

'The road's a disaster with all the construction work so I took the back track through the reserve. The storm's not helping. My other static guards are on their way and the control room called the cops. Are they there yet?'

'They got here before us,' I said.

He arrived soon after and we started to piece together what had happened.

Around 9 p.m., when the team had finished the first evening feed, five heavily armed men breached the fence, disabling cameras and cutting cables as they crept towards the carport where the security guard was sheltering from the storm. Two men attacked him from behind, dragged him into the storeroom and pistol-whipped information out of him.

When is the next feed? How many people are here? How

many firearms? What security is there? Where's the dog? Where are the horns? You lie, we kill.

The storm bucked and reared outside, drowning out his screams. They took his gun, phone, radio and shoes, tied him up and bolted the door shut. Then they waited, patient predators, biding their time until the next feed.

Axel and the volunteers had already gone to bed, five unarmed young people oblivious to the gun-and-knife-bearing thugs hiding outside in the shadows.

At 11.30 p.m., lights went on in the kitchen and the two girls on feeding duty chatted and laughed as they prepared bottles for Impi, Nandi, Storm, Gugu, Charlie, Makhosi, and the latest arrival, Isimiso. Six hungry rhino calves and a bolshie little hippo were already squealing for their midnight snack.

Within seconds of going outside, the girls were ambushed and dragged back inside. The men fired questions at them.

Take us to the boy. Where is the dog? Give us your phones. Where are the radios?

They were coerced into taking the men to Axel, who was in his room with Duma. One of the girls, Nicole, understood that the attackers might kill Duma.

'Axel, wake up! We need you,' she shouted through his closed door. 'Leave Duma behind.'

It wasn't such an unusual request. Snakes were a regular problem in the house and Axel immediately assumed the girls needed his help to get rid of one. Keeping Duma safe in the room made sense. It also occurred to him that it was probably why Duma had barked earlier.

'Sit. Quiet,' he ordered Duma as he opened the door.

Four men faced him with guns, the two stricken girls captive between them. Axel stayed calm, yanked the door shut behind him. Duma didn't move or bark.

The girls and Axel were shoved into the office where other poachers were already unplugging the data cables feeding into the CCTV video recorders. The men knew exactly where to go, what to do, to watch out for a dog.

Two weeks earlier, a drone had flown over the reserve. We have a shoot-on-sight policy for them, but the minute security was close enough to shoot, its headlights cut out and it disappeared into the darkness. We thought they were looking for Thabo and Ntombi – but now we're sure they were investigating the orphanage.

These criminals had money and high-tech equipment and had clearly been gathering information for weeks, maybe months. Ordinary thieves would have smashed the computer and video hardware, but these tech-savvy men knew that by simply unhooking cables, all links to the outside world would be dead. The team was isolated and helpless.

The men were aggressive and edgy and forced Axel into helping them round up the rest of the volunteers. One of the girls was severely assaulted while the attackers badgered the others for information about rhino horns they believed were on the premises. What horns? Permits had been granted to remove Gugu and Impi's horn stubs before they went back to their original reserves – a procedure that was also done before Ithuba and Thando left – but the dehorning hadn't yet taken place. The poachers must have known Gugu and Impi were about to leave the orphanage. Did they think their horns had already been removed? Or did they think Ithuba and Thando's horns were still at the orphanage? We'll never know.

The men dragged Axel with them as they ransacked the orphanage for the horns.

Give us the horns! Open the rooms! Why is this door locked?

'It's the manager's office. I don't have the key,' Axel replied, never raising his voice.

They struck him again and again with the back of a panga.

There must be a safe! We want the horns!

'There *isn't* a safe. We would *never* keep horns here.'

Time was beginning to run out for the poachers. They gave up interrogating Axel and tied him and the girls up with duct tape and rope and locked them in the office.

One minute the team had been getting ready to feed the calves, the next they were hostages and didn't know if they would make it out alive. Axel did his best to brief the girls on how to reduce the danger of being hurt.

'Look down. Don't make eye contact. Don't resist. Do whatever they say,' he urged.

Three men guarded the youngsters, while two others, armed with guns and an axe, headed through the darkness to the calves. I can't begin to imagine the fear the team felt for their vulnerable rhino charges and how utterly shattering the sound of the gunshots must have been.

They put a bullet into Gugu and Impi for horns no bigger than a child's fist.

Gugu died instantly, sweet Impi didn't. The poachers didn't give a damn. They held him down and hacked his face with the axe, Impi's tiny dark eyes glistening in confusion and horror. Superstitions run deep in rural Zululand; eyes see and have memories, so they did the unthinkable – they poked out his eyes.

Half an hour later, the men and their bounty were gone.

The team waited, too terrified to move, eyes glued to the clock above the door. After twenty long minutes, they nervously untied one another. They were frantic, dazed. Had the attackers really gone? Was it safe to go to the calves? What carnage would there be? A radio was found but no one was reached. One of the girls discovered a mobile that the poachers hadn't taken. They rang me, tried my assistant, phoned people outside the reserve. Desperate call after desperate call.

Unbeknown to them, the guard in the storeroom had escaped and was running barefoot through the reserve to raise the alarm. Petrified of being caught, he avoided roads and tore through the bush in the pitch dark, shredding his feet, oblivious to the rain and the pain. He reached the lodge, found the night guard and together they called the Security-4U control room – at exactly the same time as the manager from outside the reserve reached Larry Erasmus.

'It all happened at once. While I was on the phone, I had three missed calls from my control room,' he said. 'I heard about the attack from the first call, and from my guard I got the low-down and knew we were dealing with pros with serious firepower.'

A week earlier, poachers had attacked a private farm nearby and Larry had lost a man in the shootout, so he wasn't taking any chances. He unlocked his safe, grabbed weapons and ammunition, and phoned for extra reinforcements. The last thing he did was wake his wife and kiss her goodbye. He had no idea how long he would be but he knew the danger he faced.

Back at the orphanage, the team found Gugu dead, and Impi half-submerged in his wallow pool, struggling to breathe through his horrendous facial injuries, keening in pain as he tried to pull himself out of the water.

Blinded and terrified, Impi panicked at the slightest touch. No one could get close enough to help him. To this day, I can't bear to think about him and the anguish of his carers. They had hand-raised him and there was nothing they could do, not even hold him. They begged Larry to shoot him, free him from his suffering.

'I was desperate to,' Larry said afterwards, his voice raw. 'But I know how these things work. Crime scenes can't be messed with. It tortures me still that I didn't, couldn't, end his agony.'

The tragedy was that both calves had been days away from becoming wild rhinos. They were originally from different reserves and everyone had been fighting tooth and nail to persuade their owners to allow the rhinos to stay together. The owners had even been invited to visit the orphanage so they could see for themselves how strong the bond between Impi and Gugu was and how traumatized they would be if separated.

Little Impi had survived his mother's poaching then would die the same hellish way.

Tender little creatures killed for keratin that grows on our fingers.

*

I went into survival mode to keep the team and animals safe and hauled our chef Tom, who lives at the lodge, out of bed to open rooms for the girls. It was late, they were exhausted and we had to get them away from the scene of the attack.

Axel and Nicole wouldn't leave the orphans. Charlie and the four remaining calves were crying out of hunger and fear, sensing the mayhem, needing comfort and food.

More Security-4U men arrived, armed and ready for battle. Larry wasn't satisfied and woke up the area police commander to send in more support.

The weather eased. Sun spilled into the wretched night.

First thing in the morning, my assistant Kim drove the girls to the Empangeni Garden Clinic for medical care and trauma counselling. Mike Toft arrived and euthanized Impi. Vusi got hold of a local farmer to lend us his front-end loader and to help us lift the bodies out of the *boma* so that they could be laid to rest.

Those twenty-four hours are a blur. I remember it in flashes. The ashen faces of the youngsters, the explosive racket of the storm, the atrocity of Impi's injuries, the chaos in my heart.

I blocked out the pain. If I dwelt on it, it would have destroyed me. For a while, I lost faith in mankind. I lost hope in saving rhinos. Demand for their horns will never stop and they will always be in danger, as will the men and women who risk their lives guarding them. I see-sawed between being devastated that our security units hadn't been able to stop the killing and relief that they hadn't risked death by barging into the middle of the attack. It could have escalated into a full-scale hostage stand-off. If the poachers could do what they did to a live animal, they wouldn't have thought twice about killing a human being.

The orphanage sits on a hilltop, perfectly positioned for the poachers to shoot at any guard or policeman who dared to approach. But no matter how well armed and trained in high-risk situations Larry's anti-poaching men had been, they would have been sitting ducks, unable to return fire. Not with our people in the same building as the attackers.

What could I do but pick myself up and keep going? I hoped with all my heart that we would all manage to put aside our differences and be the partners we were supposed to be. Rhinos need us to fight for them, to do our best to keep them safe. But, I kept asking myself, is *anywhere* safe? What can you do against men with no fear and nothing to lose, armed to the hilt with shotguns and assault rifles? But if we don't try, more will die.

The day after the attack, I received a phone call from Megan in England. She had left soon after Ellie had died and was sickened by the killing of two little calves that she had helped care for. She knew we needed extra security to make the orphanage impenetrable to another attack and she also knew that came at a cost we couldn't afford.

'How can I help?' she asked. 'Shall I start a crowdfunding campaign? What do you need?'

'We've bolstered security but we need more, and we need urgent protection for the rest of the reserve to make sure poachers don't get in again.'

'I'll start with a goal of $6,300,' she promised.

She reached her target in five hours.

Donations flooded in from all over the world. People were

appalled and wanted to help. The outpouring of love and concern was incredible. There was so much goodwill. A Mozambican farmer *walked* to us to bring his donation.

So much goodness shone over us.

Donations sky-rocketed and within twenty-four hours over $30,000 had flowed in and continued to come in until $56,800 was raised.

We deployed round-the-clock armed guards and extra protection for staff during night feeds. We reinforced boots on the ground to create a safety net around the orphanage. We drained Security-4U of resources: every available man Larry had was at Thula Thula.

And that was just the start. I appointed Christiaan, who had military experience, to coordinate new long-term security measures for us, and to work closely with Security-4U so no stone was left unturned to keep the orphanage safe. We brought in specialists to evaluate, repair and upgrade our entire system. National and local police hunted the poachers. Wildlife authorities were on red alert. The clips of CCTV footage that could be salvaged were sent to a laboratory in Pretoria for analysis. Suspects were apprehended, two escaped, no one was arrested. The investigation is still in full swing and won't stop until the men are caught.

Dehorning the remaining calves became a red-hot priority. Everything possible was done to rush through the permits for the operation.

Three of the girls went home to their families but Axel and Nicole stayed to look after and comfort the orphans. Charlie and Makhosi were especially distressed and were put on Rescue Remedy to help them.

Thabo and Ntombi felt the danger, and for weeks they stayed close to the main house and the lodge, always sleeping within eyeshot of us. Even with full-time armed guards, they didn't feel safe in the bush and came back to the place where they were raised.

Nana and Frankie sensed the turmoil and disappeared, hiding the herd in the deepest corner of the reserve until they felt the threat had passed.

Debates raged about the future of the orphans. The outside management team wanted to move the animals to another venue which they felt would be safer. Safer? Is anywhere really safe when we can never know just how far crime syndicates will go? Some of us longed for them to stay. Others agreed that it was better for them to go. I couldn't bear the thought of the calves leaving, especially the most vulnerable ones – Charlie, Makhosi and Isimiso. The orphanage was the only home they had ever known.

In the middle of this chaos, a four-year-old white rhino was slaughtered in a Parisian zoo, the first rhino poaching in Europe. It almost broke me. Nowhere was safe. Nowhere. If rhinos weren't safe in zoos, how would they ever be safe in the wild?

I had naively believed that everyone would cooperate for the good of the animals but the opposite happened. The conflict with the outside management team worsened to the point that decisions were made without consulting me, Four Paws or the *amakhosi*.

And then I ran out of fight.

Our two older calves, Storm and Nandi, were the first to leave, going back to where they were born. I consoled myself that, given how old they were, they were ready to be making new memories and to start the beautiful process of becoming wild rhinos in the bush.

That left Duma, two rhinos and our darling hippo.

And, to my great sorrow, they too were moved.

By the end of April 2017, just ten weeks after the attack, our orphanage was an empty shell.

The days that followed were the some of the darkest of my life. I would drive through the reserve, see the orphanage up on the hill and be overcome by loss. I told myself it wasn't a failure and that we had done so much good. Four rhino calves were still frolicking, and two more, plus little Charlie, would grow into healthy animals thriving in the wild. But it was impossible to hold on to what had gone well when so much went wrong. People didn't pull together. Relationships ruptured. Friendships tore apart. Collaboration with the outside management disintegrated.

The *amakhosi* and our Austrian sponsor Four Paws felt let down and betrayed by people they believed had been partners. The accusations thrown at me about Thula Thula security almost destroyed me, but I resisted being drawn into a public squabble, and even today, I avoid going into details. There is no point. For months I lay awake at night, tormented by what had happened and the terrible fallout afterwards.

Poaching doesn't stop with us. It's bigger than us. As long as there's a market for horn and ivory, people will slaughter rhinos and elephants. Killing elephants for their ivory isn't as big a threat here as elsewhere in Africa, but it's coming.

I don't believe in the clichéd platitude that everything happens for a reason but I believe with all my heart that, when tragedy hits, we have to find a way to *give* it reason. To do our best to let good come out of it.

And for me that meant keeping the orphanage doors wide open and running it with new people who would be part of our Thula Thula team.

My way of coping with grief is to fix things and find solutions. Top of the list was protecting our animals. The money Megan raised was a godsend and every last cent went into installing state-of-the-art security aimed at preventing poachers from getting anywhere near the building again.

The orphanage perimeter fence was repaired and connected to a high-tech alarm unit. Motion detector beams now pick up the slightest movement. There are infrared night-vision cameras throughout the reserve that track activity and feed information into a cloud-based portal. If a poacher disables a camera, an alarm goes off both on-site and in an external control room. Television screens with surveillance feeds were moved from the orphanage to the off-site control room.

The harsh reality is that making Thula Thula harder for poachers to break into solves very little. The poachers will simply go to another reserve. How can we fight organized syndicates with more money than we'll ever have?

We stopped using radios to report on the whereabouts of our animals. The danger of interception was too high. Now we use only secure mobile phones. Thabo and Ntombi wear tracking collars and are never without an armed guard. Staff wear mobile panic buttons and know what to do, who to phone, how to react. We can never know what to expect but one thing is sure: we will never be caught off guard again.

It felt so good to prepare the orphanage for a new beginning. It didn't mean I wasn't hurting inside; it meant I wasn't going to let pain and trauma crush me.

It's how I survived Lawrence's death and the attack on Thabo.

Fighting for what I believe in is what gets me out of bed each morning.

26

Keeping the dream alive

The tragedy had happened so close to my home, to innocent people and animals who should be safe in our world, that it was a constant battle to stop fear and despair from over-whelming me. But I never want to lose the joy of seeing what's good in life and in people, and despite the horrific things I know humans can do, I'm still an eternal optimist who believes there are more good people than bad in the world. There will always be those who let you down or obstacles that seem insurmountable, but if you keep your goal in front of you then you'll know what to do.

Giving up isn't in my genes, even if it means starting from scratch.

Besides, I wasn't alone in this, and I was so moved by the big-heartedness of people who were as determined as I was to keep our doors open. One of them was Megan, who I phoned on the off-chance that I could persuade her to return to South Africa.

'How do you feel about coming back to help us keep the orphanage going?' I asked.

'Of course I will! And I'll stay as long as it takes for you to find a permanent team,' she promised, then immediately called her best friend.

'Vicky, bad things have happened there but it's a facility that has the opportunity to be amazing. Let's see what we can do to get it on its feet again.'

The two of them arrived a week later, rolled up their sleeves and got stuck into giving the facility a complete top-to-bottom overhaul – cleaning, fixing, painting. With youthful grit and huge smiles, they breathed life and energy into the place, and one of the first things they did was put up a big *Welcome!* sign. Their enthusiasm made everyone even more motivated to find a fresh vision for the orphanage.

Within days, Bruce joined the team. He was a stocky boxer found injured and alone in the busy streets of Empangeni and from the moment he was shown his new home, we all fell in love with him. He took his jobs of playmate to Gypsy and Gin, and bodyguard to Megan and Vicky very seriously, but that never got in the way of his afternoon snooze on the sofa.

I continued to have meetings with the *amakhosi* to slowly build their trust again and to set joint goals for the future. What the previous management team had never taken seriously was the fact that the orphanage was on tribal land – part of the original expansion that Lawrence and the five *amakhosi* had established together – and it was only thanks to these visionary community leaders that our conservation dream for an animal care centre had been possible in the first place. Their continued blessing and commitment is very important to me and they were as pleased as I was that we would be running it with an in-house Thula Thula team. Discussions have gone so well that we have even started talking about expanding the reserve with more of their land.

Our other crucial partner was Four Paws. Heli Dungler

had seen for himself how destructive the human politics had become, but he too stayed committed to keeping the orphanage open, and to my great relief he didn't hesitate to renew his foundation's financial collaboration.

'We've been thinking about creating a sanctuary for ex-circus elephants,' he said to me recently. 'Maybe this is the moment to explore taking the orphanage to a different level.'

'That's a wonderful idea,' I replied quietly. 'It fits perfectly with what we do at Thula Thula.'

'It's probably only feasible in a year or two's time, so in the meantime we'll help you keep the facility open for other wildlife needing help.'

By mid July 2017, a new joint venture agreement was signed with Four Paws and the local *amakhosi*. We were officially partners again and thrilled to be up and running. Since we were turning a page and broadening our focus, we changed the name to Thula Thula Wildlife Rehabilitation Centre.

Little Lucy, a baby duiker, was our first rescue. She was saved by vigilant policemen from poachers who were trying to sell her either as a pet, or worse, for her meat. Duikers are small antelope that get their name from the Afrikaans word *duik* – dive – because of the way they duck under cover of a bush when threatened. She was a beautiful creature, with caramel-grey colouring, a narrow pointed snout, long pixie-like ears and dark soulful eyes. She was dehydrated and so malnourished that she weighed only 2.7 kilograms.

By now, word was out that we were interviewing for a permanent team and I was receiving CVs on a daily basis. It was thrilling that, despite what had happened, there were so many young men and women who wanted to work with us.

Kayleigh and Yolandie took over the reins from Megan in October and we haven't looked back. Kayleigh is tall and graceful with gentle confidence, and with degrees in zoology and wildlife management under her belt. Yolandie is a feisty young woman with a big laugh who brought with her a decade of wild animal care.

'I always thought I would be a vet, but as I got older, I realized that I would rather protect animals than cure them,' she said at her interview.

One morning soon after they joined, I took Kathy, a local journalist I knew well, up to the rehab centre so she could write an article about its rebirth. I called Gypsy to join us. She skipped out of my general manager's office, followed closely by Gin, both looking smug.

'Has Lynda been feeding you biscuits again?' I grimaced.

Lynda walked outside, palms in the air. *Sorry*, she mouthed, not looking the least bit sorry. I don't usually take Gin with me because he's not my most well-mannered dog, but he gave me his best you-can't-take-Gypsy-and-not-me pout and I gave in. Gypsy hopped into the back footwell and Gin tried to follow but couldn't get up, balancing his paws on the edge of the car and pleading for help with desperate eyes.

'You weigh a *ton*,' I groaned. 'When we get to the orphanage, I'm going to weigh you on the new scale!'

I slid behind the wheel and, before driving off, called Siya via speaker phone.

'Morning, Siya. Where are the elephants today?'

'Don't worry. They're nowhere near you. They're at Mine Dam and it looks like they're settled in for the day.'

'That's good news, thanks. Chat to you later.'

'That sounds as if you don't want to bump into them,' Kathy said in surprise.

I smiled but didn't reply.

'You're not *scared* of them, are you?' she teased.

I mulled over the question, caught off guard, not sure how to answer.

'I love them but I also have a lot of respect for them.'

'That sounds like a roundabout way of saying you *are* scared of them,' she remarked lightly. 'That must be tough. Are you also scared of the babies?'

'Never! I *love* the little ones. I love the big ones too, but when I'm in a car, I just feel exposed and vulnerable. It goes back to a bad experience with Frankie a long time ago.'

'How bad? Did she hurt you?'

'She didn't, but she was terrifying and I always worry that she remembers what happened and is still angry with me. Maybe it's a lack of trust in myself, because I know she's a completely different elephant now to the one we ran into on the quad bike . . .' I gave a confused shrug. 'To be honest, I don't really know why I'm like this.'

'Have *any* of the elephants ever hurt anyone at Thula Thula?'

A memory of Mnumzane charging and flipping Lawrence's Land Rover in a pain-induced rage flashed before me. Lawrence and two visitors had been trapped in the vehicle while Mnumzane repeatedly battered their 4×4. I had taken Lawrence's panicked radio call.

Mnumzane's attacking us. He rolled the Landy and we're stuck inside. Get help.

I can still feel the airless cramping of my chest. Lawrence had a healthy and realistic respect for our elephants so when I heard the terror in his voice, I knew he was in catastrophic danger.

'We had a bull that tried to kill Lawrence and two guests,' I murmured. 'He was so out of control that the rangers couldn't get close to the Land Rover to get the men out.'

'Oh my God, that sounds horrific. How on earth did they get away?'

'Nana and Frankie saved them. They arrived out of nowhere and managed to jostle the bull away from the vehicle long enough for the rangers to pull them out. It was especially shocking because Mnumzane was Lawrence's blue-eyed boy and I kept thinking that if he could do that to Lawrence then what could he do to me?' I shook my head and frowned at her. 'I'd forgotten about all of this.'

'It must have been very traumatic,' she said quietly.

'It's strange, because I always assumed I became skittish around them after the drama with Frankie, but actually, now that I think about it, it wasn't then, because for years afterwards, Lawrence and I continued to go on bush drives together. The thing with Frankie gave us both a huge wake-up call, but we needed it. We didn't know anything about elephants and were so damn naive. We should *never* have gone driving around on that noisy bike, but I understood that afterwards and it made me realize how powerful and wild they were. It didn't make me scared of them though.'

I was amazed by my realization. It just goes to show how

unhealthy it is to bury fear. Until the orphanage tragedy, I had never stopped to question my bewildering anxiety about being too close to the animals I loved so deeply. Instead, I pushed it away and blamed it on Frankie. Make no mistake, she used to have a short temper, which no doubt made it easy for me to jump to the conclusion that she was angry with me.

I don't know if the trauma of the attack had brought my vulnerabilities to the surface, but for the first time since Lawrence died, I felt ready to confront it all.

'May I ask you something?' Kathy said. 'What is it you're scared they'll do to you?'

As she finished her question, gooseflesh prickled my skin. I was scared of their unpredictability. Scared they might hurt me like Mnumzane had almost killed Lawrence. It wasn't *Frankie* that had set me off, it was Mnumzane. He had gone berserk, and that terrifying switch from affectionate elephant to killing machine had triggered my fear.

It was such a powerful and unexpected insight, it took my breath away.

'Did you and Lawrence ever find out why he turned aggressive?' Kathy asked.

'He had an infected tusk that we didn't know about. It caused excruciating pain and he eventually became so dangerous that Lawrence had to put him down. It broke his heart.'

'This may be a stupid question, but if Mnumzane isn't around any more then why are you still afraid?'

I smiled at her, felt the crushing burden lift.

'There's no reason at all. The herd is happy and they trust me. I was on a game drive with Clément a while back and they were so peaceful. In fact, Frankie didn't even *look* at me.'

I fell silent, lost in thought, trying to make sense of memories that were surfacing faster than I could keep track of. Kathy was right, my fear didn't make sense. Lawrence and I had spent hours out in the bush in his clapped-out old Land Rover after the run-in with Frankie, and I hadn't been the slightest bit jumpy. Not even when we had sundowners out in the middle of nowhere. I had loved being in the wild with nothing more than bush and wildlife around us.

After Mnumzane's attack, Lawrence gave orders that no one was allowed to go anywhere on the reserve without being escorted in a proper off-road vehicle by a ranger, and that the rangers had to know at all times where Mnumzane was. It added such tension to our everyday lives.

From then on, I never again went on a game drive without Lawrence, so I suppose it's no surprise really that I pretty much stopped going into the bush after he died.

All this came together in the space of that one drive. I was astonished that I had never joined the dots before and I will always be grateful that Kathy's insightful questions helped me get to the bottom of something I had been running away from for years.

I stopped outside the orphanage gates and waited for the guard to let us in, then drove through with Gypsy and Gin going mad with excitement in the back. I let them out and they ran around in boisterous circles before racing off to say hello to Kayleigh, Yolandie, and Bruce the boxer.

'Let's test the scale on them,' I said to Kayleigh.

The scale was a recent donation – a crucial piece of equipment for checking the weight of new arrivals and monitoring their development over time. Bruce and Gypsy both bounced onto it at the same time but neither stood still long enough to get a reading. Kayleigh managed to persuade Bruce off, then she read out Gypsy's weight.

'Four and a half kilos.'

'Your turn, Gin,' I said.

He looked at me uncertainly but I nudged him on.

'*Fifteen* kilos! That's three times Gypsy's weight. Gin! You've turned into a fatty bum-bum,' I laughed.

He stepped off the scale, tail between his legs, and slunk into the corner of the room, looking at me with such reproach. I hugged him to me.

'Don't worry. We're going to get you back to the slinky Jack Russell you used to be,' I promised, patting his chunky rump.

Fifteen kilos isn't healthy for a smallish dog like him, so he went on a diet that day. What a miserable time we had. Cutting down his food was as hard for me as it was for him. A couple of weeks later, I went back to the rehab centre and took Gin with me in the hope that he had lost enough weight to stop the torture of his diet.

He refused to get on the scale.

Nothing, not even a treat, would persuade him to get on. He knew something had gone wrong the last time and wouldn't even go into the room. *He* didn't know he was fat but he knew that scale had caused him problems. I relented and didn't weigh him. It didn't seem fair to make him get on the scale when I didn't want to either!

Animals are sensitive like that. He knew we were teasing him and he was hurt. People are the same. We all have a vulnerable side that reacts when hurt or frightened, but we have the choice to do something about it.

I decided there and then to confront my fear. No more excuses, no more procrastination. My life's work had been to keep the herd safe and to keep them together, so it was high time for me to jump back on the bicycle.

A nerve-wracking issue for me was that I knew animals sensed fear and I had always been petrified that it would trigger some kind of furious reaction in them – but what if it didn't? What if they felt my fear and *understood*? What if it didn't make them angry with me but more gentle?

I loved them and they *knew* I did, despite how tense I was when they came too close. My mind was made up. I would take my fear to them and put my trust in their love.

Phone in hand, I went onto the veranda for some time on my own. It was September and the bush had erupted in breathtaking spring flowers. Slender blades of grass were pushing through the ground and the trees were a kaleido-scope of buds in every shade of green. Somewhere out there, munching on the new leaves, were my beloved elephants.

I tapped out the number of one of my most trusted rangers.

'Hi, Françoise,' he answered.

'Morning, Andrew. Please could you arrange a game drive for me?'

27

Frankie vs Frankie

11 a.m., Monday morning, 25 September 2017. The first game drive in years that I was actually looking forward to. But I was still a bundle of nerves! For all my new insights, I didn't sleep easy and tossed and turned the whole night. Just because you understand what makes you scared, doesn't make it go away. There's no fairy dust to help you get over fear; it takes good old-fashioned courage.

The sky was milky blue with a crisp bite in the air. Winter was refusing to loosen its grip over Zululand. The plan was to leave from the lodge, so I arrived early to squeeze in a quick meeting with Mabona about a wedding taking place that weekend.

Before I even parked my car, I knew the elephants were around.

'They arrived just after breakfast and have been wandering up and down the riverbank ever since,' Mabona said.

We built the lodge on the Nseleni River but at this time of the year the river is dry and the herd don't come here as often as they do in summer, our rainy season. It was hard not to read something into the coincidence of them being there. Why did they choose that day of all days to come to the lodge? I walked across the lawn to watch them with wildlife photographer Mireille, who immediately crouched low to get the best shot.

The whole herd was there – Nana and Frankie, the big boys, the little ones – ambling about in their wonderful unrushed way. Elephants are never in a hurry, whether they're going somewhere or having a meal. I've never in my life seen an elephant gulp down food quickly. The only time they know is Africa time, where today is what matters and tomorrow is another day.

I watched Mabula saunter up to a marula tree, leisurely curl his trunk around a branch and pull slowly until it snapped, then he took his time to munch the foliage.

The calves rolled and tumbled in nature's sandpit, hoovering up sand and blowing it over themselves. Even little Themba, our youngest calf, was getting the hang of it.

Frankie stood under a towering tall Cape ash quietly surveying her family. I wondered what she was thinking. Was she reflecting on how happy and carefree they were? We know elephants have superb memories, so she wouldn't have forgotten the dark days of her life before she came to us – born in Zimbabwe, sold to a game reserve in South Africa, almost ending up in a Chinese zoo. In my heart, I knew she understood how Lawrence and I had saved her and the herd, and how I continued to fight to protect them. So much water had gone under the bridge since those early days. We had both become matriarchs before our time and taken on responsibilities we never thought would be ours.

You adapted quicker than me, I thought ruefully, *but I'm getting there.*

Two calves started a chaotic game of mock charge, whirling

their wobbly jelly trunks in the air as they slammed and rammed each other, oblivious to the other elephants that they crashed into or how close to the riverbank they were.

Frankie lumbered across and put herself between them and the steep drop. The riverbed was dry but that only made it more dangerous. She didn't put a stop to their cavorting but simply stood by protectively and made sure they stayed out of trouble.

This was how I usually enjoyed our elephants – on the opposite riverbank, from the other side of an electric fence, or in the distance across a valley. I looked at my watch and felt the all-too-familiar flutter of nerves. The game drive was in an hour.

We left on time, just after eleven. I felt excited and anxious but also reassured that Andrew and Muzi were my ranger and tracker. If they were surprised that I had asked for the drive, they didn't show it.

'Frankie's going to be annoyed I'm here,' I half joked.

Muzi turned and looked at me with solemn eyes. 'She's going to love it.'

I nodded with a tight smile. Kathy, the journalist, was sitting on my right, the wildlife photographer on my left, and Clément sat behind me with two guests. We drove out of the lodge gates in a cloud of dust. I stared down at my hands, heart hammering. I always felt like this on game drives but today was especially loaded with emotion. I so badly wanted it to go well.

'There they are,' Andrew murmured.

My head snapped up. The elephants were spread out on

either side of our Land Cruiser and in front, blocking our way. I searched for Frankie. There she was. On my right, a good ten metres away. She didn't acknowledge us but the fluttering of her ears gave her away. She knew we were there. I took a deep breath, sat back and relaxed.

They ambled about, doing what they do every day: eating, strolling, touching, communicating, just living their lives, radiating contentment.

Gobisa crossed the road and paused, gazing at us with his old-soul eyes.

'Watch out. He's looking for you, Clément,' Muzi bantered.

'That's okay. He knows where to find me,' Clément shrugged with a grin.

Gobisa dawdled on, chewed on a couple of acacia branches, then sauntered over to where Mabula and Ilanga were eating.

'Watch,' Andrew said quietly. 'They're Frankie's boys and they're not too keen on her boyfriend.'

Both young bulls trumpeted loudly at Gobisa, swaying their heads in annoyance. He paused, a gracious old man taken aback by the rudeness of the younger generation. It was seven years since Lawrence had brought him in as a father figure to help guide and control the adolescent bulls, but since then Mabula had become bigger and stronger than him and had eventually ousted him as dominant male, no doubt fuelled by a fair amount of animosity about his relationship with his mother. Ilanga took his cue from his big brother and was just as stroppy. Neither wanted Gobisa anywhere near them. He moved off to the side and approached the tree from a different angle but Mabula ran up and headbutted him away.

Ilanga swaggered after them, bursting with attitude and resentment.

Not in the mood for a face-off, Gobisa left his intolerant stepsons and drifted back across the road to Frankie. He didn't look particularly troubled but I felt sorry for him. Blended families obviously present problems even in other species. Frankie caressed Gobisa's neck with her trunk, then they strolled off side by side, bodies touching, legs in step.

I felt Clément's hand on my shoulder and turned.

'*Ça va?*' he smiled.

I nodded that I was fine, and it was the truth. I was so happy to be with the herd and it felt as if I was rediscovering old friends, ones I hadn't seen in a very long time but where the trust and love and pleasure at being together had never gone away. I even asked Kathy to swap seats with me so I could sit on the outside of the 4×4.

Elephants have an exceptional sense of smell and at the first sign of danger, they will raise their trunk to locate any threat. In Kenya, they're known to be able to pick up the difference between two tribes – the Maasai who hunt them and the Kamba who don't.

Frankie *knew* I was in the Land Cruiser and if she didn't want me there, she would have made it clear, but her trunk hadn't periscoped up to sniff the air and she hadn't even looked my way, as if purposely ignoring me.

I stared at her, stunned. That's *exactly* what she was doing. My heart almost burst with gratitude. She wasn't angry with me. She didn't hate me being there. She wasn't going to take advantage of my fear. She was letting me know that my being there made no difference to her whatsoever.

I can only describe the energy enveloping me as pure, almost divine. For a moment everything seemed to stop. It felt as if every cloud, leaf, bird and insect was bathing me in peace. My heart was so open and serene and I felt deeply humbled by the herd's gentle welcome.

When you live with fear as long as I did, it is incredible to be freed of it. My anxiety had stemmed from real events but had become a monster with a life of its own. Of course our elephants are still capable of behaving unpredictably, but the difference between today and almost twenty years ago is that back then they were wild and dangerous, whereas now they are wild and in harmony.

'Françoise,' Mireille said urgently, pulling me out of my reverie. 'Something's wrong with Susanna. Her trunk is too short.'

Susanna is one of the young calves and she was standing just to the left of the Land Cruiser. Depending on how an elephant holds its head, the trunk tip usually dangles very close to the ground. Her trunk hung a good forty centimetres above it.

'*Haibo!*' exclaimed Muzi.

'Andrew? Muzi? What do you think?' I asked.

'Snare injury. She must have got her trunk caught in one but somehow pulled herself free,' Andrew grimaced. 'And in doing so the wire must have sliced off the bottom part.'

I was sick to the stomach. No one said a word. The trunk is one of the most delicate and sensitive parts of an elephant and her pain must have been mind-blowing. She stood in a dazed stupor next to her mother. I felt so helpless and so angry at the men who had set the traps.

Mireille quickly flicked through her photos and shook her head in dismay.

'Look. Her trunk was intact this morning before we left the lodge,' she said.

This is the horror of snare poaching for you. At 10 a.m., Susanna was a happy young calf without a care in the world, and by midday she had a life-threatening injury. It was even more heartbreaking because she had already suffered a snare trauma when she was tiny that had shredded part of her ear.

One minute, we're savouring being so close to these evolved, gracious creatures and the next, we're in code-red mode to help a calf with a horrendous wound.

It's such a reminder about life itself. We can never know what's around the corner and it makes it all the more urgent to relish precious moments of peace when they come our way.

We raced back to the lodge and sent Mireille's photos to the vet for his advice. Mike was worried, but the fact that the injury seemed to be a clean cut without badly ripped flesh and muscle was very much in her favour.

'It means she has a better chance of it healing without scar tissue that could block her nasal passages,' he explained. 'And she still has enough trunk left to grasp branches and suck up water. I've heard of worse trunk injuries and I'm sure she'll learn to adapt to her disability. Right now, you need to watch out for septicaemia. Call me if the rangers see the slightest hint of inflammation or infection.'

We debated whether she needed preventative antibiotics to stave off potential complications, but decided against it in favour of monitoring her closely. First priority was to make sure she was eating and drinking.

But by the end of that day, the herd had split into two and gone underground and we had no way of knowing how Susanna was.

Every available 4×4 and ranger was out looking for Susanna the next day. It always astonishes me when we can't find the herd. Twenty-nine is a lot of elephants to go missing, but I've learned with them – if they don't want to be found, they won't be.

I was beside myself with worry. What if her wound had become infected? How would we know? How could we be sure she was eating? Fortunately, she was still feeding from her mother and wouldn't need her trunk to suckle. The milk would provide her with essential nourishment to keep up her strength while her wound healed.

But I wasn't taking any chances – until we had *seen* her suckle, I couldn't relax.

The herd stayed in hiding the whole day. Twenty-four hours and the clock was ticking.

At dawn the next morning, Siya and Muzi headed back into the bush to look for them. I was on the verge of calling in an aerial search party when they radioed in the fantastic news that the herd had reunited and was down in the valley where the grass was softer and easier for Susanna to eat with her damaged trunk.

'The herd has surrounded her and formed a protective circle,' Siya reported.

'Does that mean you haven't actually seen her eat?' I asked anxiously.

'Sending pics now.'

My phone beeped and I clicked open the image he sent – Susanna suckling, forehead nestled against her mother's side, her wounded trunk curled high out of harm's way. I swallowed hard. Forty-eight hours since we had last seen her and she was eating. I gripped my phone, fighting off tears.

'Thank you, Siya.'

Susanna wasn't out of the woods yet, but the fact that she was feeding was a huge relief. Not only for the nutrition, but also for the comfort that suckling would give her.

Only then did the full impact of the herd's presence during my game drive hit me. Susanna had just been injured and yet Frankie only led the herd into hiding *afterwards*.

Elephants have an extraordinary ability to sense things. Often when Lawrence had been away from the reserve, they would come to say hello, arriving at almost the same time as he did, and once even turning back when he missed a flight.

Had Frankie sensed the significance of that game drive for me? I believe she did. That's why she kept her distance and ignored me the entire time we were there. And why, a few weeks later, she brought the herd and Susanna to my home and didn't leave until the next day – an unheard-of length of time for them to stay in one place.

It was only when I saw they were still there the following morning that it dawned on me she was doing the *opposite* of ignoring me. She looked up at the house, looked directly at me with her wise, gentle eyes, engaging with me in her elephant way. Quiet rumbles filled the air, echoed in my heart. I walked across the lawn towards her and watched her slide her trunk between the wires to sample the spring flowers on my side, as if sharing a meal with me.

She shows me again and again what an amazing leader and teacher she is, and how she lives every day with compassion, insight and kindness, whether it's keeping an eye on the little ones near a river, leading Susanna to grass that's easier to eat, or quietly nibbling on the flowers in my garden to remind me that I have nothing to be afraid of.

Afterword

2 March 2018

It is six years today since Lawrence died. So much has happened, so many lessons learned and obstacles overcome.

We have survived against all odds and I couldn't have done it without the hand-in-hand loyalty and commitment of everyone at Thula Thula. Together with volunteers, guests-turned-friends, donors and contributors, we keep the passion alive and do everything we can to ensure the survival of our fragile environment.

Our herd has grown to twenty-nine elephants and counting. Susanna's trunk healed beautifully and she has adapted well to life with part of her trunk missing. Thabo and Ntombi are nine years old and a happy, inseparable couple – and I'm impatiently waiting for them to make me a rhino granny! Our rehabilitation centre now has three orphans, with a baby kudu and baby wildebeest joining little Lucy at the beginning of January.

We are turning Lawrence's vision of creating a huge conservation area into a growing, sustainable legacy for generations to come, and there are already two expansion projects on the horizon. The first is with private neighbours for an additional 1,500 hectares, which will tick the box for the wildlife authorities in terms of our land-to-elephant ratio *and* give us enough space to bring in lions, making us a big five reserve at last.

The second very exciting development is that the five *amakhosi* have agreed in principle for us to expand onto 3,500 hectares of tribal land – magnificent bush that isn't suitable for cattle but is ideal for conservation. A feasibility study is in progress, but in the meantime we have already raised half the amount needed to fence this area, and the day that we drop the old fence is getting closer and closer.

We are in the middle of a research project to evaluate the social and emotional impact of our contraception policy on the herd. Elephants flourish in a family environment and it worries me that we're inhibiting this primeval part of who they are.

I have my own dreams for Thula Thula. We have opened a volunteer camp near the rehabilitation centre where people from all over the world, along with youngsters from local communities, will come to live in simple tents that will bring them close to nature and wildlife, and where we will teach them the ways of the bush so they can learn the value of conservation for the well-being of themselves and their planet.

And I am going to dust off Lawrence's old Land Rover and have it fixed. It will be *my* 4×4 for reconnecting with the bush I love so much.

As I celebrate thirty years in South Africa, I have learned never to give up, to hold on to my dreams, always to search for a silver lining, and that by looking forward, the difficulties of the past eventually fade out of sight.

Thula Thula is, and always will be, my home.

Françoise Malby-Anthony
Thula Thula, South Africa

Picture Acknowledgements

All photographs are from the author's own collection, with the exception of the following:

Page 1 top © Roy Watts
Page 1 bottom © Karen Sandson / *Saturday Star* newspaper
Page 3 top and bottom © Bella Marques
Page 4 top and bottom © Kim McLeod
Page 5 top © Luke Hatfield
Page 8 top left © Christopher Laurenz
Page 10 top © Thula Thula Staff Photos
Page 10 bottom © Kim McLeod
Page 11 top © Thula Thula Staff Photos
Page 11 bottom © Kim McLeod
Page 12 top and bottom © Kim McLeod
Page 13 top © Kim McLeod
Page 13 bottom © Mark Kitchingman / Mark Kitchingman Photography
Page 14 bottom © Katja Willemsen
Page 16 top left © Mark Kitchingman / Mark Kitchingman Photography